Growing Songwriting

Praise for *Growing Songwriting*

"This utterly refreshing book is sure to inspire not only those who are at the beginning of their journey through songwriting pedagogy, but seasoned practitioners too. Full of fantastic ideas for engaging and developing students' skills and knowledge, based on the author's extensive experience in classrooms. Highly recommended for anyone involved in contemporary songwriting pedagogy, music education in general, or indeed for students themselves who could learn much from this book."

—**Lucy Green**, author of *How Popular Musicians Learn*

"Clint Randles presents an entirely fresh approach to nurturing the unique abilities in individual student songwriters. His musical examples are spot on. Other books on songwriting provide academic exemplars and exercises, but this book directly connects to the creative nature of songwriters. There aren't many books in music education that break boundaries. Bennett Reimer's *A Philosophy of Music Education* was one. Lucy Green's *How Popular Musicians Learn: A Way Ahead for Music Education* was another. Clint Randles's *Growing Songwriting* is a third."

—**John Kratus**, Michigan State University

"*Growing Songwriting* offers an intriguing view of contemporary songwriting! Randles details how songwriting is currently practiced and offers a compelling view of what cover songs accomplish as a part of creative musical processes. Students progress from covering songs, to remixing, to songwriting as they grow their creative capacity. This is an enormously practical volume, highly readable yet well connected to the science of creativity."

—**Mark Runco**, Director of Creativity Research and Programming, Southern Oregon University

"Dr. Randles here continues his work of many years to promote music education that is open, creative, playful, and attentive to music that really engages students. He draws on his experiences and experiments, along with stories of major artists creating, to give teachers support as they help their students tap into songwriting as a way to understand the music they love and their imaginations."

—**Matthew D. Thibeault**, Associate Professor of Cultural and Creative Arts, the Education University of Hong Kong

"For music voices to flourish creatively, Clint Randles has written another magnificent book for making this happen, suggesting a set of starting points (seeds), stories of others (water), and inspiration ideas (sunlight). In doing so, he has skillfully added an additional set of critical ingredients: nutrients—the furtive soil full of resources and techniques—to allow learners and teachers alike to make beautiful music blossom in their lives."

—**Peter Webster**, University of Southern California and Northwestern University

"This excellent book is innovative and forges forward in an area often overlooked in music education. Songwriting is essential to music. Reading about how songwriting manifests in learning environments is eye-opening and intriguing. The agricultural metaphor and the many colorful illustrations and lesson plans help provide great examples for future practical use."

—**Radio Cremata**, Chair of Music Education, Ithaca College

Growing Songwriting

Student Creativities in the Classroom and Beyond

CLINT RANDLES

OXFORD
UNIVERSITY PRESS

OXFORD
UNIVERSITY PRESS

Oxford University Press is a department of the University of Oxford. It furthers the University's objective of excellence in research, scholarship, and education by publishing worldwide. Oxford is a registered trade mark of Oxford University Press in the UK and certain other countries.

Published in the United States of America by Oxford University Press
198 Madison Avenue, New York, NY 10016, United States of America.

CIP data is on file at the Library of Congress
ISBN 978–0–19–769322–3 (pbk.)
ISBN 978–0–19–769321–6 (hbk.)

DOI: 10.1093/oso/9780197693216.001.0001

Paperback printed by Marquis Book Printing, Canada
Hardback printed by Bridgeport National Bindery, Inc., United States of America

This book is dedicated to John Kratus.
We all stand on the backs of giants.
There is no greater giant in songwriting in music education than Dr. Kratus.

Contents

Illustrations

Boxes

Figures

Tables

Acknowledgments

I cannot express in words how important John Kratus was to the development of the ideas in this book. I worked hand in hand with John as one of his students at Michigan State University for my master's and doctoral degrees in music education from 2003 to 2010. From the first class that I took with Dr. Kratus, I was inspired. He told me that it was okay to think things that I had always thought about music education. He provided me with a license to consider things differently that I carry with me to this day. John walked the walk and talked the talk. He is a songwriter. He taught a songwriting class at MSU, one of the first of its kind in higher education. He is an eminent scholar and researcher in music education. He is a person for me to aspire to be like. Thank you, John.

My colleagues in music education at the University of South Florida have provided me with freedom to learn how to be a progressive music education pedagogue. David Williams has been a constantly supportive brother-in-arms in providing leadership to the profession on how to teach the next generation of music teachers to be different—better than the ones that we were and/or had. David is the best music administrator that I have ever known. Victor Fung has been a dedicated and always excellent researcher colleague, modeling flexibility and depth in his research practice. He truly is a wonderfully balanced person who exercises vision, kindness, and *junzi* (Fung, 2018) through his interactions with students and colleagues. I could not ask for better colleagues. And to many of my other USF School of Music colleagues, I have succeeded in spite of your efforts and desires to keep me from doing so. May grace and peace abound in your hearts. I forgive you.

The world of music education is full of people who like me have wanted to create alternate pathways for curricular expansion. I think most notably of my colleagues at Arizona State University who are well known for being distinct and educating students with different ways of thinking and doing in music education practice. In the early 2000s when I was doing my graduate schoolwork, the places to be for big ideas and doing things differently in practice were Michigan State University and Northwestern University. I have great admiration for those schools and the Big Ten. There are Modern Band promoters and social change advocates out there who do work in a similar vein as mine. I have been teaching teachers contemporary musicianship skills that celebrate multiple musical creativities since the fall of 2010. There were not many models for how to do that when I started. I have had to forge my own paths in many ways, learning along the way as I made mistakes and worked through challenges. I am thankful for all of my colleagues around the world who do similar such work. It's getting better, isn't it? People are starting to come around as we hoped they would. [smile]

If you know me, you know that my family means everything. My older kids are nearly adults now. Pearl is finishing her degree in education and will be the world's best elementary school teacher very soon. Calvin is trying to discover the person that he wants to be when he grows up. Henry is preparing to apply to art schools. Harper is blossoming as an empathetic and curious human being in middle school. And Arianna, our beautiful little foster daughter, is learning how to speak in sentence fragments as she begins to make sense of the love that we shower on her every day. It really is a wonderful life—with all of the pain, joy, and exuberance that comes along the spectrum of human experience. I would not trade it for anything under the sun.

I have fallen in love with songwriting over the years. It is my hope that you will be able to feel that love in these pages. It was a joy to write this book. From beginning to end it took me a little over 100 days to write and it flowed easily like no other project that I have ever worked on. It almost seemed as if the project had ideas and desires of its own—wanting to come out, eager to be born, aspiring to change lives. I seek to honor all the students that I have taught by putting these ideas out into the world. As I revere the great songs that have been a continuous part of my experience thus far, I look forward to the songs that you and your students will write. As you read this book and desire to grow songwriting in your classroom, know that you and I are a couple of pieces of a massive puzzle that encompasses us and many others like us. While any one of the pieces alone does not seem like anything very significant, when considered together with all others it emerges as part of a picture that is intense, profound, and awe-inspiring—the voices in unison of all of the lives that will be touched by an abiding love of music because of our efforts. This is important work. Lean into it now.

—Clint Randles

Prologue

There are many different ways that I could have organized this book. I wanted to create something that would be helpful for anyone off the street who wanted to get started writing songs. That was very important as I planned for and then started working on this project. Some books in the field of music education look nothing like the real world of music-making. I felt that a good book on songwriting should reference in large part the greater world of music and connect the dots in as many ways as possible to that world and the world of teachers and schools and/or community centers. The focal point is the creative practice of professional songwriters, producers, and engineers. This work plays nicely with *Music Teacher as Music Producer* (Randles, 2022) and *Sound Production for the Emerging Music Teacher Producer* (Randles, Aponte & Johnson, forthcoming). In fact, this book might be considered Book 2 in a trilogy that starts with *MTMP* (1) and will conclude with *SPEMTP* (3). Like George Lucas's original *Star Wars* series, I have plans to continue the saga. [smile]

After an introductory chapter, the book is organized into three parts:

Part I: Covering Songs
Part II: The Middle Ground
Part III: Songwriting

To properly introduce the idea of growing songwriting, I start with an understanding of what cover songs accomplish. With a clear understanding of how artists find themselves in the work of their favorite artists, you will be ready to consider the role of remixes and sampling (the Middle Ground) in the greater world of professional music-making. You will then be ready to practice your skills as a songwriter. These three parts are worthwhile endeavors that should not be considered as a linear progression. A student could land on one of these and find an endless well of inspiration that will fuel their lifelong love of being musical. In my professional experience, though, very few people become songwriters without first covering songs. So, you should start there! I have provided you with starting places for doing that.

After an introductory chapter for each main section (Covering Songs, the Middle Ground, and Songwriting) that presents ideas, skills, and techniques from the literature on songwriting, I provide you with beginning, intermediate, and advanced lesson seeds. These seeds are a starting place for developing lessons in these three areas that collectively support growing songwriting in your classroom. I also provide you with water and sunlight. Here is what seeds, water, and sunlight accomplish for you:

- **Seeds**: Starting points for you to develop lessons on Covering Songs, the Middle Ground, and Songwriting. These are not meant to be prescriptive. Rather, they are seeds that will grow as you plant them and provide . . .
- **Water**: Stories of how songwriters have navigated creative processes that have led to Covering Songs, the Middle Ground, and Songwriting. We learn best by examining other peoples' stories as we hold them up to our own. Creative processes are best furthered by providing . . .
- **Sunlight**: Inspiration that has helped other people navigate similar such creative processes. When you plant a seed, water it, and provide sunlight, things grow. That is what we are after here.

Can you see the analogies here? The metaphor is rich with possibility and potential in the hands of artist teachers. That is where you come into the exchange!

The theme of growing songwriting as in (1) the presence and prominence of the practice and (2) a metaphor of how it is best practiced with students in classrooms borrowing from an understanding of nature can be seen across the pages of this work. By focusing our attention on building skills and nurturing practices with potential to grow without us in the future, over time as people continue to see the cultural capital that this activity affords, we will grow songwriting as a curricular offering. The proof of the value of all of this is how well our plants look as they grow. They give off a beautiful green hue, produce fruit, and display gorgeous flowers that bless them and the plants around them. Of course, I speak of plants here as people.

The ideas presented here are nothing without the work of Master Gardeners. That's you! It takes the work of artist teachers to plant these seeds, offer up water, and provide optimal conditions for sunlight, so that songwriting can grow. I have seen these ideas in practice. They work well. You have that going for you as you get started or continue your work. You will need to grow the presence of songwriting in your own life as you seek to put these ideas into practice in your life. You don't have to be Grammy-nominated as a songwriter to get the songwriting lives of hundreds of people in your care started on a growth trajectory that will mean the world to them for decades to come. This is important work that you are doing. It builds on the soundtracks to their lives that have been going on since before they took their first breaths. It authentically leverages all of the world's music. Songwriting is smart work. It is timely and necessary. It elevates the status of the more traditional ways that music education has been doing in schools and community centers. Doing this work puts you on the cutting edge. Soak in the sunlight as you work.

INTRO

1

An Orientation to Growing Songwriting

WATER: When Inspiration Comes

The Rolling Stones toured North America from April 23 through May 29, 1965. On May 6, 1965, they were in Clearwater, Florida, for their 9th show of the tour. Guitarist Keith Richards woke up in the middle of the night with some musical ideas in his head. Instead of going back to sleep, he got up out of bed, picked up his Gibson Hummingbird, and recorded about 60 seconds of a guitar part and then fell back to sleep.

The next morning, he inspected the tape and found that it was at the end of the tape recorder; he remembered having inserted a new tape in the previous night. Upon playback, what he discovered was the rough idea for the main riff (along with 40 minutes of snoring). When we are inspired, we have a little bit of time to capture those bits of inspiration before they are lost. Take the time to capture them. It makes all of the difference in the world to our lives when we do this.

It's about Growing

Hello reader, thank you for picking up this book. Songwriting is one of the final frontiers in music education at the moment. If the 18th-century music educator Lowell Mason were a leader in the field today he would be advocating for songwriting experiences for students at every level (Mark & Gary, 2007). Technologies for music creation have never been as intuitive and inviting to both teachers and students as they are right now. Trailblazers in music education curriculum development recognize the scalability of music-making that leverages the impact of working with students on cover and original songs that can be both performed live and recorded. School by school and student by student, we are making the world just a little better than it was before our efforts.

Except for a few articles and the work of a handful of pioneers in music education (Green, 2017a, 2017b; Kratus, 2016; Reinhert, 2019; Reinhert & Gulish, 2020; Tobias, 2013), songwriting has been a musical gold mine that the profession has underexplored in school and community music settings. Great research questions and meaningful studies (Draves, 2008; Hughes & Keith, 2019) are sure to follow a large and widespread adoption of songwriting as an essential component to the

Growing Songwriting. Clint Randles, Oxford University Press. © Oxford University Press 2024.
DOI: 10.1093/oso/9780197693216.003.0001

music education of all students. I would like to do my part with this work to help make this possible. To grow songwriting as a curricular offering (Baker, 2016), we need as a profession to first think of it as a large process that involves three closely related elements:

1. Cover Songs
2. Middle Ground (remixes and samples)
3. Original Songs

Each of these pieces is a unique pathway to musical fulfillment and a lifelong love of learning. I have divided this book into these three content areas where I provide seeds, water, and sunlight for you to literally grow songwriting in your classroom. This is the most exciting time in the history of music to be a music teacher. [smile]

In order for us to be successful, we need to get a few things straight so that you understand what this book is (and what it is not).

What this book can do for you:

1. It situates *cover songs as the necessary first focal point* of curricular efforts in live performance and recording in your classroom. No other songwriting book that I have seen starts with ideas on how to cover songs. My approach matches the professional world of music that I live and work within.
2. It gives you *starting points for lessons* where students cover songs, work in the Middle Ground, and work up original songs in your classroom. From the sample starting points that I provide you will be able to create your own. The seed ideas come from the real world of my teaching practice. They are scalable.
3. It *connects the worlds of live performance and recording*, two separate but related areas of curricular focus in your classroom. These two areas have rarely been considered alongside one another, or as two sides of the same coin. However, thinking this way will make our curricular efforts look more like the real world of music-making (Cremata et al, 2017). Again, this looks like the world of professional music-making that I live and work within.
4. It will provide you with *ideas for how to have your students create, perform, and respond* to music, in accordance with the National Association for Music Education's (NAfME) efforts to help teachers develop curriculum in the United States, or whichever organizational support group that you find in the country where you teach music or study music education. This book is *not only for teachers and students in North America*; it is for the greater world of music education practice and research.

What this book will probably not accomplish for you:

1. It is *not a book of set-in-stone prescriptions.* Your students bring a unique chemical reaction to your classroom. You will need to respond in the moment

to and interact with them constantly. The classroom is an exciting place where a complex improvisation occurs between what you have in mind for lessons and what students bring. Lessons are not linear. Rather, they are beautiful unfoldings and unwrappings of musical lives in time and space.
2. My goal is *not to provide you with worksheets to copy* and give your students. You are an artist teacher. You will be able to determine what makes sense for your students and your classroom and to create worksheets if that makes sense in your classroom creative process (I avoid worksheets).
3. This is *not a book about technology*. However, technology will facilitate the success of both you and your students. *Music Teacher as Music Producer* (Randles, 2022) sets the stage for beginning to understand the technology that you use all of the time in this type of classroom. *Sound Production for the Emerging Music Teacher as Music Producer* (Randles, Aponte & Johnson, forthcoming) will help you with the technology related to making your recorded tracks sound better.
4. *This is an ideas-to-practice book*. I am someone who has experience in the separate but related worlds of music teacher education and musical performance. Good ideas in the hands of artist teachers are extremely valuable. My goal throughout is to give you great ideas that you can transform and grow in practice, without being too prescriptive.

There are some good resources for songwriting that accomplish quite a lot for developing your understanding about how to best teach songwriting in your class. Here are a few of them:

1. *Great Songwriting Techniques* by Jack Perricone (Oxford, 2018)
2. *Teaching Music through Composition* by Barbara Freedman (Oxford, 2013)
3. *Songwriting: A Complete Guide to the Craft* by Stephen Citron (Hal Leonard, 2008)
4. *Using Technology to Unlock Musical Creativity* by Scott Watson (Oxford, 2011)
5. *Electronic Music School: A Contemporary Approach to Teaching Musical Creativity* by Ethan Hein and Will Kuhn (Oxford, 2021)

My favorite among this group of books is *Great Songwriting Techniques* (Perricone, 2018). It is full of tested techniques that you can use in your classroom without being too prescriptive. I like that. If you are a teacher who is thinking about bringing more experiences of songwriting into your classroom, then you are going to need a variety of different resources.

I wrote *Music Teacher as Music Producer* (Randles, 2022) as a primer to the different type of classroom and different type of teacher that will be required to teach songwriting for live performance and recording. It would be good for you to consult that book first if possible. It is not impossible, however, for you to jump right in with covering songs and songwriting along with your students, to learn along with them as you go. Be transparent with them about what you can do and what you cannot do. Develop an environment where it is okay to fail. Performing along with them, even when you are not perfect, will go a long way toward developing the right kind of atmosphere in your classroom for student success.

SUNLIGHT: Finding Your Sound in the Sound of Others

When searching for what you want your song to sound like, you listen to other people's music. Over time, we assimilate the music that we love into our subconscious musical well, the one that we draw from to create our own music. When you are stuck in the process of musical creation, make a catalogue of musical elements of songs that you love. Here is a catalogue of the musical elements in Beyoncé's "Formation." Start your song by borrowing from the musical elements of your favorite songs.

"Formation"
Beyoncé

Tempo: 122 BPM
Harmony: Key of Cm, then F
Form: Verse-Chorus
Sound Elements: 808-styled drums, bassline FM-ish, lead synth
Rhythm: Four on the floor drum beat
Production: Diverse adds and fills, synth embellishments and creative panning

SUNLIGHT: The Power of Being Vulnerable

You need to be vulnerable in front of your students. We can learn a lot about this important aspect of our being from people who study vulnerability:

> Owning our story can be hard but not nearly as difficult as spending our lives running from it. Embracing our vulnerabilities is risky but not nearly as dangerous as giving up on love and belonging and joy—the experiences that make us the most vulnerable. Only when we are brave enough to explore the darkness will we discover the infinite power of our light. (Brene Brown)[1]

Your students will appreciate your being human in front of them. You are going to need to share your darkness as much as you are going to need to share your light. Of course, there are dark subject matters that aren't appropriate for school settings. However, we all hurt, we all fail, and we all benefit from knowing that we are not alone in feeling and behaving this way.

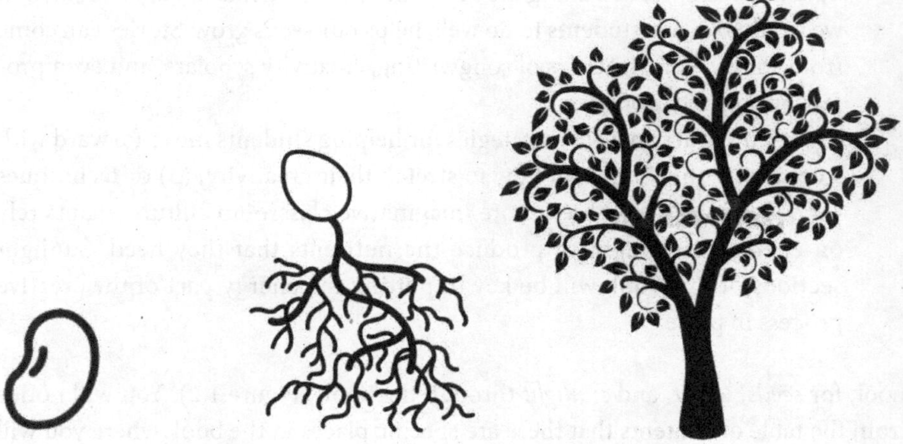

Figure 1.1 Metaphor of a lesson seed

This book is about ideas for how to get started with projects. When I refer to lesson seeds here, I refer to places to begin. A good lesson seed is an orienting idea or collection of ideas that will allow you to insert a high degree of your own skills and passion equal in dose with the interests and desires of your students—for their success. You don't need checklists. When I have a good idea, I can grow it in the fertile soil of my classroom. Just like you can't predict how a seed will grow and the shape that it will eventually take, you cannot predict or force-feed a lesson to be something before it takes root and begins growing. You take a seed, plant it, provide adequate water, make sure that your seedling gets enough sunlight, and try to keep the weeds away as best as you can. If you do that, you will see your seeds grow into massive trees before your eyes, trees that grow roots deep into the soil and grow for decades (long after they are in your care) (see Figure 1.1). That is what we want!

Think of yourself as a master gardener. The more you plant, water, keep your soil full of nutrients, and provide sunlight and other optimal conditions for growth, the better your plants will grow (McIntyre, 2008). You wouldn't want to try to predict the final shape and form of a plant before you plant it. To get started, you simply need a seed. That is what I want to provide for you in this book—a collection of seeds for you to plant and watch grow in your classroom. Along with seeds, I will provide you with sunlight and water. Let me explain how I use the metaphor of a master gardener to help you be a better teacher of songwriting. I'll start with some definitions:

Seeds: Places to start lessons that ignite student creativities. Remember, my goal is not to prescribe. You are an artist teacher. You will learn the most by trying things out for yourself—experimenting. More on that idea in the next section.

Water: Stories about how professional songwriters have navigated the creative process of songwriting. Stories illuminate our path. Knowing how others have lived and worked doing the thing that we would like to do, the thing that we would like our students to do well, helps our seeds grow. Stories can come from songwriters, teachers of songwriting, creativity scholars, and even professional music producers.

Sunlight: Sunlight can be (1) strategies for helping students move forward with a composition; (2) tips on how to stretch their creativity; (3) or techniques for developing a healthier, more imaginative classroom culture. Plants rely on energy in sunlight to produce the nutrients that they need. Sunlight sections of this book will be key to putting the energy part of the creative process in place.

Look for *seeds*, *water*, and *sunlight* through the book (Figure 1.2). You will notice from the table of contents that there are specific places in the book where you will find seeds. Conversely, water and sunlight can be found opening each chapter, and scattered throughout the book for good measure. When you come to these segments, stop . . . soak in the nutrients, absorb the energy, be fed so that you can know how to help your students in the same way in class. Plan on doing these same

Figure 1.2 Seeds need water (songwriting stories) and sunlight (inspiration for continuation) to grow

exercises for your own benefit. If you are not currently a songwriter, here is your chance to become one. Practice and grow your own skills along with your students.

SUNLIGHT: What Makes Gardening So Rewarding?

Here are some of the many benefits of gardening. Think of them analogically as benefits of growing songwriting as a part of your curriculum, AND of becoming a songwriter yourself:

1. **It connects you with nature.** There are a lot of rewards to being out in the elements. To be truly alive is to connect fully with the earth that sustains us. Songwriting helps us tap into the well of the human condition that has existed since there have been humans.
2. **It gives back to the earth.** Gardening produces products that make life better for the people who populate the planet. Apples and bananas. Songs and instrumentals. These make life better for all of us.
3. **It allows you to build relationships with other people.** Sharing our songs with others provides a platform for us to share our lives and learn more about the people around us. We come together in class to listen, share, respond, and celebrate. There are many rewards to be had for doing that.

Being and Becoming a Master Gardener

Being a gardener is healthy, beautiful, and rewarding. A master gardener is a gardener who is interested in both the art and science of gardening. The art—*expression or application of creative skill and imagination*—and the science—*systematic study of the natural world through observation and experiment*—of tending to your garden is where the heart of high-quality teaching is found. I am part of a movement, a collection of music educators whose goal foremost is to create educative experiences for students and teachers within a growth mindset. Education is and should be all about *the process* of growing. Our assessments should be *formative* and *tentative*.

Artist teachers go about each day looking for ways to exercise their own creative imagination. They are musicians themselves who stretch themselves in new and interesting ways, always looking to grow and move forward. They have come to realize the power of creative activity in their lives and work to nurture it. That excitement is viewable by their students who would like themselves to actualize their creative potential. They begin to see a person who in some cases they would like to be just like, in other cases someone who is flawed but compelling enough in ways to follow and learn from. It's important to be vulnerable. Artist teachers understand the value of their being creative along with their students.

Scientifically minded teachers look constantly for ways to improve their teaching and undertake daily reflection about how things are going, while constantly experimenting with better ways of doing what they do. *Everything is an experiment* with these types of teachers. They use their artistic powers of creative imagination to help them discover the best questions to ask with regard to daily practice. In this way, art and science combine to propel them to the best practices for their students.

The Health of Your Plants (Students) Is Priority One

The seeds of lesson plans, water, and sunlight presented throughout the book will help you get started teaching songwriting as a regular part of the classroom experience of your students. Songwriting promotes musical health and well-being. It leverages their creative imagination. It taps into their human experience. It fulfills a longing that we all have to take simpler things and make them more complex, to put our signature on something that we have made. We seek to grow songwriting as a curricular practice. We seek to grow our skills as songwriters. I hope that this book helps you do both of these things.

Our goal is to plant and provide the right conditions for seeds to grow while they are in our care, so that they continue to grow when they are no longer in our presence. Growth is the singular goal. There are lots of ways both quantitative and qualitative to measure growth. We need to become experts in ways of doing this. I have provided MANY ways of doing that here, and you will have to always be on the lookout for more refined ways that fit well the culture of your classroom and the specific interests of your students.

In some cases, you will have to tend to removing the weeds that can grow around your plants. Weeds take the shape of self-doubt and discouragement at times, while other times weeds can be personality conflicts among band members of bands in your care. You will have to think of both the short term—"How can I help this group finish a song without damaging their creative vision?—and the long term—"How can I provide feedback on a particular song that will provide forward momentum for a songwriter who is graduating or moving to another state?" The best predictor of long-term success and continuation is healthy success and continuation while in your classroom.

WATER: Stevie Wonder's Baby Ruth Candy Bars

Part of your job as a teacher in a classroom where nurturing creativities is priority one is making sure that your students' needs are being met. Sometimes that need a snack. Blind since birth, little Stevie Wonder knew by feel which knob on the Motown Studio A candy machine would deliver a Baby Ruth bar, so staff made sure the nutty nougat was always in the same spot (see Figure 1.3). Baby Ruth remains Stevie's favorite candy bar to this day, and the now-vintage machine—complete

Figure 1.3 Stevie Wonder's Baby Ruth candy bars in a vending machine at Hitsville U.S.A.

with candy bars leftover from the 1960s—remains featured in Hitsville U.S.A., the Motown Museum in Detroit. Wonder could write songs and be inspired when his snack needs were met.

Skill-Building: Part of Your Focus

In order for your students to become good songwriters, they will need some time-honored strategies for how people have written songs. This book taps into the professional working lives of professional songwriters, the working lives of practicing music teachers who have taught songwriting, and the working lives of music teacher educators to work to teach pre-service music teachers to do this. I am partly all of these things in my job as a professor, but I don't have all of the answers. So here I gather many of the best ideas from the best sources that I have used over the years.

Remember foremost that songwriting and creativities, for that matter, resist linear paths. Start with cover songs. Use preexisting forms and write original lyrics. Use improvisation for motivation and inspiration, check out the Middle Ground as I have described it here, then follow the joy of your students. Break down the task of writing a song to:

1. discovering grooves
2. finding harmonic progressions
3. discovering melodies
4. writing lyrics

These are the areas that you will need to help your students with (see Figure 1.4). I will be coming back to these four skill areas throughout the book. Let me unpack what these four look like briefly now.

WATER: Ben Gibbard Treats Songwriting Like "Going to Work"

Death Cab for Cutie front man Ben Gibbard treats songwriting like he's going to work. This is echoed again and again in the literature on creativities in music education (Randles & Burnard, 2022). Gibbard says:

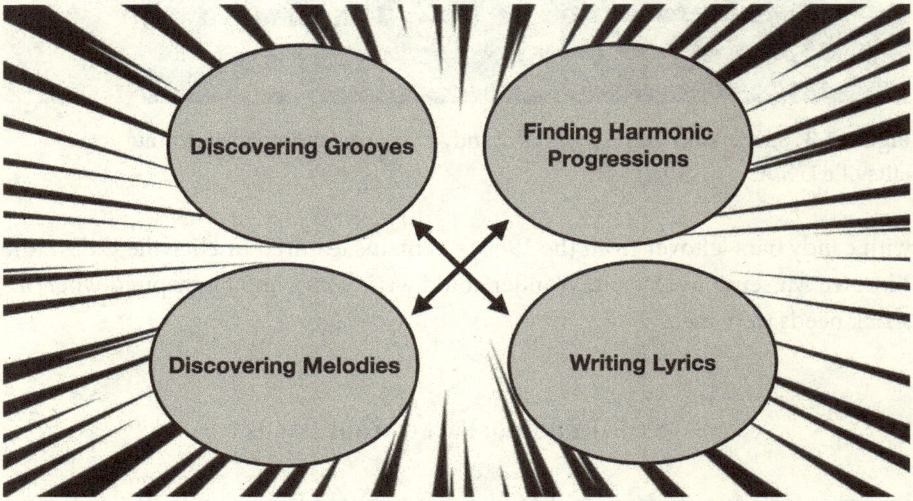

Figure 1.4 Songwriting skills to focus on

I try to keep a very regimented schedule of writing. I treat it like a job. I literally have an office in downtown Seattle and with a small pro-tools rig, a couple of small amps and a piano, and I treat going there like I'm going to work and writing music. It's frustrating that you can't do it when you want to do it.

Gibbard's words about his work schedule push against the romantic notion that you can't control when songs get written, or the idea that having a set time that you write can work—like a set time for a class during a school day! By treating the task of songwriting like a job, an autoworker going to the factory, clocking in, welding quarter panels onto Mustangs on an assembly line, we are able to accomplish our goals. We are able to grow. That is what we want for our students.

A Process

Notice how I did not say "the process." This is "a process." Songwriting is nonlinear and actually resists linearity. That is why checklists and simple assessments tied to national content standards are not a good idea, not when our foremost goal is to water and provide nutrients for growing seeds that we plant and nurture in our classrooms. The ideas suggested here can be intersected with such things, but that is not the reason we do or are interested in them. This is a music thing. It starts with groove.

1. **Discovering Grooves: Improvisation.** There's no substitution for jamming around. Improvisation is the key that unlocks the whole music-making enterprise. You need to allow your students the time that it takes to jam around with ideas, really listen to each other, and direct their music-making and learning in real time.
2. **Finding Harmonic Progressions.** When you are free to mess around through jamming, you come up with particular harmonic progressions that work and sound good to you. You then share those progressions with your band and then jam around with the ideas. Discovering a groove and finding harmonic progressions go hand in hand.
3. **Discovering Melodies.** With a general groove established and some harmonic progressions to hang your hat on, you are ready to play around with melodic ideas. Some people like to hum along and riff on melodic ideas while the band jams. The Ch33rios (a band that I used to work a lot with) tended to write around a table with acoustic instruments, while working on lyrics and melody simultaneously. Sometimes individual members brought in their own more fully fleshed out ideas. They kept their ideas on their phones primarily and shared those ideas via a group text.
4. **Writing Lyrics.** One of the most effective strategies when I'm helping people write songs is to start with *object writing*. You just need a prompt, a seed. "Bad

dreams," "crazy baristas," "pocket lint," and so forth can be prompts that start what is basically a brainstorming session for ideas around these prompts. Set a timer and have them write anything and everything that comes to mind. Lines do not need to rhyme at this stage. You are after just getting as many ideas out there. Generate without the extra layer to being critical. That will come later. At this point you just want to produce as many ideas as you can.

At the end of your object writing time, have the group share their ideas while someone (this can be you at first) takes notes. You will have a page of ideas that will help you write lyrics. Then, go back to your groove, harmonic progressions, and melodic ideas and look at your object writing ideas. Something will emerge in the form of lyrics. Pay attention to the vibe and flavor that emerge. Let their creativity be your guide. Keep good records of what emerges. Take pictures of notebooks and phone screens and keep tracks of those files. Make recordings of your song ideas all during the process. It is easy to forget what you did in prior sessions, so making recordings is key.

WATER: 10 Tips on Songwriting from Bob Dylan

Bob Dylan won a Nobel Prize for Literature in 2016. He is one of the best songwriters of all time. Here are some tips from him on how to write a good song gathered from interviews that he has done with *Rolling Stone*, the *New York Times*, *USA Today*, and the *Song Talk Interview*:

1. The best ones are written quickly
2. Immerse yourself (but don't copy)
3. Keep your ears open
4. Write the songs you want to hear
5. The right environment can bring out a song
6. Sort out your thoughts
7. Access your subconscious
8. Don't think too much
9. Make it yours
10. Follow your path

Doing all of these things won't mean that you will automatically write great songs. However, isn't it nice to know a few tricks about doing it well from someone with good ideas to spare? Which of them makes sense for you today as you write your own songs? How can you use them to help your students write their best songs? As I write this morning, I have *The Philosophy of Modern Song* (Dylan, 2022) open in front of me. It is Dylan's first book on songwriting in the nearly two decades since

Chronicles: Volume 1 (Dylan, 2005). It is cryptic and brilliantly crafted as Dylan writes poetically about 66 songs from the past 100 years of music. Important for you, the practicing music teacher producer, is how Dylan analyzes the songs. Make it a daily practice of listening to and analyzing songs for their organizational structure, lyrical content, musical uniqueness, and propensity for telling stories of the human condition. Dylan does a masterful job of it in this book. Check it out. You won't be disappointed by reading either of the Dylan books on songwriting. There is something there for everyone.

SUNLIGHT: Five-Minute Thinking

Here is a strategy to assist your students in their creative thinking. It goes hand in hand with object writing as an exercise for generating ideas. The idea can be found in *The Innovator's Dictionary* (Buchholz & Aersson, 2020). The strategy relies on timing yourself to do three tasks in five minutes. Here are the tasks:

1. Set goal and task to solve (one minute)
2. Expand and explore (two minutes)
3. Contract and conclude clearly (two minutes)

Phase 1 lasts a minute and deals with the actual question. Phase 2 gives you two minutes to discuss different known and new solutions (idea generation). Phase 3 is the evaluation stage for the idea(s) generated. Remember that idea generation and the evaluation of those ideas are two separate processes.

In a classroom, you might use this strategy to get students to think about a focal point of their song: setting, characters, vibe, emotions, and so on. If you run out of time before they come up with a solution it means that your task or problem was not clearly defined. You as the teacher need to be the timekeeper. You will need to explain why you are doing this—to help them come up with an idea quickly. Just do one of these sessions at a time. Don't give up on the idea of five-minute thinking if it doesn't catch on the first time you do it.

Discovering Grooves: Opening the Door to Their Creativities

When your students improvise, they let their creativity lead. They experiment with rhythm, melody, and learn to listen to each other very well. Jamming is done on the spot, but the roots of being able to jam run deep and require years to nurture. There is really no substitution for it. It takes a considerable amount of time. Improvisation is at the same level of importance as knowing your multiplication tables in the development of your math competency or knowing how to write with a pencil/pen to your writing competency. It is essential. Upon saying it here, I realize that it is one of the first things left out of an education in music. That is so sad. We are starving our students of the magic of music by not giving them space to improvise. We must change how we think and act.

Improvising does the following things for them:

1. It is built on self-expression and emotion and therefore draws it out of them
2. It encourages their creativities by focusing on music in its most natural form
3. It provides a way for even the not-so-great music readers to get an equal chance to create and perform
4. It is a living breathing conduit to originality and authenticity in music (which is why it is among the most important things that we can have them do in our music classes)

Improvisation is the key that unlocks the door to being and becoming a musician. We naturally as small children improvise without effort or even giving it a thought. As time goes on, our music teachers show us by time allotted for various activities that improvisation is less important than note reading. It's like our music teachers forget that many professional musicians around the world don't even know how to read music yet thrive communicating their art through sound to audiences. Sound before the sight of sound. Let's recapture the joy in music-making by reconnecting to what is most important.

I have seen growth in musicianship like you would not believe when students are given a chance to jam with each other regularly. You feed these exercises at the beginning, demonstrating riffs and musical expressive ideas while playing along with them. They then learn way more than the things that you've shown them and set out on a path to learn the music of their heroes. You encourage this activity because you know that it is a natural step in finding their own voice. Through the structure, musical elements, groove, and all other characteristics of their favorite music, students find a well that springs up and spills over into a musical world that is exciting and self-sustaining. That is what we want. Music will be a forever friend to them, a companion to help them live a life well-lived.

WATER: The Decline of Improvisation in Classical Music

Moore (1992) writes of the decline of improvisation in classical music at the end of the 19th century into the beginning of the 20th century. He believes that as improvisation declined as a common practice in the development of musicianship in the academy that teachers, performers, and musicians lost track of it as something that builds essential skills for being and becoming a musician. We still today suffer from this trend. As music teachers, we have a responsibility to all of music to bring it back, put it back where it belongs—the heart of what it means to be musical. Bach was said to have been an EXCELLENT improvisor. We should bring back the centrality of improvisation in music in the music teaching and learning that happens in schools and community centers.

SUNLIGHT: Improvisation Can Change Who You Are

We can learn a lot from the world outside of music about the value of improvisation. Here we learn lessons from theater. In theater improvisation, dialogue and action are made up on the spot. Here are some of the things that you learn by practicing improvisation in the theater realm:[2]

1. You learn to own your own power
2. You learn to embrace your fear
3. You develop better listening skills
4. You learn the value of collaboration
5. You learn to adapt and be agile
6. You learn to build a great ensemble troupe
7. You learn the importance of creativity and discovery
8. You learn to lead and to follow

Now, sit back and look at these points through the lens of music education. Do we want our students to learn their own power, embrace their fears, learn to adapt and be agile, learn to lead and follow? Think about it. Improvisation can take us there. There are so many benefits. It just takes time. Start today.

Finding Harmonic Progressions

Songs are equal parts melody, rhythm, and harmony. You can get to writing good songs from each of these musical areas. It's nice when they come together easily somewhere in the middle. As a teacher you need to make sure that you are giving your students water and sunlight in each of these areas. Harmonic progressions (or chord progressions, said another way) and the rhythmic harmonies that animate them are the musical framework upon which the rest of the musical aspects of the song hang. It is true that some songs bypass harmonic progression at times in favor of riffs of melodic hooks that serve as landmarks for the listener. However, a lot can be gained by trying to understand how harmonies fit together and work in progression to support the other aspects of the song.

In my experience, the students that I work with find and create harmonic progressions when they improvise. Again, they need to have time to improvise in every class session! It is the most important area of development in their journey to become musically independent—our ultimate end goal. As they mess around with harmonies, play around with the harmonic progressions of the songs that they love, alter the harmonic progressions to their own liking, transpose them, and try them out in different inversions; they will stumble upon and own their own progressions. There is no shortcut to knowing your way around the landscape of harmonic progressions. You have to play a lot of different songs (cover songs) to internalize the way that artists use harmonic progression to help them tell a story in a song.

The same harmonic progressions can sound dramatically different when played on different instruments, in different inversions, at different dynamics, in different timbres, and by different performers (with different feel). So how do you know when you have a good one? It will work well with the other aspects of the song, and in so doing create a good vibe that makes you want to hear the song (or play the song) again. We know that music is saturated with I–IV–V chord progression songs. With a harmonic vocabulary that includes those three and ii and vi, you can cover a lot of ground with your harmonic progressions. The I–V–vi–IV chord progression is imprinted in our brains because of songs like "I'm Yours" (Jason Mraz) and "Don't Stop Believing" (Journey). You have to give your students lots of examples of chord progressions to feed their appetite for harmonic progression. Look for these types of lessons throughout this book.

WATER: "Smells Like Teen Spirit"

The song is modeled after a F–B♭–A♭–D♭ chord progression, where the main guitar riff consists of four power chords played in a syncopated sixteenth note strum by front man/guitarist Kurt Cobain. It sounds like the riff of Boston's "More than a Feeling" or The Kingsmen's "Louie Louie." These chords make sense maybe only if you think about how they lie easily under your hands on a guitar neck. You play the F and then move your hand down to the next higher string and play B♭, slide up three frets to A♭ and then, like the F to B♭, you move to the next higher string and play the D♭ chord. The second and fourth chord are a short distance from the first and third chord. Sometimes chord progression fall out of specific instruments. In the case of "Smells Like Teen Spirit" the progression falls out of the guitar (a Fender Mustang, to be precise). I have said in other publications that particular guitars produce particular progressions, riffs, and variations. They are not all alike. They feel different in your hands. Each type of guitar will unlock something else in your musical subconsciousness. The same thing can be said about sitting down at an actual Fender Rhodes organ, a Hammond B3 organ, or a Mellotron. You play differently and you think differently in and through sound.

SUNSHINE: Thinking of Your Own Chord Progression

Here is a process that might work for you as you're trying to think of a harmonic progression. Consider these sequentially . . . or not:

1. Choose an instrument
2. Choose a key
3. Choose to be minor- or major-centric
4. Choose the second chord
5. Choose the feel of your music
6. Add another chord
7. Create a rough demo
8. Try making your progression more interesting by choosing chords out of the key
9. Try to simplify things by choosing fewer chords

How is this helpful? How doesn't it work for you? How would you change the process. Do that! Reflect. Repeat. Reflect. Repeat. [smile]

Discovering Melodies

Melodies might be the most elusive musical building block to try to come to terms with. Melodies of course (1) move up and down as far as pitch is concerned and (2) are propelled forward by some sort of rhythmic cadence, flow, and groove. Melodies are what envelop our lyrics. They are the thing that gets stuck in our ears, the thing that we hum and sing when we lay our heads on our pillows at night. Here are three types of melodies:[3]

1. Chord-based melodies
2. Scale-based melodies
3. Monotone melodies

Let me unpack what each of these are, how they are born, and how to think of them along with the others.

Chord-based Melodies. These types of melodies follow and flow through particular chord changes. The melody notes can often be found within the notes of the chords and move along with the changes. To write a chord-based melody, you play along the chords of the progression that you are working with and hum around with the notes in the chord. In reality you might wander into a scale or mode that works with the harmony that your chord creates, but you are keen to follow the chord progression most of all. Many melodies seem to fall out of playing chords on a particular instrument.

Scale-based Melodies. This variety of melody follows a scalar or modal pattern. The notes come from a particular melodic series. When you sing around in a particular scale or mode, the rhythm, cadence, and flow will animate how you make use of the possible notes of the scale or mode. In practice, it helps to also be making use of a chord progression, but that is not always that case. In fact, there are a number of songs, "Hey Ya!" by Outcast, "Blitzkrieg Bop" by The Ramones, and "De Do Do Do, De Da Da Da" by The Police, that are more or less chant songs in portion. Chord-based and scale-based melodies are close friends and work very well together.

Monotone Melodies. This type of melodic writing is most prominent in hip-hop and hip-hop varieties/crossovers of diverse musical genres. With this variety of melodic writing a rhythmic pattern sung, spoken, or otherwise performed serves as the melody for a section or for the entirety of a song. Where monotone varieties of melodic writing are concerned, the rhythmic aspect of the melody becomes the most important. Monotone melodies can jump out of the other two forms of writing, especially when particular rhythmic and lyrical fluency are present. Good monotone melody writers are lyrical geniuses who pour their imaginative and creative energies into the rhythmic aspect of the craft of melody writing. They are aware of the other two and often move in accordance to sections of the music that tend to be marked by chord-based changes and are made up of scale-based material.

In Practice. Melodies flow out of improvisational practice, jamming, and/or messing around with these three types of melody. Finding a good melody is the result of trying out a bunch of other ideas that didn't work. Just as babies babble and play around with the sound of their voices, we play around with musical melodies—singing and/or playing them on an instrument—until we find something that we can take away and use as building blocks of a song. The earworms start as happy accidents, moments in time that we decided to remember in our ongoing musical improvisations.

WATER: Paul McCartney and "Yesterday"

The song "Yesterday" was written at 57 Wimpole Street, London, where Paul McCartney lived in attic rooms at the top of the family home of his girlfriend, the English actress Jane Asher. Paul says that he wrote it in his sleep: "I woke up with a lovely tune in my head. I thought, That's great, I wonder what that is? There was an upright piano next to me, to the right of the bed by the window. I got out of bed, sat at the piano, found G, found F sharp minor seventh—and that leads you through then to B to E minor, and finally back to G."

He spent some time not quite believing that he had in fact written it. He would play it to everyone he met, asking if they recognized it, thinking maybe it was some obscure old standard. Of course, nobody did. "Eventually it became like handing something to the police. I thought that if no one claimed it after a few weeks then

I would have it." He recalls, "I started to develop the idea: 'Scram-ble-d eggs, da-da da.' I knew the syllables had to match the melody, obviously: 'da-da da,' 'yes-ter-day,' 'sud-den-ly,' 'fun-il-ly,' 'mer-il-ly,' and 'yes-ter-day,' that's good. 'All my troubles seemed so far away.' It's easy to rhyme those 'a's: say, nay, today, away, play, stay, there's a lot of rhymes and those fall in quite easily, so I gradually pieced it together from that journey. 'Sud-den-ly,' and 'b' again, another easy rhyme: e, me, tree, flea, we, and I had the basis of it." So, a tune that started as "Scrambled Eggs" became one of the most-covered songs of all time and one of the most memorable songs in The Beatles catalogue.[4]

SUNLIGHT: 9 Tips for Writing Melodies

Here are nine tips for writing memorable melodies from the Masterclass series:[5]

1. **Follow chords.** Start your writing process by improvising on a set of chord changes, and let your melodies fall out of those chords.
2. **Follow a scale.** Major scales and minor scales form the basis of most pop melodies, but if you want to push further, try a dominant scale, an altered scale, or a mode.
3. **Write with a plan.** Try writing your song's chorus melody first and then work backward. Think about what kind of verse or pre-chorus melodies would best serve the chorus. You can even add an intro section with its own melody that never shows up elsewhere in the song.
4. **Give your melodies a focal point.** A focal point is a high note that a melodic line touches once but never again—or at least not in that section of the song. Make sure that the highest note falls within your range. Sometimes making your focal point the lowest note is the best way to go.
5. **Write stepwise lines with a few leaps.** Most vocal melodies follow stepwise motion; this means that most notes are followed by a note that's only a half step or whole step above or below. Great songwriters then mix in leaps (two whole steps or more), which stand out from the stepwise motion.
6. **Repeat phrases, but change them slightly.** If you come up with a short musical phrase, repeat it, altering the notes or rhythm slightly each time. Try inserting one different note on each repeat, or add some syncopation to the rhythmic pattern.
7. **Experiment with counterpoint.** Instead of writing one single melodic line over a chord progression, write two melodies and interweave them. If you have digital audio workstation (DAW) software on your computer, you can lay down one melodic line and then experiment with a second one layered on top of it.
8. **Put down your instrument.** Writing away from an instrument is a great way to generate creativity or push past writer's block. Try singing vocal lines into a

recorder app on your smartphone. Then, return to your instrument and transcribe what you sang.

9. **Get inspired by your favorite artists.** Analyze your favorite songs and try to identify what it is about their melodies that hooks you. Then, borrow some of their techniques, whether that involves certain scales, leaps, or rhythmic patterns.[6]

Writing Lyrics

There are a lot of ways to approach writing lyrics in your own songwriting practice and in what you do daily in your classroom. After more than 20 years of helping people write songs in K–12 settings and in the music teacher preparation realm, I can say that lyric writing is the most difficult thing for people who come from more traditional music education backgrounds to grasp. It's simply the thing that we do the least in our regular practice. Unless we have experience with creative writing, composing lyrics is something very foreign. Fortunately some people have thought long and hard about lyric writing and have shared their strategies for practice that we can translate into classroom settings. I will start with *Song Maps* by Hawkins (2016).

WATER: Asbury Park, NJ

Bruce Springsteen recalls writing the song "Blinded by the Light" for VH1's Storytellers (2005).[7] He had turned in his first album *Greetings from Asbury Park, N.J.* to record producer Clive Davis of Columbia Records, when they decided that although the material was really great the album didn't have a hit song on it. So, Springsteen locked himself in an apartment above an old abandoned beauty salon in Asbury Park, NJ, and sat in his bed with a rhyming dictionary in one hand and a notebook in the other hand. He recalls that the rhyming dictionary was on fire as people from his life and their circumstances jumped onto the pages of the notebook. A lot of the references are personal, including people he knew or had met on the Boardwalks, or people he had grown up around:

> "Madman drummers bummers"—Vinnie "Mad dog" Lopez, the first drummer in the E Street Band.
>
> "Indians in the summer"—Bruce's little league baseball team as a kid.
>
> "In the dumps with the mumps"—being sick with the mumps.
>
> "Boulder on my shoulder"—a "chip" on his shoulder.
>
> "Some all hot, half-shot, heading for a hot spot, snapping fingers clapping his hands"—Being a "know it all kid growing up, who doesn't really know anything."

"Silicone Sister"—Bruce mentions that this is arguably the first mention of breast implants in popular music—a dancer at one of the local strip joints in Asbury Park.

We learn from the example here of one of the best songwriters of all time that a rhyming dictionary is a good thing to have around as you write songs, that the dictionary itself can turn a song in many different and interesting directions. For certain, teachers can make use of them in classroom settings with students.

SUNLIGHT: Tips for Writing Better Lyrics

Here are some tips for writing better lyrics:[8]

1. **Show, don't tell**: It can be tempting to simply describe to your audience what happened and how you felt about it, but good storytelling suggests that you proceed more subtly. Think of your senses and then use sight, taste, smell, feel, and hearing to describe what is going on in your song.
2. **Make use of imagery**: We use our imagination to create pictures and/or scenes in our minds. Using imagery creates an immersive experience that we take the listener on, a journey through our created life conditions. It helps to draw upon actual lived experience when we do this, of course.
3. **Don't overuse metaphors**: There is a difference between using simplistic metaphors and ones that are more subtle and intentional. When using metaphors, stick to just a few, and make sure they fit the same theme or relate to each other somehow.
4. **Avoid lyrics that are clichés**: One of the worst things you can do for your song is fill it with overused lyrics. What do you want to say? How can you say it in a way that has not already been said? "I love you": "You elevate me" "You complete me" (that one has already been taken) "I delight in you" "You and me = Endless joy," and so forth.
5. **Find new ways to say the same thing**: This is a great tip to use whenever you want your lyrics to be more interesting or captivating than the things that you have already heard. Saying something in a way that people do not normally hear in everyday life grabs the listener's attention.
6. **Try new rhyming schemes**: Mix up your rhyming schemes. We typically use ABAB or AABB. However, you can even create your own rhyming scheme by altering or combining the schemes you already know. Take AABB and turn it into ABCC, for example. The first two lines don't even have to rhyme as long as the last two do. Or take the ABCC structure and repeat it in the next stanza (a group of four lines) to create ABCC ABCC. Experiment with lyric-writing exercises in class. Pose a problem scheme that students have to populate with their own lyrics.

7. **Don't force rhymes:** One of the biggest signs of poor songwriting is forced rhymes. This happens when you set your heart on a perfect rhyme and come up with the rest of the line to help make that rhyme make sense. Resist the temptation of doing that. Maybe you need a different rhyme scheme instead of forcing one that doesn't work.
8. **Prioritize your message:** To avoid frustration with the notion of what your song is going to be about, try to make a short plan that you will try to unpack over the course of a song. When it comes to songwriting it is essential to prioritize the message. What do you want your song to say? Write in prose what your story is going to be about, or write a few lines that you would like to include. Then, build the song around those lines, and use all of the above techniques to turn the prose into lyrics.

Object Writing

One of the best tools that I know of to help jump-start the creative process around songwriting is to engage your students in object-writing sessions where they free write around a topic, an idea, a sentiment, a person, a place, a thing, an action, and so on, for a timed duration. I set the timer for five minutes when I object write with students, and ten minutes when I do it myself in practice. Five minutes is generally enough time for them to come up with interesting talking points, but not too long that they start to find more interesting things to do with the time.

It does not matter what that thing is actually that you have them write around. What is important is the process of coming up with interesting descriptions of the objects being studied. One of the most interesting songwriting sessions that I did with students was on the object "pocket lint." "It's always there." "How does it get there?" "It feels funny." "It smells fresh." These ideas around the object then become the building blocks to begin thinking of what your song might be about. Object writing precedes any notion of rhyming scheme or overall theme. It is an essential well (the water variety) that you will locate through the process of object writing and return to when looking for inspiration for what your song is about. You will look to the results of your object-writing sessions to help you create rhyming schemes that are new and innovative for you and your listeners.

Object writing is too easily skipped by songwriters who think that they have to hurry up and cut to the chase. My undergraduate students are notorious for skipping this step and cutting straight to writing lines that rhyme. They only cheat themselves when doing this. In your classroom, make it a general part of practice to object write around interesting objects. Have your students choose them. That is good fun. The pocket lint idea came from a first-grade student.

They will guide and inspire your journey with object writing. It is as important for songwriting with lyrics as improvisation is to the entire enterprise of being a musician—including of course being a musician where creativities are concerned.

Song Maps

Song maps are ready-made plans that you can use when writing your songs and helping your students write theirs. What follows are some of the song maps that I have used with my students, starting with a general lyric writing order that commercial writers tend to work within. I have used *Song Maps* by Hawkins (2016) for years to help me help my undergraduate students write better songs. The pre-service music teachers that I work with have an idea about musical elements like harmony, melody, and phrasing from their other classes in the school of music where I work. However, lyric writing is something brand new altogether. Therefore, it requires the most help from us! Here is a lyric writing order:

<u>Lyric Writing Order</u>
Chorus (ideally identical each time)
Pre-Chorus (if appropriate)
Verse 1 (maybe a double verse)
Pre-Chorus 2 (if not the same as Pre-Chorus 1)
Verse 2
Bridge
Outro

People don't stick to this order all of the time. It is, however, a good place for you to start when teaching people how to write songs. The chorus tends to be (but isn't always) the main point of the song. It's the part that keeps coming back—the punchline. Many times the title is in the chorus. Hawkins (2016) suggests that a lot of songs are written in a 2D style.

<u>2D Writing</u>
Here is what we tend to start with:
Verse 1—Idea 1
Chorus—Title
Verse 2—Idea 1, different words
Chorus 2—Title
Bridge—Idea 1, different words again
Chorus 3—Title

While 2D lyric writing can work much of the time, Hawkins (2016) suggests that we can do better in thinking about lyric writing as having a narrative arc. We can think of our songs in terms of 3D writing:

3D Writing
Verse 1—Idea 1
Chorus—Title
Verse 2—Idea 2
Chorus 2—Title
Bridge—Idea 3
Chorus 3—Title

Within this train of thought and practice, there are seven different kinds of songs that we can write. Here is a list of them:

Tension/Response
Problem/Declaration
Timezones
Places
Roles
Twist
Literal/Figurative

Understanding these seven different song maps can give us a place to start when planning for the original songs of our students. They can actually be separated into individual units, lessons, or weeks of the semester, depending on what works best for your school culture. I will list each of them here in this introductory chapter, and then I will bring them back individually with the various lesson seeds, water, and sunlight that I present here throughout the book.

Map 1: **Tension/Response (Ex. Kelly Clarkson "Breakaway").** Here is the basic layout of this map:

Verse 1—How the tension is sensed
Chorus 1—The response
Verse 2—How the response is sensed
Chorus2—The response
Bridge—How I feel about the response
Chorus 3—The response

In the plan for this song, you introduce some sort of tension that is responded to in the chorus. The 3D nature of the map suggests that you state how the tension is sensed in Verse 2 and how you feel about the response in the bridge. Listen to Kelly Clarkson's "Breakaway" for an idea of how this plays out in lyrical form.

WATER: Avril Lavigne, Kelly Clarkson, and "Breakaway"

While Kelly Clarkson is known as the person who brought "Breakaway" to the public, it was Avril Lavigne along with Matthew Gerrard and Bridget Benanate who wrote the song. Lavigne worked it up for her debut album in 2002, but it was not seen fit for release from a production standpoint and so was passed along to Clarkson. The song is autobiographical from Lavigne's perspective but was also owned as being personally accurate for Clarkson. It's about a girl who leaves home and discovers herself, spreads her "wings and learns how to fly." The writers and Clarkson as she delivers the performance bring you into a world of tension experienced by the heroic figure in the song:

Grew up in a small town
And when the rain would fall down
I'd just stare out my window
Dreaming of what could be
And if I'd end up happy
I would pray

Trying hard to reach out
But when I tried to speak out
Felt like no one could hear me
Wanted to belong here
But something felt so wrong here
So I prayed (I would pray)
I could breakaway

Songs that tap into universal pockets of emotion such as in this song tend to be widely received. Have you ever felt trapped in your present ordinary everyday world? This is a song for anyone who has ever felt unappreciated.

Map 2: **Problem/Declaration (Ex. Miley Cyrus "The Climb").** Here is the basic layout of this map:

Verse 1—The problem
Chorus 1—Declaration
Verse 2—The response
Chorus2—Declaration
Bridge—What it means
Chorus 3—Declaration

In this type of song plan a problem is introduced in Verse 1. In Verse 2 a response is made. The bridge is where we state what it all means. The choruses are for the place where a specific important and essential declaration is made. Have a listen to Miley Cyrus's "The Climb" for an example of how this plays out in real time.

WATER: A Song for Hannah Montana

"The Climb" is a song written by Jessi Alexander and Jon Mabe, and produced by John Shanks. It was recorded and made famous by Miley Cyrus and the *Hannah Montana* movie (2009). However, it was not originally written for the movie. Co-writer Alexander conceived the song's melody while driving to the home of song-writing partner Mabe. When reaching Mabe's home they developed a song about overcoming life's obstacles inspired by their personal struggles in the music industry. Alexander referred to the process as a form of "therapy" and recalled:

> I was just driving to work one day. It's just a typical day, nothing really special about that day. And I just had this melody in my head. And I couldn't get to my co-writer Jon Mabe or my guitar fast enough because I just wanted to play what I was hearing. And, you know, we just kinda put it down pretty fast and didn't really think anything about it. The lyrics kinda started to come, I think for both of us, being kinda underdogs in the business. My co-writer was a songplugger, just turned songwriter, and I'd had record deals and ups and downs in the music business. I think for both of us, we just came from a place of, you know, "it's not a race."

When a song is ready, it's ready, and like Bob Dylan has told us before, the best songs sometimes are born quickly.

Map 3: **Timezones (Ex. Five for Fighting "100 Years").** Here is the basic layout of this map:

Verse 1—Timezone 1—The story begins
Chorus 1—Title
Verse 2—Timezone 2—The Story moves on
Chorus 2—Title
Bridge—Timezone 3/Payoff
Chorus 3—Title

In this type of song map a story is told in the verses of the song and the bridge is the payoff of the song. The title is in the chorus that is the main idea or sentiment of the song. "100 Years" by Five for Fighting is a great example of a timezones song!

WATER: John Ondrasik's Song about Aging

This might be the quintessential aging song for me. Five for Fighting's "100 Years" gets so many things right. First, the songwriter takes us to our adolescence:

I'm 15 for a moment
Caught in between 10 and 20

And I'm just dreaming
Counting the ways to where you are

Who is the person that the writer is referring to in the line "to where you are". We don't know, and are left to wonder. That leaves the door up to interpretation, and in songwriting that's usually a good thing.

I'm 22 for a moment
And she feels better than ever
And we're on fire
Making our way back from Mars

This is a young love verse and the joys of self-discovery.

I'm 33 for a moment
I'm still the man, but you see I'm a "they"
A kid on the way, babe
A family on my mind

A family enters in the writer's 30s. Life is moving on, with "I" becoming "they."

I'm 45 for a moment
The sea is high
And I'm heading into a crisis
Chasing the years of my life

The thing about aging is that we will always have regret. That makes this song universal. If we age (instead of the alternative) we will have regrets. This is good writing. It taps into a universal quality of living.

Map 4: **Places (Ex. Taylor Swift "Love Story").** Here is the basic layout of this map:

Verse 1—Place 1—The story begins
Chorus 1—Title
Verse 2—Place 2—The story moves on
Chorus2—Title
Bridge—Place 3/Payoff
Chorus 3—Title

In this type of song, the story begins in Verse 1, continues in Verse 2, and we experience the payoff in the bridge. The title of the song and main point is in the chorus. Each verse represents a different place. Have a listen to Taylor Swift's "Love Story" for ideas about how this map works in practice.

WATER: Romeo and Juliet for Real

Taylor Swift recalls the origin of the song "Love Story": "It's actually about a guy that I almost dated," she said. "But when I introduced him to my family and my friends, they all said they didn't like him. All of them! For the first time, I could relate to that Romeo-and-Juliet situation where the only people who wanted them to be together were them." So, it's a true story that she tells in the lines of the song.[9] At the time, she was only 19 years old. She recalls it as being one of the most romantic songs that she's ever written. So your students can write on sensitive subject matter such as love in a way that can be important for them now and for a very long time into the future.

We were both young when I first saw you
I close my eyes and the flashback starts
I'm standin' there
On a balcony in summer air
See the lights, see the party, the ball gowns
See you make your way through the crowd
And say, "Hello"
Little did I know

That you were Romeo, you were throwin' pebbles
And my daddy said, "Stay away from Juliet"
And I was cryin' on the staircase
Beggin' you, "Please don't go," and I said

Romeo, take me somewhere we can be alone
I'll be waiting, all there's left to do is run
You'll be the prince and I'll be the princess
It's a love story, baby, just say, "Yes"

Map 5: **Roles (Ex. Third Day "I Need a Miracle").** Here is the basic layout of this map:

Verse 1—Role 1
Chorus 1—Title
Verse 2—Role 2
Chorus 2—Title
Bridge—Role 3/Payoff
Chorus 3—Title

In this type of song, each verse represents a different role of the main character or characters in the narrative. The bridge is a special place where the payoff might occur. The title is repeated in the choruses. Have a listen to Third Day's "I Need a Miracle" for an example of this song map in practice.

WATER: A Literal Miracle

According to Third Day frontman Mac Powell, the idea for "I Need a Miracle" came from a post-concert meeting with a New Jersey couple. They told them a story of their son and how he had been depressed and drove deep into the woods planning to kill himself. He turned on the radio and heard "Cry Out to Jesus" (from Third Day's 2005 album *Wherever You Are*), which gave him encouragement to keep going. In this case hearing a song literally saved his life.

Verse 2:
He lost his job and all he had in the fall of '09
Now he feared the worst, that he would lose his children and his wife
So he drove down deep into the woods and thought he'd end it all
And prayed, "Lord above, I need a miracle"

Verse 3:
He turned on the radio to hear a song for the last time
He didn't know what he was looking for even what he'd find
The song he heard gave him hope and strength to carry on
And on that night, they found a miracle
They found a miracle

Chorus:
Well no matter who you are and no matter what you've done
There will come a time when you can't make it on your own
And in your hour of desperation
Know you're not the only one, praying
Lord above, I need a miracle
I need a miracle

Map 6: **Twist (Ex. Michael Bublé "It's a Beautiful Day")**. Here is the basic layout of this map:

Verse 1—Meaning 1
Chorus 1—Title
Verse 2—Meaning 2
Chorus2—Title
Bridge—Payoff
Chorus 3—Title

This type of song uses the bridge as the payoff and each verse to tell different meanings that contribute to the narrative arc of the story. The title is in the choruses, as in a number of the other song maps. Have a listen to the twist idea in practice by listening to Michael Bublé's "It's a Beautiful Day."

WATER: Better When She's Gone

Bublé wrote the song with his longtime co-writer and musical director Alan Chang and his producer Bob Rock, who was also responsible for his *Call Me Irresponsible*, *Crazy Love*, and Christmas albums. He recalls: "I thought this is a great concept," he added. "I am going to write this song about a guy whose girlfriend thinks she's the greatest and dumps him. And he realizes that once she is gone, his life gets so much better."[10] Bublé told *Parade* magazine that he considers the song to be a "revenge" track. "Yeah, it's revenge! I wanted to write a song that empowered anyone going through that and give them hope," he said. See if you can understand the payoff.

> I don't know why
> You think that you could hold me
> When you couldn't get by by yourself
> And I don't know who
> Would ever want to tear the seam of someone's dream
> Baby, it's fine, you said that we should just be friends
> While I came up with that line and I'm sure
> That it's for the best
> If you ever change your mind, don't hold your breath
> 'Cause you may not believe
> That baby, I'm relieved, hmm
> When you said goodbye, my whole world shines

Map 7: **Literal Figurative (Ex. Kelsea Ballerini "Peter Pan").** Here is the basic layout of this map:

> Verse 1—Literal
> Chorus 1—Title
> Verse 2—Figurative
> Chorus2—Title
> Bridge—Payoff
> Chorus 3—Title

This type of song type plays on our conceptions of literal and figurative, flipping back and forth between them across the verses of the song. The title is repeated in choruses. There is typically a payoff in the bridge.

I have seen these maps work as places to start with countless students in countless classes. Knowledge of them will be helpful throughout this book as I provide you with seeds, water, and sunlight to aid in the creative processes of you and your students.

WATER: Off to Neverland!

"Peter Pan" is a country pop song about lost love. It is known as one of Kelsea Ballerini's most emotional ballads. The song has been noted by critics for showcasing a greater emotional depth than Ballerini's previous releases in terms of both lyrical complexity and performance excellence.

> Verse 1:
> The smile, the charm, the words, the spark
> Everything, you had it
> I guess I had a I heart
> 'Cause boy I let you have it
> You said I was your only
> I never thought you'd leave me lonely
>
> Verse 4:
> And you're always gonna fly away, just because you know you can
> You're never gonna learn there's no such place as a Neverland
> You don't understand
> You'll never grow up (oh, you'll never grow up)
> You're never gonna be a man

Ballerini does an excellent job of mashing the figurative and literal together so that you have to think of which one she's trying to build on at any particular moment. This works very well for her in this song that tore up the country music charts when it was released in 2015.

Assignments built around teaching each of these various song maps should be developed. Use them as a template from which to build lyrics that tell a story through song.

The Addiction Formula

Friedemann Findeisen writes (2015) in his book of the same name as this section that we should write songs on the basis of an addiction formula that he states has two parts:

1. Gratification: Getting something that hooks you.
2. Anticipation: Waiting for more gratification.

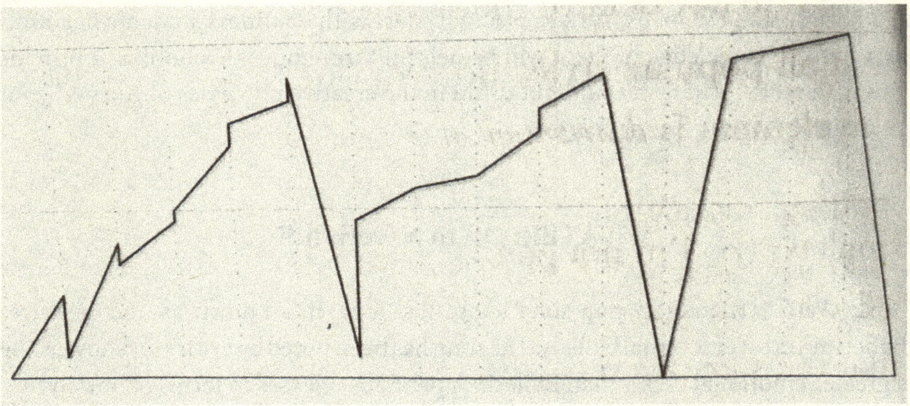

Figure 1.5 Energy curves across a song

Good songs then move between these two things: anticipation and gratification. The absence of gratification means that we are anticipating its return. Both of these terms' functions proceed from an understanding that there is a governing principle of *energy* at play in all songs. Findeisen (2015) writes that it is the task of songwriters/producers to distribute the energy across the song in a way that plays on our sense of gratification and anticipation. The energy level of a song rises and falls across its timeline. The moments of highest energy tend to be choruses. Moments of lower energy tend to be verses that function well as anticipatory phases.

See Figure 1.5 for a visual representation of the energy curves that Findeisen (2015) writes about in his work. He provides a blank page in the back of his book that can be photocopied and used in class as a prompt for students to write their own energy curves. For visual learners, this will be very helpful as they consider the energy trajectory of their song. It functions as a way to get into their minds as well with regard to their creative process. Consider using these as part of your toolkit for helping students write better songs.

In terms of composition and composition pedagogy, we sometimes think of the terms "tension" and "release." Tension certainly works well in most settings. Stories have tension in them. We might think of tension as somewhat of an analog to energy. It isn't the same term, but tension is a descriptive word for describing what happens as far as the distribution of energy is concerned across a song. Instead of "release" or the absence of tension, Findeisen (2015) uses the term "hype" to describe what he calls the *relative energy level*. Hype is altered abruptly and happens every five to eight measures. Findeisen writes that if your song were a car, hype would be the gears. In other words, hype moves the song.

There are a number of things that can influence hype. They are, among other things:

1. arrangement (more instruments equals more hype)
2. part-writing (an instrument playing louder increases hype)
3. rhythm (intensifying the rhythm of a passage increases hype)

Tension can be thought of as the accelerator pedal that drives the engine that engages the gears. A number of musical elements can affect the tension in a song:

1. harmony
2. part-writing
3. rhythm
4. production

The energy curve of a song is created by tension working with hype. With this idea in mind, you can map out the energy curves of a song.

Findeisen (2015) also uses terminology from screenwriting to talk about how songs tell stories. He does it like this:

1. Act I—Set-Up
2. Act II—Confrontation
3. Act III—Resolution

This basic three-part structure reminds me of *The Hero's Journey* that I have liked to describe in my work through the years (Randles, 2020). It is based on a three-part progression of:

1. Separation
2. Initiation
3. Return

The fact that some stories over time have endured more so than others says something about the quality and character of those stories. Joseph Campbell, a professor of literature at Sarah Lawrence College in New York, studied comparative mythology and comparative religion. His book *The Hero with a Thousand Faces* (2008) has influenced artists, screenwriters, and scholars from diverse backgrounds since its first publication. It can help us write better songs.

The plight of the hero in following his or her bliss is very similar to the life of the practicing songwriter. Campbell identifies the monomyth, a cycle that follows the basic pattern: separation, initiation, and return. Heroes leave the normal world for a special world where they are tested and tried. Eventually, they return to the ordinary world transformed in some way. Campbell's work is most usefully interpreted by Vogler for professional writers (2007) (see Figure 1.6).

Every song contains characters who can serve as heroes. We become concerned with their well-being to the point that we care about their lives in the ordinary world. We sympathize with them as we have felt stuck in the ordinary world and have longed for a call to adventure ourselves. We understand what it means to cross the threshold into new worlds (relationships, new places, new experiences as we get older, etc.). There is an uncertainty to our success that is inevitable . . . and it also

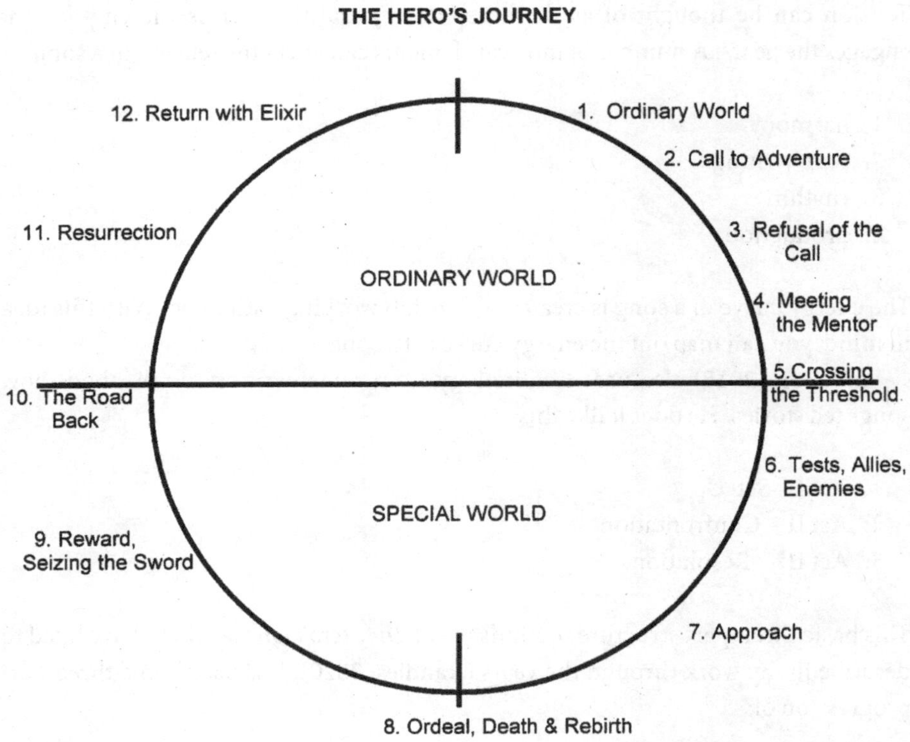

Figure 1.6 The hero's journey

makes for a good story. When we (or the characters in our songs) succeed, we (they) receive a reward that changes the story, seals the deal, and/or breaks new ground in some way. Heroes are changed and return to their ordinary worlds in much better places than they were before. That type of resurrection is what we want. Indeed, that is what the world needs and what good songs can give them.

Lessons from Jeff Tweedy

Wilco frontman Jeff Tweedy wrote a wonderful book that was released during the pandemic called *How to Write One Song* (Tweedy, 2020). It is full of wisdom that I will be bringing you in part throughout the pages of this book. You should go right to the source at some point and get your hands on that book because it is very good. Tweedy suggests, and I will echo this over and over across the pages of this book, that songwriting is a habit—something that people should do every day like going to work. When you make the things that I talk about here the daily regimen of your classroom, over time your students will become really good songwriters.

Tweedy champions the following exercises to develop our lyric-writing skills:

1. Use word exercises to loosen your mind up to creative use of words, lists of nouns and verbs
2. Hum a melody over and over and then open up a page of a book and sing bits of the words of the book to your melody until you find some words that you like
3. Print some words that you have been working on. Cut up the words into phrases or words and then creatively arrange the words in some different order
4. Make a list of nouns and adjectives. Same as Exercise 1, borrow from each list to create some pairings in lyric form
5. Record some of your conversations with people. Analyze what you said and consider borrowing some of the language and style within your songs
6. Create lists of rhyming words that are unattached to songs
7. Write from someone else's perspective—not your own

I write each of these strategies into lessons that appear over the course of this book as seeds. There is so much wisdom in these strategies for getting outside of ourselves with language. Tweedy writes in such a conversational way that draws me into reading his books. He also has a wonderful memoir called *Let's Go (So We Can Get Back): A Memoir of Recording and Discording with Wilco, Etc.* (2019) that is full of stories about how songs were born. Tweedy writes books like he writes songs—and I would imagine how he converses with friends. He's honest and forthcoming. That's a wonderful quality to develop as human beings who would like to share stories in song form!

Tweedy has other suggestions for being and becoming a songwriter that I have taken into consideration when writing this book:

1. Become a listener of music on a grand scale. There is no shortcut or substitution for continuously taking in new music through careful listening.
2. Set a timer when you are writing. Coming up with ideas on a time crunch can help you focus and complete your big projects.
3. Loosen your judgment of yourself. It is okay to not be perfect.
4. Look for chord progressions, samples, and melodies that you can steal and use in your songs.

These suggestions will make their way into Part I of this book on starting with cover songs. We all stand on the backs of giants—our heroes in the world of storytelling through song. We have to study them: beg, borrow, and steal . . . always giving credit where credit is due. This is how every songwriter who has ever written a song got started. They were inspired to write by hearing and performing songs that they love. We will start there in Part I.

Sweden and Popular Music: A Model for Music Education

The country of Sweden has become a hotbed for songwriting and production talent in popular music over the past 30 years, cranking out number 1 hit after number 1 hit across that span. Johansson (2020) calls it the "music miracle." Max Martin is the most prolific of the songwriter/producers to come from the country and is ranked number three of all time for number 1 hits, outdone only by John Lennon and Paul McCartney in that category. That's some pretty amazing company to be in! He has written songs for Britney Spears, Backstreet Boys, NSYNC, P!nk, Taylor Swift, The Weeknd, and especially Katy Perry (see Figure X). Sweden has been a model of what focused and sustained energy in a particular arena can mean for global prominence and success for a country. Johansson (2020) builds on three areas of theory when explaining the success of Swedish songwriters/producers. They are (1) the global circulation of music; (2) a favorable reputation in the global music industry; and (3) a global-local hybrid. Let me unpack how these might relate to music education at this point in time.

Global Circulation of Music

Sweden. Different aspects of the music-making process are being delivered by people in different parts of the world, where it might have happened in one geographical location only decades earlier. Musical ideas and particular sounds have places of origin that are shared by people everywhere in constant "feedback loops" (Johansson, 2020, p. 5). Every music-listening human being on the planet has the ability to internalize these stylistic sources of inspiration and adopt them or use them meaningfully in their own work. Johansson (2020) writes that people within particular areas develop reputations for being able to do things that people around the world borrow, adapt, and assimilate.

Music Education Practice. Individual schools can be thought of as places where innovative music teaching and learning happens. Teachers can be thought of as individuals who create classes, performances, and recordings of students' original music. The reputation of particular teachers can be and will be seen more and more as music education grows songwriting's place among the musical things that students do in school. A "feedback loop" of our own will develop from school to school as particular schools and regions create music with a local as well as global flavor.

Favorable Reputation

Sweden. Sweden has turned into a place where major artists go to collaborate with songwriters and to record their music with producers. It was not always this way in Sweden. When ABBA took the world by storm in the 1970s, winning Sweden's first

Eurovision music competition in 1974, Sweden was thrust into the international Pop music spotlight. That success carried into the 1980s and early 1990s with bands like Roxette and Ace of Bass. Johansson (2020) suggests that this success was furthered in part by ABBA's choice to sing their song "Waterloo" in English instead of Swedish in 1974. While not accepted but quite a large portion of Swedish society, ABBA's success inspired the next generation of singer-songwriters and producers there.

Music Education Practice. In every major curricular turn in the history of American Music Education, there are early adopters and late adopters (Mark & Gary, 2007). The Wind Band movement as a part of the early industrial revolution period is full of stories of how wind bands came to be in schools. Motivated to sell instruments, Conn and Selmer sold the idea of contests and competitions to see which school band was the best. They invented the required list, march, and selected number idea in the 1920s. Fast-forward to the early 2000s and the Modern Band movement and you can see the same thing—early adopters and late adopters. The constant though is that we changed our practice. Early adopters are more known and have an esteemed reputation for having seen the potential and benefits for students that the newer curricular innovations would bring.

A Global-Local Hybrid

Sweden. In Sweden a particular kind of pop music was born that was global and at the same time uniquely Swedish. The world loved lines like "Hit me baby one more time," from the song "Baby One More Time," written by none other than Sweden's Max Martin. What does that line mean, though? It sounds a little like domestic violence. Why are the lyrics in a pop song? Well, the answer to this question might be found in the use of English as a second language. Does "hit me baby one more time" mean the same to a Swedish writer as it does a North American one? Hmmm . . . Well, there's something about it that the world liked. It was a number 1 hit in 1999. That song is only one of the 25 number 1 hits that Martin has written in his lifetime. Do you know the others? Take some time and dig a little deeper into what can be learned from the country of Swedish popular music.

Music Education Practice. As you introduce songwriting to your classes, because you are going to be shepherding the collection of music in your classes, your school will develop a unique sound that will be recognizable in certain ways. In much the same way that there was a sound to Sun Studios in Memphis and Motown Studio A in Detroit, there will be a sound to your school. You can and might very well become a Max Martin kind of figure in your town, in your school, in your region of the United States. This is the most exciting time in the history of music to be a music teacher (Randles, 2022). Dig in and see where your own songwriting and music production skills can take you. The end will most likely be a music reality in 50 years that looks back at this period as the time when songwriting and music production entered the list of ubiquitous school music offerings.

A Few More Big Ideas before Getting Started

Keep a Journal

Errico (2022) suggests that keeping a songwriting journal is the most important thing that budding songwriters can do. It is the well that you will keep coming back to day after day as you come up with ideas for work. I have been keeping journals since I started my master's degree in 2003. In the pages of my journals you can find ideas that are years ahead of making their way into published papers and books. Drawings line the pages of my journals that later become much more refined and end up in some sort of published form. Songwriting is like this too. You sketch all kinds of ideas, object write, pair words, collect metaphors, and write prose, poetry, and some nonsense. Journaling is essential. Start one yourself and have each of your students start one. There's no substitution for doing this, really. We make voice memos and sometimes jot ideas down on napkins and letter envelopes, but your songwriting journal will be the essential tool in your tool song-crafting kit.

Study the Mechanics

It is time to start carefully studying the songs of your heroes. It is the primary way that you learn how to write songs that are personally meaningful to you. Within the structure of the musical elements of your favorite songs are the building blocks of songs that will be personally meaningful to you. Part I of this book (the next section) is full of ideas for studying the songs that you love so that you can cover them. Understanding why you love the ways that your heroes craft their songs goes a long way toward your being able to do the same. How do they group words? What sorts of imagery do they evoke with their lyrical content? Where do their melodic fragments come from? Can you replicate them on an instrument? How are their songs arranged? What gets added/subtracted on the verses/choruses? Which harmonies do they use? Are there catchy riffs? Where do those come from? How long are there songs? How quickly do the songs move into the chorus? What do they do for introductions/outros? There are so many things to study in the music of our favorite artists. We just have to get started.

Get Help from People Who Are Smarter than You

We are constantly on the lookout for ideas about how to write better songs. There are a plethora of good tips from books that have come out over the past ten years or so on how to do this. In this book, I have brought together many of them in a way that will be very helpful to you and your students. Discovering new ways of approaching the daily practice of songwriting is never-ending and endlessly rewarding. I'm hoping that this book will provide the best place for you to go for the day-to-day practice and teaching practice of songwriting. I have no doubt that if we were in the same room today, working on our own songs, I would learn something from you about how to do what I do better. You will learn SO much from your students. They will be your constant daily teacher.

Keep Trying to Figure Out "Why?"

The pursuit of "why?" is never-ending. Why do I respond the way I do to this song that I love? How much of why I love it is wrapped up in the memories that attached themselves to my subconscious when I heard it for the first time? What about this music lit up my life like a 4,000-Watt bulb because of musical elements that I can study and replicate? Why do I salivate every time I hear a particular guitar timbre (Pavlov's guitar effects)? Are there particular production elements that would help me write better in the style of my favorite songwriters? Songwriting and production are very close allies these days, and we need to do them both to be able to make it as independent songwriters. Songwriting is one of the final frontiers in music education at the moment. It is the cutting edge in many ways. Being and becoming better songwriters is one of the most important tasks on our collective tables at the moment. It is worth our best efforts to understand for ourselves and our posterity. This is so exciting to me. I hope that you can use this book to help you and your students discover pathways to songwriting, to grow a beautiful curriculum that is wild and strong, able to withstand the test of time. Let's work together to achieve this goal!

Resources Worth Exploring

Source	Expertise	URL
Song Exploder	The creative process of songwriting along with production	https://songexploder.net/netflix
VH1 Storytellers	Chronicles the songwriting process of some of music's most iconic artists	https://www.amazon.com/Welcome-Vh1-Storytellers-Various-Artists/dp/B00004STQB
This Is Pop	Recounts some of the most important waves of popular music creation	https://www.imdb.com/title/tt14155414/
Amazing Grace	Here's the story of Aretha Franklin and her 1972 iconic performance	https://www.npr.org/2018/11/14/667440842/aretha-franklin-touches-the-infinite-in-the-long-delayed-film-amazing-grace
Montage of Heck	The story of Kurt Cobain and his creative journey	https://www.imdb.com/title/tt4229236/
Homecoming	The creative process leading up to Beyoncé's Coachella performance	https://www.imdb.com/title/tt10147546/

PART I
COVERING SONGS

2

Borrowing from Our Heroes

WATER: St. Vincent's Musical Heroes

Annie Clark, also known as St. Vincent, is one of rock 'n' roll's shape shifters in the same vein as David Bowie. Her musical influences are far-reaching: Miles Davis, Steely Dan, experimental rock, chamber rock, electropop, soft rock, and cabaret jazz. She works the way Bowie did to be uncategorizable, which I suppose puts her in a special category of uncategorizable musical artists. Her music is noted for its complex arrangements utilizing a wide array of instruments. St. Vincent is the recipient of various accolades, including three Grammy Awards. Study your heroes. You, like Annie Clark, will find yourself there.

SUNLIGHT: Think about the Elements

Music exists at one level as a collection of elements. Think about the elements as they pertain to your musical heroes as a way of understanding your favorite songs. Understanding the elements through your favorite music will prime you for writing your best songs.

- Sound (overtone, timbre, pitch, amplitude, duration)
- Melody
- Harmony
- Rhythm
- Texture
- Structure/form
- Expression (dynamics, tempo, articulation)

How do these elements each play out in the music of your heroes? What is the progression of their development as artists? Have they evolved? Where did they start? Are there pivot points in their style trajectory? What sort of musical environment influenced them initially? How about now? Many of these clues can be found in VH1 documentaries and other internet content. Have you seen the *Masterclass* series?

Growing Songwriting. Clint Randles, Oxford University Press. © Oxford University Press 2024.
DOI: 10.1093/oso/9780197693216.003.0002

It All Starts with the Music We Love

As a music teacher in Michigan, I coached one rock band at a time. Students came to me for guitar lessons that would always start with learning the music that they love—the riffs, the chord progressions, and the timbral choices that created the foundation of songs that inspired them. These ventures would sometimes lead to their singing particular songs that we were working on, and other times not. In the case of one particular student, we had worked on some cover songs and dabbled with an original song that he could not actually sing and play at the same time. We multitrack-recorded him playing the guitar track, and then followed with recording him doing the vocal part. As it turned out, he ended up being a finalist in a state songwriting competition, which meant that he would need to perform the song live.

I quickly accessed my music teacher skill set. I taught K–12 music at a school in Michigan, and so had access and knowledge of around 700 musicians (K–12), including the general music students whom I taught at the elementary level. I decided with his permission to recruit a singer for a band that he would assemble from among his friends. I chose a fourth-grade female vocalist who was a part of a choir that I taught as well as being in general music class with me. The decision was not all that popular with the fifth-grade boys that made up the band. She was a fourth grader . . . AND a girl . . . Two strikes. However, she joined the band, performed with them at the state music education conference, and just recently informed me that she had begun a master's in vocal music performance degree at the University of Michigan—she was really good, I could see that very early on!

A lot of great things are possible in our musical lives when we start covering our favorite songs. The pathway of working up a song is lined with hurdles both technically and musically that need to be jumped over. What key works best for our voice? If we are playing guitar, do we need to use a capo? When do we copy a song note for note, and when do we take artistic liberty in realizing our own unique version? Cover songs are a gateway into the world of songwriting. They are also good in and of themselves. Someone need not become a songwriter for them to glean positive and incredibly meaningful experiences from the process of covering songs. Let me start this chapter with a discussion of some key points that you should have for students when you are helping them work up cover songs.

WATER: Elvis Presley's Musical Influences

The music of one of pop music's most popular artists of all time, Elvis Presley, was heavily influenced by African American blues, Christian gospel, and Southern country. He was most inspired by blues, gospel, and rhythm-and-blues, being a regular listener to Memphis radio shows hosted by local disc jockeys B. B. King and Rufus Thomas, who both sang live during their radio broadcasts. He was a consummate student of these musics: begging, borrowing, and yes . . . stealing it at times. Some of Elvis's biggest musical influences were:

1. Sister Rosetta Tharpe (the "Godmother of Rock 'n' Roll")
2. Little Richard (the "Architect of Rock 'n' Roll")
3. B. B. King (the "King of the Blues")
4. Jimmie Rogers (the "Father of Country Music")
5. Fats Domino (the "Real King of Rock 'n' Roll")

Notice that only one of these people is White. The person whom many remember as the "King of Rock 'n' Roll" was a White version of his favorite Black artists. He studied them. He copied them. He wanted to be just like them. Make a list of your influences and then do the same.

SUNLIGHT: Daily Listening

What will you do to reinforce the daily listening routine of your students? You will have to model it yourself, for sure. Here are some tips to get out of your same old listening habits:[1]

1. Listen to streaming services that give you things to listen to based on unique algorithms: Spotify, Apple Music, Pandora Radio, and so on.
2. Check out music review websites:
   a. Pitchfork: They write reviews on mainstream and indie artists, which is the perfect way to diversify your listening habits.
   b. *Atwood* magazine: Each Friday, *Atwood* staff shares what they have been listening to that week and compile lists into an article detailing the intricacies of the music and how it impacts them.
   c. The Luna Collective: They produce a quarterly editorial magazine and consistent online content that spotlight young, lesser-known artists.
3. Here are some music review YouTube and TikTok channels:
   a. The Needle Drop: Anthony Fantano creates music review videos on a range of genres from rock to R&B. His sarcastic, dry-humored personality paired with his expert analyses of albums makes watching this enjoyable and insightful regarding new albums.
   b. Mostley Music: This TikTok account is dedicated to giving music recommendations from artists that the youngest generation would want to listen to. The user creates videos titled "New Music Friday" and reports on music news in a new, creative format.

c. Spectrum Pulse: Another classic music reviewer on YouTube, Spectrum Pulse gives insight into new albums and even does a video series titled "On the Pulse" where they review multiple albums at once.

We have to plan and build in time for the most important activities in our music classes. Along with improvisation, our students need to be listening to music daily. I have heard from researcher friends that adolescents listen to music on average for 3.5 to 5 hours per day. With a little persuasion and encouragement, they might use that time specifically to help them make their cover and original songs better.

Guiding Principles

1. Let them choose their songs most of the time.

It is essential that your students themselves be the ones to choose the songs that they will cover. That is not to say that there might be times when you strongly suggest songs for them or provide guidance when particular songs are not working. Having choice in the learning process is empowering. You want to give them the power of choosing the music that they perform. It is the same power that you would like them to exercise when they finish learning in your class. It is the sticky music education that John Kratus (2007) speaks of (see Figure 2.1).

There are times when it would be better for our students if we choose the music for them. The more we understand where their musical inspiration comes from—their heroes, preferred musical styles, and genres—the better we will be positioned to bring in a song choice selection that they might really enjoy. For the vast majority of the time, however, students should choose their own music.

Figure 2.1 John Kratus teaching at Michigan State University

SUNLIGHT: The Power of Choice

Choices give us control over our life. Having choices, or the ability to make choices ourselves, puts us in the driver's seat and therefore ensures our survival. Sure, having options may not directly increase our chance for survival, but it is positively correlated to more access to resources that consequently heightens our odds of survival. One of our most powerful unconscious drives is to continually seek out ways to control all aspects of our lives. We need our daily lives to be predictable in order to stay sane. Our routines and habits are a byproduct of attempting to stay in control and are a symptom of our trying to make sense of the world. When people stray too far from what they know, what is predictable, they tend to become anxious, fearful, and even insane. Having no choice is not a good thing. It decreases our possibility of survival and our overall contentment in life. So, give your students choices in your classes.

2. Try to understand the genres, styles, and artists that make up your students' musical universe.

As soon as a student enters your classroom you have the task of trying to learn their musical interests (see Figure 2.2 for examples of genres/musical interests). You do this by engaging with them in conversations and writing seeds around their musical inspiration—favorite artists, genres, video games, movies, YouTube channels, Instagram musicians, performers, performances, TikTok trends, Twitter (now "X") posts, and the like. The world of social and other medias is massive and growing

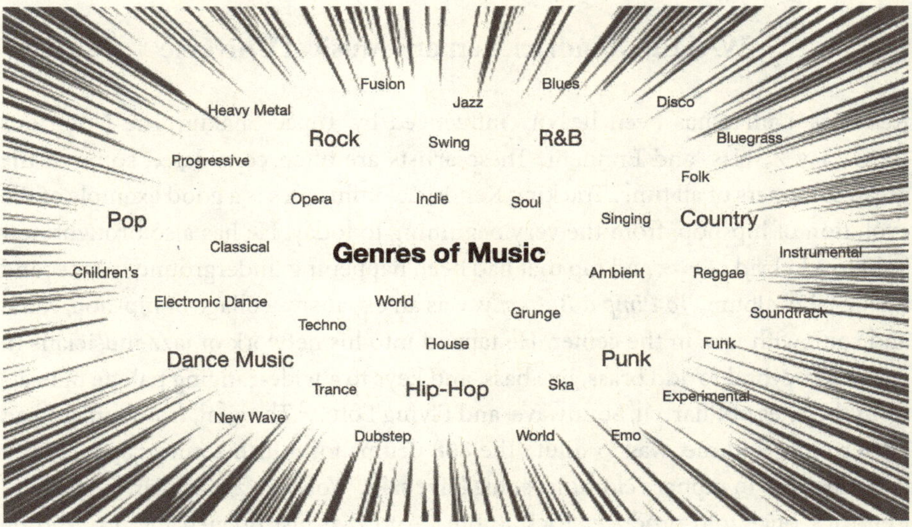

Figure 2.2 Examples of genres/musical interests

all the time. These outlets are full of musical meaning for our students. We have to know and understand them as best we can. Our students will teach us about them, if we let them. They know more than we can possibly know about the latest outlets for music consumption. We just need to listen as we provide avenues for sharing.

Our students can be found all over the map with regard to their musical interests. Try not to make assumptions about what kinds of music they like. You need to let them tell you. Just because you teach in an inner-city school with a strong percentage of African American students does not mean that they are all going to favor hip-hop. They may. However, don't assume that is true. Ask them. Be open, honest, and transparent with them. Listen. Understand. They will know right away if you care. Create a safe place for sharing. Have them give you artists and songs. Search them on a music-streaming service. Look the songs up and play them on YouTube. You might be shocked at the video content of the songs. You might be shocked about lyrical content as well! You might also want to screen songs before you play them for the class. Have students tell you their favorite music, then screen the ones that you want to share with the class.

As you can see from Figure 2.2, the list of musical genres is long and complex and getting more complex as the years go by. For proof of this claim, visit everynoise.com and see how the thousands of genres are related. It will kind of blow your mind how many there are and how very specific the labels are. In the figure that I have provided, the size of the genres matters, as the bigger ones are more commercially successful as of the printing of this book. Hip-hop, rock, and R&B are fairly large, while classical, emo, and bluegrass are relatively small. My point here is that our students love a lot of different genres of music. We need to be sensitive to what they love so that we can help them realize their musical aspirations. We need to be ready to go where they lead us. Start listening outside the box.

WATER: Kendrick Lamar's Musical Universe

Kendrick Lamar has been heavily influenced by Tupac Shakur, The Notorious B.I.G., Jay Z, Nas, and Eminem. These artists are often considered some of the greatest rappers of all time. Tracking Kendrick's influences is a good example of the evolution of hip-hop, from the very beginning to today. He has also brought new light to a hybrid of jazz and rap that had been happening underground. His second major-label album, *To Pimp a Butterfly*, was an expansive collage of hip-hop, funk, and soul, with jazz in the center. He tapped into his network of jazz musicians in L.A. and beyond to add brass, live bass, and keys to a wide-ranging palette of beats from the likes of Pharrell, Sounwave, and Flying Lotus.[2] The goal, trombonist Ryan Porter once told me, was to dilute the 808 drums for a lush soundscape. He is a jazz musician in rapper's clothing, some have said. "You a jazz musician by default," Kendrick once told producer Rick Rubin. "And that just opened me up. And he just started breaking down everything, the science, going back to Miles and Herbie

Hancock." What can you do to get outside your own listening practice and rediscover the great music in other genres? The effort might prove substantial for your own work.

Here is a list of some of the best hip-hip albums of all time. How well do you know them?

1. The Notorious B.I.G., *Ready to Die* (1994)
2. Outkast, *Stankonia* (2000)
3. Jay-Z, *The Blueprint* (2001)
4. Public Enemy, *It Takes a Nation of Millions to Hold Us Back* (1988)
5. Kendrick Lamar, *To Pimp a Butterfly* (2015)
6. Kanye West, *My Beautiful Dark Twisted Fantasy* (2010)
7. Missy Elliott, *Miss E . . . So Addictive* (2001)
8. Wu-Tang Clan, *Enter the Wu-Tang (36 Chambers)* (1993)
9. A Tribe Called Quest, *The Low End Theory* (1991)
10. Lauryn Hill, *The Miseducation of Lauryn Hill* (1998)

3. Know that your students' songwriting style will in many ways begin with their musical heroes.

The trajectory of this book is to take students from being anywhere from beginning, intermediate, and/or advanced music makers and make them better—augmenting their skills and providing them with opportunities to practice and improve from wherever they are. We start with covering the music of our heroes and then add creating original songs (see Figure 2.3 for the most popular artists of all time). We

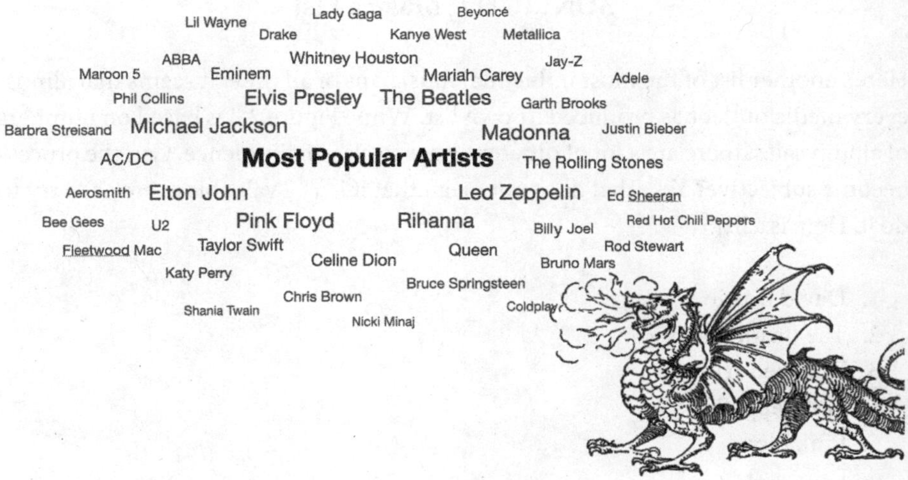

Figure 2.3 Most popular artists of all time

can do these two separate-but-intricately-related things simultaneously. However, the narrative arc involves them moving into songwriting at some point along the way. We use cover songs as a way of finding ourselves musically as we develop as songwriters. There is a lot to that statement.

Songs have structure, form, harmonic progression, melodic content, and timbral distinction, among a host of many other qualities. Artists employ various strategies to put all these qualities to work in their songs. By analyzing songs, we gain knowledge—a window into the creative process employed by songwriters. Covering songs includes being a student of the conventions of the craft that they employ. In order to cover a song well we demonstrate the ability to do these things at a reasonable level of rigor. When we are able to pull off something that sounds close to the original or takes a song in a new direction, we achieve some approximation of that. We become acutely aware of how our favorite artists do the thing that we are trying to learn how to do.

You will notice from Figure 2.3 that The Beatles, Madonna, Rihanna, and Michael Jackson are some of the most popular artists of all time as measured by record sales. The musical heroes of our students are going to come out of their favorite genres. With every genre comes the work of artists that transcend other artists' work within that genre. Some music always rises to the top of the heap. Know those artists within the genres that your students love. Again, they will lead you to where you need to be looking. Music Teacher as Music Producer classrooms center on the musical interests of students. That means that the musical heroes that we spotlight will change with every group of students that we teach. It is important, however, for us to recognize musical heroes who seem to rise above historically from all the rest. Figure 2.3 gives you an idea of who those people are as of the writing of this book. Try to keep up on how this data changes.

SUNLIGHT: Make a List

Here's another list of the most influential musicians of all time. It seems that almost every media outlet has produced its own list. While Figure 2.3 is based on numbers of album sales, there are a lot of different ways to classify influence. Can the process become subjective? Yes. That does not mean that it isn't a valuable exercise to try to do it. Here is a list:[3]

1. David Bowie
2. The Beatles
3. Jimi Hendrix
4. Led Zeppelin
5. Pink Floyd
6. Prince
7. Kate Bush

8. Bob Marley
9. Kraftwerk
10. Madonna

You should stop right now and make your own list. Whom do you include? Who just barely gets bumped off your list? Who is at the top of your list? This is a valuable exercise, one that will tell you a lot about your students' listening world.

4. As they find their niche and as you begin to understand where they come from musically, expose them to artists and sounds that might have inspired their style.

As the person in the room who has lived beyond high school and into the world of professional music-making, into the world of higher education music, you are nonetheless not poised to be the expert on all things musical. Rather, you are very well positioned to be someone that your students can bounce ideas off of. They need to know that they have the final say regarding musical decisions. And they need to know that you have their backs. You know things that they don't. They know that. That is part of the reason that the school hired you to do the job you are doing. However, your students have really strong, highly developed musical ideas that are worth your attention and respect. Their musical ideas matter more than yours do in your classroom—one focused on their creativities. Did you get that?

You are a very valuable sounding board, though (Randles, 2009a, 2009b). Peer feedback is the strongest form of feedback for them. After peers, you are incredibly valuable to them as they form and reform their music. You are another set of informed ears. Your ability to internalize their musical worlds will help you be the best sounding board that you can. Once you have earned their trust, they will be more likely to allow you to help them. What you should avoid at all costs in a classroom centered on student musical creativities is one where students feel as if YOU are the person directing their musical choices. They will do mediocre work if they feel you are just going to derail them in the end. The power needs to be clearly with them if they are going to give you their very best creative effort.

Connecting them to musical worlds that didn't exist before they came to you is important too. You focus squarely on understanding their musical worlds first, facilitating and many times producing their music in your classroom. After that working arrangement is in place you will need to connect them to artists and genres that inspired their musical universe. That takes a smart and intuitive music teacher who listens outside of band, choir, and orchestra music. You need to be a real-life Pandora radio station, keen to musical trends and styles, always looking to grow your own understanding of the roots of musical styles.

Figure 2.4 Discovering our musical roots

Another important aspect of your job in this vein is connecting students to African and Native American musical heritage and their links to popular musical styles. The links are substantial, and the roots run deep (see Figure 2.4). Rock 'n' roll, country, funk, jazz, rhythm and blues, hip-hop, and other genres have roots in African and Native American populations whose participation gets overlooked sometimes in our accounts of musical history. Connect students to the music of women in each of these genres as well. Their contribution is profound and helps tell the complete story of how musicians have come to function and practice in the world. This is your chance to do your part to encourage diversity and inclusion in your classroom. The work of members of the LGBTQ+ community is also substantial. Be inclusive in your recommendations to students for extension and growth.

In Figure 2.4 you will see some of the artists whom you might focus and zoom in on in your teaching. In a world where White men are championed above all others, a healthy and concerted effort to diversify the artists we spotlight is very much welcome and encouraged. Start to familiarize yourself with artists who might be on the fringe of what is frequently spotlighted and go there often in your musical examples. Do you know the impact of Sister Rosetta Tharpe on the history of rock music? Have you experienced the hard-blowing presence of Vi Redd's saxophone playing? Have you ever watched a video of Chaka Khan's funky stage presence on display as the frontwoman for the band Rufus? We need to demonstrate in every way we can how the roots of the music we love go deep into the working lives of historically underrepresented and appreciated musicians. It is part of our collective mission as a profession.

WATER: It Might Get Loud

One of my favorite music documentaries of all time is the film *It Might Get Loud* (2008). It is a 1 hour and 38-minute tribute to the electric guitar that features three of my favorites: Jimmy Page, The Edge, and Jack White. Each of the guitarists gets a section of the film dedicated to him, complete with back story, influences, and a window into their practice life. The film starts with Jack White building a guitar out of a block of wood and a single-coil pickup and then playing it on a front porch in the country for a bunch of cows. [smile]

One of the central messages of the work is the love that each musician has for the instrument itself. Jimmy Page is the quintessential pioneer of the electric guitar, having started and produced one of the most popular and commercially successful bands of all time—Led Zeppelin. Jack White likes to play instruments that are less than perfect so that he has to fight a little bit with them, and the struggle helps him produce musical art that is honest and authentic. The Edge is all about the sonic qualities of the guitar and seeing what technology can do to extend the capabilities of the instrument. Each of these musicians teaches us things about being a musician. If you can, stop reading this book right now and go watch the movie.

Lessons learned include:

1. Jimmy Page—we learn to be entrepreneurial about the music around us, to be studious of music production tips and tricks as we work to perfect our musical craft. He was in the right place at the right time to take his most cherished form of music—rock 'n' roll—to the next level. Page created colossal chords and riffs and captured them cleverly in the studio. He was a product of talent, drive, and intuition.
2. The Edge—we learn that new technologies can alter the course of our sound and that new paths can actually alter the course of all of popular music. U2 has created some of the most amazing sonic textures—many times aided by the visionary work of Brian Eno. The sound of The Edge's guitar takes center stage in that work. He has never been afraid to go to the end of the musical road in order to find the perfect use of any given technology. It is something that gives him great pleasure.
3. Jack White—we learn that you don't need all the technology in the world to say something new with the guitar. All you need to do is drop your pail into some of the oldest storytelling wells and be diligent to hoist it up. White likes to mine the past to uncover keys to the future. He's known to record on reel-to-reel tape and champions the raw sound of vinyl over digital. In many ways, White is a reaction against the technology-centric sound of The Edge (at least in the video). His work since the documentary embraces more and more of what The Edge utilized in the film.

Who are your musical influences? What sorts of lessons can they teach you?

5. Help them find keys for the songs that fit their vocal range.

The amateur thing to do is only perform songs in the key that a particular artist did the song in. Your students search a song and find a lead sheet. They then work at learning how to play the chords on an accompanying instrument. They often do not consider what would happen if they moved the tonal center up or down a half or a whole step or more. Sometimes just a little movement either way results in songs having quite a lot more impact than they did before. Singer vocal range is a huge consideration in choosing cover songs (see Figures 2.5 and 2.6).

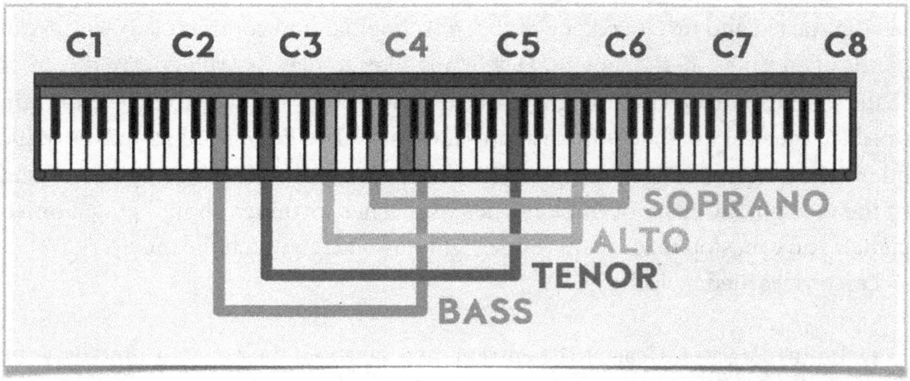

Figure 2.5 Vocal ranges

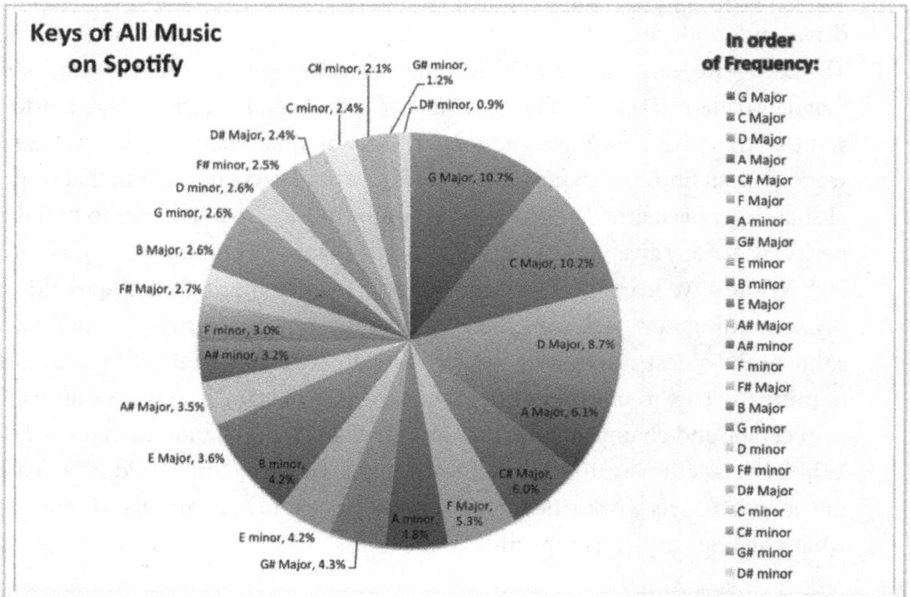

Figure 2.6 Most utilized keys

Know that guitars can be capo-ed and electronic keyboards can be transposed easily to account for performance in different keys. Capos and keyboard transpositions many times do not even require playing chords differently. You just need to know that these techniques exist and are used readily in the wide world of music—including in the music of many of our students' favorite artists. Doing a song in a key different from that of the original artist or iconic performance can also go a long way in making a song sound original, fresh, and innovative.

SUNLIGHT: Vocal Range

The Average Male Vocal Range

About 1.5 to 2 octaves, while for others it can reach 4 (Freddie Mercury) or even six (Axl Rose and Mike Patton).

Male Bass Vocal Range Exemplars

Johnny Cash, D♯2–B5
Barry White, C3–A4

Male Baritone Vocal Range Exemplars

Elvis Presley, F♯1–A5
Corey Taylor, F1–G5
David Bowie, B1–E♭6
Chris Cornell, C2–A5

Male Tenor Vocal Range Exemplars

Freddie Mercury, F2–F5
Robert Plant, G2–C♯6
Brendon Urie, D2–C7
Paul McCartney, A1–E6
Bruno Mars, C3–C6
Prince, F2–C7
Charlie Puth, C♯2–G5

The Average Female Vocal Range

About 2 to 3 octaves, but for some artists it can reach further, such as Mariah Carey, who has a 5-octave vocal range.

Female Alto Vocal Range Exemplars

Amy Winehouse, D3–E♭6
Cher, C3–F6

Fiona Apple, D3–E5
Tina Turner, D♯3–F♯5
Lana Del Rey, B♭2–C♯6

Female Mezzo-Soprano Vocal Range Exemplars
Janis Joplin, D3–A5
Beyoncé, C3—F6
Alanis Morissette, D♯3–G7
Lady Gaga, A2–G5–B5

Female Soprano Vocal Range Exemplars
Ariana Grande, D3–E7
Billie Eilish, D3–G5
Christina Aguilera, C3–C7
Aaliyah, G2–E6
Floor Jansen, C3–F6
Whitney Houston, A2–C♯6 (A6)

6. Help them discover better ways to perform the chords and riffs that are required of particular songs.

When your students go about learning instrumental parts for their cover songs they will need your instrumental performance expertise. If you are a teacher who is relatively new to this performance space, you need to make sure that you get started developing your skills in this area (Randles, 2022). Electric guitar voicings are different from acoustic guitar voicings. Both instruments are tuned similarly, and essentially they can accomplish the same results. However, they are utilized in practice in much different ways. Acoustic guitars tend to be used to accompany voice and for rhythm function. Acoustic players tend to make use of capos quite a lot of the time, while electric players tend to play lead lines and do not make use of capos. Abbreviated versions of chords exist for both of those functions and can really make a difference for someone trying to approximate a version of a particular performance or someone trying to create an amazingly innovative version of a particular song.

Drumbeats can have an endless degree of variation and still get musicians where they need to be—creating satisfying performances. Riffs can be played on different instruments for creative impact and for ease of use for performers. They can be moved up and down the neck of a guitar or left or right on a keyboard to achieve various results in different keys. Timbral choices can be made to diversify the feel of particular pieces (Randles, 2022). Musical ideas can be sampled and performed with a MIDI trigger or tablet. When your students are searching for something else, something different, a way to solve their musicals dilemmas, you become a very important asset. It is times like these when all the other key points in this section come together. The result is a music teacher producer who is effective, valuable to the creative process, and sought after by students for help.

WATER: Unique Ways of Playing

Wes Montgomery

The most influential jazz guitarist ever, Montgomery developed unique playing styles out of sheer desire and necessity. His wife and neighbors complained that his late-night practices were too loud, so he would play with his thumb instead of a pick.

Maybelle Carter

The Carter Scratch is a style of guitar playing popularized by Maybelle Carter. While holding down a chord, the higher strings are strummed while a melody is picked out on the lower strings. She popularized this technique and created a style that many who followed have emulated.

Alan Holdsworth

Holdsworth is referred to as the greatest technical guitarist to ever live. He developed a unique way of playing chords and in the process defied traditional harmony for the guitar. His unique playing style also involved wide stretches that would be unattainable by most hands.

Eddie Van Halen

Van Halen displayed a visceral technique and touch and made the world experience a ferocity that rock had not seen. Through the unique use of tapping and other techniques, he showed the music industry that you could be a virtuoso guitarist and play extremely catchy rock songs at the same time.

Jeff Beck

Jeff Beck is one of the most imitated guitar players ever. The way he combines the use of the volume knob with his pick and thumb is truly unique. The ways in which he uses his pick are even more unique. Add to this an unorthodox use of the whammy bar, slide, and an extremely musical mind, and you have one of the most unique playing styles ever.

Jimi Hendrix

Jimi Hendrix's use of feedback, distortion, wah, and even teeth were unprecedented when he exploded on the British scene in the 1960s. He is the guy that made impossible sounds become possible. Besides the technical stuff, Hendrix was also unusually charismatic (especially for a guitar player). And he was the most introverted person when he was off the stage.

The contribution of each of these unique guitar players is immense. They were bold. They were different. We recognize their playing right away. How much will you allow your students to be and do completely different?

7. Help them in any way that you can realize their vision for their cover songs.

Your students will come at cover songs somewhere on a spectrum of trying to exactly replicate what an artist did on a particular recording or live performance to their merely using the structure and harmonic content of a song as a place to start as they jam around and come up with something interesting and new with a song. Understand that some of your students are wired in a way that an exact copy of a song is the only benchmark for excellence, while others will push for coming up with their own way to play a song and will be turned off by the people who try only to make an exact copy. These differences stem from the multitude of different ways that human beings experience the world.

There are times to celebrate complexity and other times when less is more. We all have to figure this out for ourselves in our music. You as the teacher are a valuable set of ears in your room. As you build your students' trust they will come to you more and more for lots of different things. You first try to understand their vision for the song. Their musical heroes and listening habits will provide you with clues to their vision. There is not a recipe for being able to do this well, but I have found that I get better at it the more that I practice. You first need to listen well to what they say. Try to imagine what they might do if they knew all the things that you do about how music works. Don't ever assume that your version of reality is more important or correct than theirs. You are there to help them when they need your help.

SUNLIGHT: Five Tips for Making a Song Your Own

Here are some tips to help you make a song your own. They have been tested and tried over many years. Here you go:

1. **Find ways that you can relate to the song.** If a song is about a protagonist's pain, draw from your own well of pain to make the words come to life. The longer we are alive on the planet, the more pain and suffering that we have internalized. Be honest and authentic with a song by really feeling the pain and suffering.
2. **Take the song back to its roots.** From where did the inspirations for a song come? Take a new version of the song to places where the song came from. Are the roots in country? Try an Americana type of flavor for the song. Are the roots in gospel? Channel your inner gospel musician.
3. **Covering a song doesn't have to mean copying the artist.** Try changing the tempo, reimagining the feel, singing in a different style completely, or doing it in another genre. Be yourself. Who are you as a person? As an artist? What are you comfortable with? Stretch yourself.
4. **Change the key.** One of the most profound things to do to change the feel and overall vibe of a song is to change the key. Here is a list of keys and what they have sometimes meant to composers/musicians in the past:[4]

   C Major Pure. Its character is: innocence, simplicity, children's talk.

   C Minor Declaration of love and at the same time the lament of unhappy love. All languishing, longing, sighing of the lovesick soul lies in this key.

   D♭ Major A leering key, degenerating into grief and rapture. It cannot laugh, but it can smile; it cannot howl, but it can at least grimace its crying. Consequently, only unusual characters and feelings can be brought out in this key.

   C♯ Minor Penitential lamentation, intimate conversation with God, the friend and help-meet of life; sighs of disappointed friendship and love lie in its radius.

   D Major The key of triumph, of Hallelujahs, of war-cries, of victory-rejoicing. Thus, the inviting symphonies, the marches, holiday songs, and heaven-rejoicing choruses are set in this key.

   D Minor Melancholy womanliness, the spleen and humors brood.

   E♭ Major The key of love, of devotion, of intimate conversation with God.

   D♯ Minor Feelings of the anxiety of the soul's deepest distress, of brooding despair, of the most gloomy condition of the soul. Every fear, every hesitation of the shuddering heart, breathes out of horrible D# minor. If ghosts could speak, their speech would approximate this key.

E Major Noisy shouts of joy, laughing pleasure and not yet complete, full delight lies in E Major.

E Minor Naïve, womanly innocent declaration of love, lament without grumbling; sighs accompanied by few tears; this key speaks of the imminent hope of resolving in the pure happiness of C major.

F Major Complaisance and calm.

F Minor Deep depression, funereal lament, groans of misery and longing for the grave.

F# Major Triumph over difficulty, free sigh of relief when hurdles are surmounted; echo of a soul that has fiercely struggled and finally conquered lies in all uses of this key.

F# Minor A gloomy key: it tugs at passion as a dog biting a dress. Resentment and discontent are its language.

G Major Everything rustic, idyllic, and lyrical, every calm and satisfied passion, every tender gratitude for true friendship and faithful love—in a word, every gentle and peaceful emotion of the heart is correctly expressed by this key.

G Minor Discontent, uneasiness, worry about a failed scheme; bad-tempered gnashing of teeth; in a word: resentment and dislike.

A♭ Major Key of the grave. Death, grave, putrefaction, judgment, eternity lie in its radius.

A♭ Minor Grumbler, heart squeezed until it suffocates; wailing lament, difficult struggle; in a word, the color of this key is everything struggling with difficulty.

A Major This key includes declarations of innocent love, satisfaction with one's state of affairs; hope of seeing one's beloved again when parting; youthful cheerfulness and trust in God.

A Minor Pious womanliness and tenderness of character.

B♭ Major Cheerful love, clear conscience, hope aspiration for a better world.

B♭ Minor A quaint creature, often dressed in the garment of night. It is somewhat surly and very seldom takes on a pleasant countenance. Mocking God and the world; discontented with itself and with everything; preparation for suicide sounds in this key.

B Major Strongly colored, announcing wild passions, composed from the most glaring colors. Anger, rage, jealousy, fury, despair, and every burden of the heart lie in its sphere.

B Minor This is as it were the key of patience, of calm awaiting one's fate and of submission to divine dispensation.

5. **Change the instrumentation.** If the instrumentation of the original song was complex, try something markedly more simple. Take some clues from

artists who have reinterpreted their own songs. One of my favorites lately is Paul Simon's *In the Blue Light* (2018). The album consists of re-recordings of lesser-known songs from Simon's catalogue, often altering their original arrangements, harmonic structures, and lyrics. The songs were recorded with guests including the instrumental ensemble yMusic, guitarist Bill Frisell, trumpeter Wynton Marsalis, and Bryce Dessner. It is a wonderful example of all of the tips that I offer here.

6. **Change the tempo.** Changing the tempo can have an astoundingly transformative effect. Take Gary Jules's cover of "Mad World" vs. the Tears for Fears version. Also, The Flamingos' "I Only Have Eyes for You" vs. the Busby Berkeley–choreographed version in *Dames*.

8. Be prepared to play any parts that are missing to help them realize their vision for the arrangement of a song.

Over the years I have played all the various instruments found in a modern band for my students when they needed my help. This has included accordion, trombone, and melodica as well. Your knowledge of the technological world of timbre, effects, and sounds will help you to help them realize their vision for songs, as unique sounds can be a part of the performance of any and all instruments found in a classroom of this variety. How is your practice routine for jamming on the instruments in your room? Are you able to find major and minor keys on keyboard and guitar? Are you able to pick up a bass and quickly find three places to play a "D" note? Do you know about the octave jump that is easy to perform on an electric guitar and/or bass guitar? Do you know how to navigate the sound library of your keyboard? These are all important things for you to practice as you assist students in your classroom.

The most important thing to think about with this key point is "where are my skills on all of the instruments found in my classroom?" This is true of music teachers in diverse contemporary as well as more traditional settings. When you teach clarinet and saxophone, you should be working on your skills as a clarinet and saxophone player. The more proficient you are playing the instruments in your classroom, the better prepared you are to offer advice and suggestions for performance, and the better positioned you are to sit in on an instrument that they might be looking for in their song. It is wise to work your practice of these instruments into your class time with students. When I'm teaching songwriting, I tend to use an acoustic guitar that allows me to walk around the room. Other times I'm using a keyboard. When I demonstrate skills and share songs, I practice on these instruments. This is easier to do around younger students if you are a beginner teacher in this type of environment. Be brave. Your students need you to practice along with them. Make it a valuable part of the experience—"we are all learning and practicing together."

WATER: Performing Along with Your Students

When one of my students, Ross Reynolds, was selected as a finalist in the Michigan State Honors Composition Competition I helped him put together a band. It was difficult to find a person in our school community who could play the guitar part to his song, so I jumped in and covered the part. I highly recommend that if and when you are given a chance to perform for your students, take the opportunity. It provides an example for them of a person who is musical their entire lives (you are OLDer than they are and still eager to perform). It also demonstrates that you care enough about them to provide a support role for their music-making. They will feel empowered that you would play in a group where they call the shots. That's a very special dynamic that is difficult to experience any other way.

I have performed alongside my students time and time again over the years, in diverse settings and in various music education teaching settings. I did this when I was a K–12 teacher in Michigan, and it is something that followed me as I became a college professor in 2010. The dynamic changes a bit when you become a professor who works with young adults. There are boundaries and limits to what you can do, and how you can help in collegiate settings. Those were all things that I had to learn on the job. Regardless, it is a great idea to play alongside your students, helping them realize their vision of their cover and original songs (see Figure 2.7).

9. Think about what your students' emerging style based on their musical interests might mean for the community that you serve.

Communities of learners have a common DNA. When I taught in Coopersville Area Public Schools in Michigan, I worked to understand the community. They were a hard-working blue-collar farming culture—a place that Norman Rockwell would have enjoyed painting. They appreciated my efforts. Music had a strong presence in the schools there for over a hundred years. I was aware of the various places where my students' talents could be featured. When I was invited to direct the basketball pep band, I saw an opportunity to get a vocalist involved and bring in more electric guitarists than we needed at the time. Basketball games were well attended there. It was a chance for my students to be heard.

What places in your community would lend themselves well to small groups performing cover songs? We live and work around restaurants, wineries, breweries, band shells, churches, and other places that can serve as venues for musicians to play. Can you arrange with those places to allow your students to perform there? Cover songs tend to be the way in, as these places are most often open to live musical performances. Work with the owners of these places to come up with a plan that would benefit all involved. In that way the music program would be very visible to the same people who support the arts in schools. We desperately need these

Figure 2.7 The author as a professional musician in Tampa, Florida

bonds to be strong as we work to create excellent music education experiences for students and the communities that we serve.

SUNLIGHT: Community Music

The value of music in a community is profound. The school music program is one of the main avenues for music-making in a community. However, programs exist for populations of people beyond the K–12 years. Here are some things to think about when considering what music can do for a community:

Amateur Music-Making Is Good for All Ages

Guitar, keyboard, ukulele, banjo, and other instrumental classes are an excellent way to promote lifelong learning in a community. School music programs that include these classes can continue for members of a community after people graduate and become working members of society. Djing and Turntable performance, when a part of school music programs, can then be taught and offered in community music settings as well. As hip-hop music is the top-selling genre of music at the moment, it would be an excellent idea for music educators to include opportunities to make music this way in both school and community music settings.

Ensemble Musical Experiences Are Powerful

Band, choir, orchestra, and modern band are all ensemble experiences that are good for both in school and out-of-school music-making experiences. Music educators need to create places for all of these forms of music-making beyond high school to help promote lifelong learning in music. Civic functions, holidays, and diverse aspects of community life can benefit from these types of ensembles. The same type of pride that can come from a fine community concert band can come from an excellent modern band presence. We have to look at each type of ensemble as a potential place for growth and flourishing of musical engagement.

Music Intervention Programs and Positive Effects

When the title character of *The Music Man* (1957) declared "There's trouble in River City . . .," he preached the power of music to help young people turn from wicked and wasteful ways. There was actually some truth to Harold Hill's declaration! Classical music, when played in areas where crime is an issue, actually deters criminals from carrying out their offenses. That's using strings and winds as a weapon in the war on crime! After-school programs that incorporate music and the other arts provide a constructive way for students to positively occupy their time in a way that supports their own livelihood and keeps them off the streets where they might fall ill to the sins of society.

The Needs of Diverse Learners

Music is an excellent tool for giving diverse learners a pathway to success and fulfillment. All learners deserve a customized music-making experience that fits their unique needs and desires. The students with disabilities space is an excellent place where this has been happening quite well in community music settings. I work with a group called Arts4All Florida that provides programs for students with exceptionalities in the state of Florida (see Figure 2.8). By serving on their board, I am able to direct ideas for programs and services that the school of music that

Figure 2.8 Sarah Hardwig performs as a part of Arts4All Florida's Young Performers Program

I work in can provide for the program to Tampa Bay community that I live in, and also to various places around the state. The rewards are massive and far-reaching.

10. In what ways can you celebrate and use their heroes to teach the rest of the class something of value?

When I taught general music in Michigan I was constantly on the lookout for what was trending in the lives of my students. Social media nowadays would be very helpful in accomplishing this task. If a student walked in the room with a Beyoncé shirt, I would take the opportunity to play some of her music. If the Grammys were held and there was a memorable cover song performance of a song from our collective past, I would play the original and talk about where it came from.

The singer-songwriter Del Shannon, who made the song "Runaway" popular in 1961, was from the town, Coopersville, that I taught in. I made sure that I talked about how Del Shannon toured in the UK in 1963 and The Beatles opened for him. They opened for him! Imagine that?! We had a community car show and festival every year in Coopersville. I made sure that I played and we discussed the music of Del Shannon. That meant a lot to the community that I served and was a point of pride for the school and community.

Another thing that I liked to do every year was write musicals with my students that included some of their musical heroes. I have written Madonna, Kid Rock, Johnny Cash, The Rolling Stones, The Beatles, Elvis Presley, and many more into scripts based on the interests of my students and the communities that I have served. It always made good sense for me to do this, as it is the community that supports my efforts to serve them. If I could show them something special, do good things for their kids, they always supported me. Introducing creativities into the curriculum and large ensembles went a long way to help me do something special. Many times I would use the music of their musical heroes to assist in accomplishing this end goal.

WATER: The Musical Influences of Michael Jackson

Michael Jackson was heavily influenced by R&B, pop, and soul from the 1950s on. He had been influenced by the work of contemporary musicians like James Brown, Jackie Wilson, Diana Ross, Fred Astaire, Sammy Davis Jr., Gene Kelly, David Ruffin, The Isley Brothers, and the Bee Gees. His iconic dance move, "the Moon Walk," was said to have been based on the routine of mime artist Marcel Marceau. He was a big fan of Broadway musicals such as *West Side Story*.

Michael's biggest influence and his favorite performer was the "Godfather of Soul," James Brown. Michael was blown away by James's energy and charisma on stage. He loved the way James danced and was endlessly taken by the way he so effortlessly moved his feet when performing. As a child, Michael would watch James on television, eagerly trying to learn his dance steps. He would get very angry when the camera man wouldn't show James's feet. Michael Jackson was 100 percent original, but built on the legacy of his heroes when developing his own style. He provides us with a study into how to help our students find their own style and voice.

Benefits from Learning Cover Songs

The following benefits of working on cover songs have been gleaned from the work of Amy Saari,[5] who calls herself an interfaith music minister. Here we learn that cover songs are a sort of lifeblood of the gigging musician. As a music educator, you would like nothing more than your students finding a source of meaning making in and through music that can sustain them for an entire lifetime. Covering songs can do that for them. It is a rite of passage for people wanting to become songwriters, and it is also a worthy end goal in and of itself. Here are ways that Saari suggests that cover songs help musicians:

1. **Cover songs help you test yourself.** And not just for skill but for interpretation, artistry, and presence. What's the highest difficulty level I can master while delivering a performance that really communicates something?
2. **You get to learn other styles.** That way, I don't have to be boxed in by any particular one, and I expand my skills.
3. **You get to learn YOUR style.** Cover songs are not meant to be carbon-copied, so I don't have to kill myself trying to duplicate every nuance of the artist's original. At worst, I'll sound like a hack or a fake. Sometimes I'll more truly discover what my personal style is by learning a song that goes against the grain of it. How would I communicate this idea?
4. **You get to generate more listenership.** Especially if it's an open mic or another forum where I get to meet a new audience, I have a much easier time connecting with listeners by way of a song they already know than by throwing out my quirkiest original composition. If I perform well, they will remember me well and probably also dig on my original work if it's included in the same package.
5. **You get to work more with others.** One of the easiest ways to get other musicians to play with you is to offer up a cover song you can play together. This happens a lot at open mics, where a handful of musicians will play with each other for long sequences because the whole thing has turned into a festival of songs not unlike a campfire under the stars. And it's just as magical. Musicians learn about each other best by playing together, and doing so on a commonly known song is the fastest way to experience their magic, and for them to experience yours.
6. **Cover songs help you get gigs!** Many bars, clubs, and restaurants have customers who just don't prefer new music, and that's okay; they will still pay to have musicians come and do their favorite songs. Right now I'm working in a cover duo called Windfall Prophets and we've had all kinds of fun playing over 50 years' worth of popular favorites in more sedate restaurant settings. It helps me keep my chops up and keeps me connected to listeners.

Ultimately, what I get from learning cover songs is flexibility, the ability to bend without breaking. It's given me the ability to be more myself, not less, and that sustains me through everything I do in music: playing, singing, communicating, promoting, teaching, networking, and the rest of it.

A Process for Covering Songs

Covering songs, like being a good human being, requires honesty and authenticity to be pulled off successfully. There is a kind of honesty in songwriting that comes from writing about the things that you know and have experienced. You should choose cover songs that you can sing honestly. Can you be the main character in the song? Do you know that character well enough to be able to tell their story? These are important questions.

What makes music meaningful? That of course is an important question. There are plenty of exceptions, but time and time again the music that ends up resonating with audiences and pushes genres forward is made by musicians who express their creativity in original, authentic ways. Authenticity is HUGE to us as we work with songs. We play with social/emotional fire when we tell stories through our cover and original songs. They become the sparks that ignite the flame of our lifelong love of music and provide us with necessary fuel for our sonic lives. While a perfect process for covering songs does not exist, the following one suggested by Cover Band Central[6] is good enough to get you started:

1. Learn the Song Correctly

People in the crowd will expect to hear certain signature parts, including guitar solos, melodic riffs, rhythmic patterns, and especially lyrics. It's imperative that you, the cover band musician, learn the song the correct way in the beginning.

2. Respect the Original Artist

More often than not, you'll be playing a song that was a big hit for an artist or band, and the time and care that was put into creating the original recording deserve to be respected.

3. Learn the Lyrics

Even if you're not the singer, and you have no backup or harmony vocals, it's a good idea to learn the words. This will help you in remembering your own parts, as well as with communicating with the rest of the band at rehearsal.

4. Watch Live Performances

Most artists will put a little bit of a spin or twist on a song that has attained success when they perform it live. In fact, some songs have gained even more popularity from a live recording.

5. Practice with a Metronome

Timing is important for every instrument, including vocals. Get yourself in sync with the tempo, and it will pay off handsomely for your own musical growth.

6. Practice a Lot

There is a quote that I happen to love: "Amateurs practice until they get it right, professionals practice until they can't get it wrong."

7. Record Yourself

There are free and/or inexpensive apps that you can download to your smartphone for audio recording purposes. Record yourself and listen. It will alert you to things that you might be overlooking and it will help the quality of your performance.

8. Make It Your Own

It's very important to play a song correctly. I think it's also equally important to inject your own style and personality into your chosen instrument.

9. Use Transpositions

Once you've learned a song where you can play it with comfort, test yourself to see if you can play it in a different key without making a mistake. Once you master this skill, you'll be prepared for anything.

10. Play It Like It's the First Time Every Time

Dig from your social/emotional well each time you get up to perform your songs. You owe it to that person in the room who just might be hearing the song for the first time, or is having the worst week of their lives and needs your performance to get them back on the right track. You could bring healing, and you should try.

I hope that you share this process with your students. Maybe you will adjust it so that it makes more sense for your particular school environment. Completing the items on this list takes time. You are going to have to provide them with that time. Can this all happen in time allotted for music each week? Yes. Remember that creativity needs parameters and deadlines to be actualized. We can provide that in school settings. Start thinking like a music producer. That is what they will need from you.

Writing Your Best Music Starts with Covering the Music That You Love

You work side by side with your students in your classroom to assimilate the best of their musical worlds into performances and recordings. Their interests lead and guide you to discover the best ways forward regarding genre and song selection. You have all of the major success stories in music to use as a guide as far as connecting what you do with them covering songs and what you will eventually do with them with original songs. These two musical practices work best intertwined like the threads of a rope that will tie them from what they have done to what they might accomplish in the future when your class is done and they are on their own.

You should practice your own craft as a coverer of songs along with your students. Practice performing songs with various accompaniment instruments. The most common are guitar and keyboard. The ukulele is also a very popular choice for an accompaniment instrument. I recently did an open-mic night with a friend where a guy got up and sang "Wonderful Tonight" by Eric Clapton accompanying himself on the accordion (see Figure 2.9). It was a good enough performance to be accepted well by the audience and novel enough—utilizing an accordion instead of a keyboard—to be set apart in a good way from all other performances.

Celebrate their successes and share them often within your community. Start your own school-wide open-mic nights. That's a great way to bring other students

Figure 2.9 "Wonderful Tonight" with accordion accompaniment

into your music classes. Allow spoken word and other art forms as well. Doing this will put your music class on the radar for students and community members who might not know that these types of musical activities were being celebrated in the school. You will have to educate them. That is part of why you are there in the first place. You serve them, and many times you will show them what they need before they know that they need it. I can say for certain that an open-mic night will go over very well and will support the type of classroom where music teachers serve as music producers for their students' cover songs and original work.

Grow the community of teachers doing these types of activities in their classrooms. Be the change that you wish to see. If you don't know any teachers around you who serve as music producers for their students, and work on cover and original songs with their students, be the first one. Then, search out friends who might be willing to join you in offering classes for students to do similarly. The idea of providing this avenue for student music-making is a good one, and is part of a much larger movement in music education to allow for such experiences to exist, grow, and thrive. Once you show your community what you can provide for students, and show them performance and recording examples that demonstrate excellence, they will be willing to support you in any way that you desire them to. This style of practice is just what communities are longing for currently.

Remember as you open up opportunities for students to cover the songs of their favorite artists from all genres you are partnering with the read from notation only primarily Western classical music tradition that is ubiquitous in music education at the moment. Our goal has never been and will not be to replace those activities. Rather, we seek to make our practice look more like the real world of music-making, with a balance that favors much more reading and comping parts from lead sheets coupled with creative group arranging. There is room for a music education that de-centers read-from notation only and Western classical music. It should most definitely, however, NOT be the focus of all that we do in the education of the masses in and through music.

Resources Worth Exploring

Site	Expertise	URL
Most-Covered Songs	Spotify	https://open.spotify.com/playlist/1WbsYAbvxIqhKH3mdHV4Hm
Sister Rosetta Tharpe	NPR	https://www.npr.org/2017/08/24/544226085/forebears-sister-rosetta-tharpe-the-godmother-of-rock-n-roll
Tips for Covering Songs	Berklee	https://online.berklee.edu/takenote/how-to-cover-a-song-on-youtube/
Recording and Selling Cover Songs	Tune Registry	https://www.tuneregistry.com/blog/how-to-legally-record-and-sell-a-cover-song-in-3-steps

Site	Expertise	URL
Legally Performing Cover Songs	LinkedIn	https://www.linkedin.com/pulse/cover-songs-performing-recording-them-legally-sue-basko/
30 Best Cover Songs of All Time	Time Out	https://www.timeout.com/music/best-cover-songs
Top Ten Cover Songs	*Rolling Stone* magazine	https://www.rollingstone.com/music/music-lists/rolling-stone-readers-pick-the-top-10-greatest-cover-songs-12792/

SEEDS FOR COVER SONG LESSONS

3
Beginner Cover Song Seeds

A Song That Makes You Happy

Materials

- A room full of accompaniment instruments including but not limited to: guitar, keyboard, bass guitar, drum kit, drum sequencer, and ukulele, and so forth. You can use a digital audio workstation (DAW) with various keyboard and pad controllers as instruments as well. You can also use homemade instruments and/or body percussion.
- Access to the information universe via phones, tablets, computers.
- Optional: The ability to print lead sheets.
- Audio recording capabilities that make use of software like GarageBand/Logic, FL Studio, Audacity, Soundtrap, Abelton Live, ProTools, and so forth on a computer/tablet/phone.
- Computer connected to a video projector.
- Optional: Computer connected to audio interface with a pair of condenser microphones to capture live audio.
- Sound system that contains speakers to amplify your computer's sound.
- Optional: Video camera to capture live student performances.

Context

When you teach in a classroom where the core of your curriculum is helping students create the music that they love, you simply need lesson seeds to get things started. In this case you are going to ask them to find a chorus of a song that makes them happy. Certain songs trigger particularly happy emotions from us. Pretty much anything produced at Motown Studios in Detroit in the 1960s triggers a happy response from me. Your students have many of these triggers themselves. You are going to ask them to think of a chorus of a song, just the chorus. You can, of course, have them cover the entire song. However, the beginner nature of this plan hinges on their ability to find a chorus that they enjoy. You will have to teach them a little about song structure for them to know what the chorus of a song is. Then, you will have to give them time to search for songs. This is very much a task that involves social bonding, identity sharing, and the expression of

Growing Songwriting. Clint Randles, Oxford University Press. © Oxford University Press 2024.
DOI: 10.1093/oso/9780197693216.003.0003

cultural capital. The process of searching for and sharing songs that make you happy goes a long way in solidifying and validating music's valuable place in your life. Celebrate your students' excitement about this lesson because they will be happy to be involved with it.

SUNLIGHT: Some of the Happiest Songs Ever Made

Here is a list of some of the happiest songs ever written:

1. "Let's Go Crazy" by Prince
2. "I Got You (I Feel Good)" by James Brown & The Famous Flames
3. "Don't Stop Me Now" by Queen
4. "Good as Hell" by Lizzo
5. "Walking on Sunshine" by Katrina & The Waves
6. "Tightrope" by Janelle Monáe
7. "Three Little Birds" by Bob Marley & The Wailers
8. "You Make My Dreams" by Hall & Oates
9. "I Wanna Dance with Somebody (Who Loves Me)" by Whitney Houston
10. "Sir Duke" by Stevie Wonder
11. "Dance to the Music" by Sly & The Family Stone
12. "Happy" by Pharrell Williams
13. "Don't Worry, Be Happy" by Bobby McFerrin

Do an analysis of the elements of some or all of these songs. What is it about them that makes them happy? Is it the tempo? Is it the key? What is it about the lyrical content? Is it the melodic content? How do these artists create a good vibe that makes us happy when we hear them? Also, how have people done covers of these songs? Do a search for covers on YouTube to find such examples.

WATER: "Summertime": The Most Covered Song of All Time

The most covered song of all time is George and Ira Gershwin's "Summertime," with at least 25,000 different versions existing in the world of recorded music. Written in 1934, "Summertime" was one of the first compositions George Gershwin worked on for the opera *Porgy and Bess.* The jazz-inspired song is a lullaby for Clara to sing to her child, and it is reprised several more times throughout the opera. George Gershwin came from a musical theater background and *Porgy and Bess* was his first opera. The song was covered famously by Billie Holiday in 1936, Ella Fitzgerald and Louis Armstrong in 1957, Miles Davis in 1959, and Janis Joplin in 1968. Listen to the different versions of the song. How does each artist treat the song similarly?

How do they add their own artist stamp on it? How might you add your own creative personality to it?

Lesson Time

This lesson can take place in one 45-minute class. However, you will most likely have to extend it over multiple classes if you decide to have them learn more than the chorus of the song, and depending on how well they take to the seed. You will need to allow time for this lesson to emerge. It is a seed that will take you in many different directions if you allow it to. That is the goal of this book—to give you many places to start a creative lesson. You could make this an individual lesson or you could have the students self-select their own group. If you have the ability to put them in small bands with differing instrumentation, that would be best. See *Music Teacher as Music Producer* (*MTMP*) (Randles, 2022) for ideas on how to configure your classroom space to allow for these small ensembles. Figure 3.1 depicts a sample class layout for you to consider that makes use of a traditional band, choir, orchestra room layout.

Lesson Instructions

Preparation (10 minutes)

Gather the class and give them a short lesson on favorite songs, their value, the thoughts and prior experience that they trigger. Share with them sound bites from some of your favorite happy songs. Talk about how they make you feel when you hear them, how they can alter your mood for the better. Demonstrate how you go about searching for your favorite songs by typing the name of the song and "chords" into a search engine. Show them how some searches give songs with chords that say "capo"

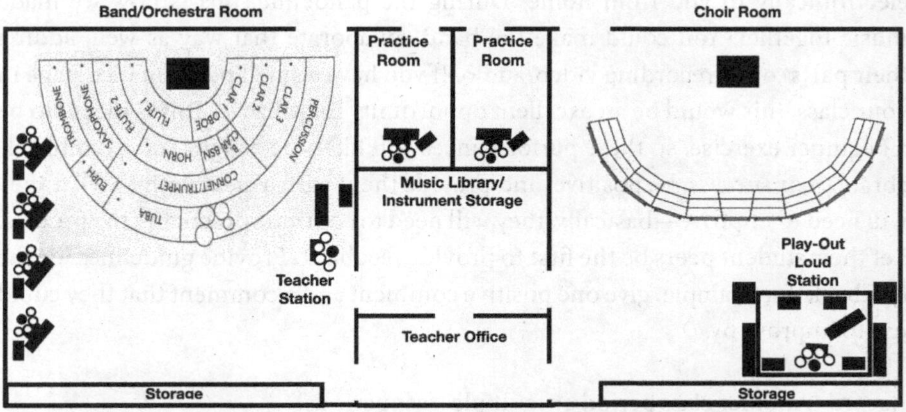

Figure 3.1 Classroom setup for small technologically mediated cover bands

for a guitar while other songs give you tablature ("tab"), a short form of musical notation for guitar players. It might be appropriate for you to teach how tab works.

Choose the Song (10–15 minutes or longer)
Give them some time to search for the song. They will have to agree on which one that they want to do. This could take a lot of time or not, depending upon the group and their dynamics. Help them only when they need your help; otherwise, stay out of the way. They come to you with diverse opinions and highly developed tastes for what they like. Let them lead the way. You will sometimes have to move them away from music with explicit content. You know your school culture and what is allowed/tolerated. Monitor the activity in the room carefully to make sure that it stays productive.

Work on the Song (30 minutes or most likely much more)
You are going to have to allow them time to work on the song. This can be complicated if they are working on band arrangements of the song in groups. If they are working on the song individually, you will have a different series of considerations. Most of your students will likely be self-conscious about their singing abilities. You will have to create a safe place to not be perfect all of the time. You will have to discuss the role of feedback and what is acceptable. Positivity needs to be the mantra in your classroom for students to feel safe singing in front of each other. Also, it is a great idea for you to model singing in front of them. It is okay for your performances to not be perfect as well. Performing in front of them goes a long way to establish a positive and supportive culture in your classroom.

Perform (Another Class Period)
Depending on how many groups/individuals you want to perform in class, you will have to leave time for all students who want to perform. You will have students with severe performance anxiety. For them you will have to create alternate performance opportunities. They could record their performances and submit them electronically to you from home. During the pandemic, this is how we made music together. You could make the band collaborate that way as well, adding their parts to the recording video/audio. If you have a small performance stage in your class, this would be an excellent opportunity to utilize it. This is meant to be a beginner exercise, so these performances will likely be rough. You need to celebrate their success, be positive, and provide them with a clear path to what they will need to improve—basically, they will need to continue practicing the process. Let their student peers be the first to provide feedback. Provide guidelines for the feedback: for example, give one positive comment and a comment that they could use to improve by.

Record (Another class period or multiple class periods)
It is nearly always worth your time and effort to record the songs/performances of your students. They learn by engaging in practice and reflection upon their practice.

There is not a better way of self-assessment for musicians than critically listening to our performances. You can be meticulous and professional about recording or not depending upon your expertise with recording arts. An audio interface with a XY-configured microphone pattern would capture the sound of a room well. If you have a computer at each station that your small groups are in you could multitrack-record their performance and engineer the audio for matching with your video. You could simply use your phone or tablet to record the performances with the built-in microphone. All of these options are available to you. You have to choose a path that makes sense for your setting and work life.

Modifications for Learners

Recording at Home Modification

For those of your students with performance anxiety, allow them to record their performances at home on their phones or with their computers with DAWs. Many times their desire to make use of this modification has nothing to do with their interest in your class or the lesson, but everything to do with their anxiety about performing in front of their peers. Allow them to record at home. Doing so still means that they are developing a connection to the real world of people making music in the world. They could come around to the possibility of performing in front of their peers when they develop a bit more confidence. You should encourage them to share their videos with the class as a way of encouraging their live performance prowess.

You Perform with Them Modification

If performing the accompaniment is too difficult a task for them, you can always sit in and perform an accompaniment for their singing. This is a widely used accommodation by me when I am working with younger students. It is not easy to play an instrument and sing at the same time. Remember, though, as you are working on developing this skill in your students that singing and playing together is wrapped up in quite a lot of cultural capital. They will gain skills that can last a lifetime with these abilities.

Learning Outcomes

- Choose a song chorus that makes them happy. Share it with their peers.
- Work on the song either independently or within a peer group.
- Perform a song chorus of a song of their choice and accompany their voice with an instrument of their choosing.
- Perform the song in front of their peers (or via a pre-recorded performance) for their peers (or not).
- Record the song performance.

- Learn what it feels like to engage in a process of covering a song that makes you happy.

Assessment Considerations

Informal Assessment. You will assess their learning for this lesson by the extent to which they engaged with the process. Are they sitting on the side and not talking? Are they leading the group? Are they taking notes on their phone? Are they smiling? Are they messing around? It is difficult to know exactly what they are getting out of a particular experience. In some cases it may seem that they are not engaged when they actually are quite engaged. You will need to have a loose set of criteria for assessing their learning. Think of assessment in this case as part performance quality assessment, part mechanics of performing their accompaniment, part mechanics of singing, part creativity of the song choice, part creativity of the performance, and part intangibles that are difficult to describe. Your assessments should be additive in nature and should avoid reduction. In other words, there should be multiple ways for them to do well on the assignment, and fewer ways that they can bury themselves in a low performance score. Failure to do any of the parts that I have outlined here could cause that. Remember, though, that learning in this setting is non-linear and that most of all you need to celebrate successes, even minor ones, to help ensure that future learning takes place.

Formal Assessment. Here is a rubric that you might use for this exercise. Rubrics like this one encourage your students to look for specific things as they grow their skills. Along with formal assessments like this, it is a good idea to give worthwhile qualitative feedback that helps your students grow in each area that you would like to see them grow.

Criteria	Ratings					Pts
This criterion is linked to a Learning Outcome "Recording"	**4 to >3.0 pts** **Expert** I love that your recording is approaching professional quality	**3 to >2.0 pts** **Practitioner** I like that you demonstrated very good recording technique (including balance)	**2 to >1.0 pts** **Apprentice** I'm concerned that the recording isn't very good	**1 to >0.0 pts** **Novice** What's up? Your recording is really difficult to listen to	**0 pts** **No Marks**	4 pts
This criterion is linked to a Learning Outcome "Musicianship"	**4 to >3.0 pts** **Expert** I love that you displayed almost professional levels of musicianship	**3 to >2.0 pts** **Practitioner** I like the level of musicianship you displayed in your performance—it's very good	**2 to >1.0 pts** **Apprentice** I'm concerned with how many errors showed up in your performance	**1 to >0.0 pts** **Novice** What's up? Your performance seems lacking in music	**0 pts** **No Marks**	4 pts

Criteria	Ratings					Pts
This criterion is linked to a Learning Outcome "Creativity"	**4 to >3.0 pts** **Expert** I love that the creativity you displayed could end up on a recording	**3 to >2.0 pts** **Practitioner** I like that you displayed a very good sense of creativity	**2 to >1.0 pts** **Apprentice** I'm concerned that your performance did not display very much creativity	**1 to >0.0 pts** **Novice** What's up? There was really no sense of creativity in your music	**0 pts** **No Marks**	4 pts
Total Points: 12						

Further Reading/Resources

- Check out Amy Schwartz, *100 Things That Make Me Happy* (New York: Abrams Appleseed, 2015).
- Check out this TED talk by Dan Gilbert titled "The Surprising Science of Happiness": https://www.ted.com/talks/dan_gilbert_the_surprising_science_of_happiness.
- Check out Clint Randles, *To Create: Imagining the Good Life through Music* (Chicago: GIA Publications, 2020).
- Check out Gretchen Rubin, *The Happiness Project* (New York: Harper, 2009).
- Check out Dalai Lama, Desmond Tutu, and Douglas Carlton Abrams, *Book of Joy: Lasting Happiness in a Changing World* (New York: Avery, 2016).
- Check out Taylor Swift's song "Happiness": https://www.youtube.com/watch?v=tP4TTgt4nb0.

Songs about Being Sad

Materials

- See first cover song lesson (see page 77)

Context

Some songs focus on the pain of being sad. Because at all times we can feel both happy and sad, over time human beings have produced a lot of sad songs. Both you and your students can share the pain that you have experienced in your lives and the songs that helped you deal with that pain. You are going to ask them to think of a chorus of a sad song, and as with the happy song lesson, you will just ask them to learn a chorus. You can, of course, have them cover the entire song. However, the beginner nature of this plan hinges on their ability to find a chorus that they enjoy from a sad song. You will have to teach them a little about song structure for them to know what the chorus of a song is. Then, you will have to give them time to search for songs. As stated in the previous lesson, this is very much a task that involves social bonding, identity sharing, and the expression of cultural capital. The process of searching for and sharing songs that make you sad goes a long way in solidifying and validating music's valuable place in your life.

SUNLIGHT: Some of the Saddest Songs Ever Written

Here is a list of some of the saddest songs ever written:

1. "Tears in Heaven" by Eric Clapton
2. "Hurt" by Nine Inch Nails (and the cover by Johnny Cash)
3. "Everybody Hurts" by R.E.M.
4. "Cats in the Cradle" by Harry Chapin
5. "Something in the Way" by Nirvana
6. "He Stopped Loving Her Today" by George Jones
7. "Black" by Pearl Jam
8. "Sam Stone" by John Prine
9. "Nutshell" by Alice in Chains
10. "I'm So Lonesome I Could Cry" by Hank Williams

Do an analysis of the elements of some or all of these songs. What is it about them that makes them sad? Is it the tempo? Is it the key? Is it the melodic content? How do these artists create a vibe that makes us sad when we hear them? Also, how have people done covers of these songs? Do a search for covers on YouTube and see how people have covered these songs.

WATER: The Story of "Everybody Hurts"

Put simply, R.E.M. wrote "Everybody Hurts" to save people's lives. Everything about the song was designed to stop teenagers from committing suicide; from the straightforward lyrics to the dramatic string arrangements to the beautiful melody, the song hits directly where it counts—the heart.[1] "Everybody Hurts" appeared on the band's 1992 album, *Automatic for the People*, and is one of the record's strong points, if not of the band's entire back catalogue. Surprisingly, the drummer Bill Berry is credited as the primary songwriter for the track, although the entire band was involved with completing the song, as well as producing it, alongside Scott Litt.

Guitar player Peter Buck stated in an interview that " 'Everybody Hurts' is similar to 'Man on the Moon.' Bill brought it in, and it was a one-minute long country-and-western song. It didn't have a chorus or a bridge. It had the verse . . . it kind of went around and around, and he was strumming it." Buck then proceeds to go into detail about how the band approached the first draft and how they completed it: "we went through about four different ideas and how to approach it and eventually came to that Stax, Otis Redding, 'Pain in My Heart' kind of vibe. I'm not sure if Michael would have copped that reference, but to a lot of our fans, it was a Staxxy-type thing. It took us forever to figure out the arrangement and who was going to play what, and then Bill ended up not playing on the original track. It was me and Mike and a drum machine. And then we all overdubbed."[2]

Lesson Time

This lesson can take place in one 45-minute class. However, you will most likely have to extend it over multiple classes if you decide to have them learn more than the chorus of the song, and depending on how well they take to the seed. You will need to allow time for this lesson to emerge. It is a seed that will take you in many different directions if you allow it to. That is the goal of this book—to give you many places to start a creative lesson. You could make this an individual lesson or you could have them self-select their own group.

Lesson Instructions

This is very similar across cover song lessons. Check out the lesson on page 79 for a detailed breakdown.

Modifications for Learners

This is very similar across cover song lessons. Check out the lesson on page 81 for a detailed breakdown.

Learning Outcomes

- Choose a song chorus from a sad song. Share it with their peers.
- Work on the song either independently or within a peer group.
- Perform a song chorus of a song of their choice and accompany their voice with an instrument of their choosing.
- Perform the song in front of their peers (or via a pre-recorded performance) for their peers (or not).
- Record the song performance.
- Learn what it feels like to engage in a process of covering a sad song.

Assessment Considerations

This is very similar across lessons. Check out the lesson on page 82 for a detailed breakdown of both informal and formal assessments ideas. There is also a rubric that you can use there.

Further Reading/Resources

- Check out how listening to sad music is actually good for your health: https://pittnews.com/article/168858/opinions/opinion-listening-to-sad-music-isnt-bad-for-you-its-actually-healthy/#:~:text=Listening%20to%20sad%20music%20is,of%20empathy%2C%20nostalgia%20and%20tranquility.
- On the pleasures of sad music https://www.frontiersin.org/articles/10.3389/fnhum.2015.00404/full#:~:text=As%20previously%20stated%2C%20sad%20music,Taruffi%20and%20Koelsch%2C%202014.
- Sad music can make adolescents who are already sad . . . sadder: https://journals.sagepub.com/doi/full/10.1177/0305735619849622.
- Here are six reasons that we enjoy listening to sad music: https://www.psychologytoday.com/us/blog/science-choice/201905/6-reasons-why-we-enjoy-listening-sad-music.
- Check out Holly Chisholm, *Just Peachy: Comics about Depression, Anxiety, Love, and Finding Humor in Being Sad* (New York: Skyhorse, 2019).
- Listen to "Everybody Hurts" by R.E.M.: .https://www.youtube.com/watch?v=5rOiW_xY-kc

4

Intermediate Cover Song Seeds

Work Up Your Favorite Song

Materials

- See first cover song lesson (see page 77)

Context

When it comes to our favorite songs, we have ownership and multiple reasons for making particular songs our favorites. The stories behind why some songs make it to the top of our list are worth telling as they are intricately connected to who we are as human beings. Our favorite songs are a part of our identity. So, right away, when you ask someone to come up with a cover song version of their favorite song, you are asking them to share a large part of who they are with members of your school music community. That is an incredibly meaningful use of your time.

SUNLIGHT: Your Favorite Artist's Favorite Songs

Have you ever wondered what your favorite artist's favorite songs are? You can get a little bit of history of your favorite music by understanding the favorite songs of your favorite artist. You should stop everything that you are doing right now and do a search for the favorite songs of your favorite artist. What did you find out? Were they what you expected? Were there any surprises? Here are the favorite songs of Jack White, my favorite artist at the moment:

1. "Grinnin' in Your Face" by Son House
2. "Crazy Hazy Kisses" by Flat Duo Jets
3. "Whole Lotta Love" by Led Zeppelin
4. "Electricity" by Captain Beefheart
5. "You're Looking at Country" by Loretta Lynn
6. "Mother of Earth" by The Gun Club
7. "Shelter from the Storm" by Bob Dylan

Growing Songwriting. Clint Randles, Oxford University Press. © Oxford University Press 2024.
DOI: 10.1093/oso/9780197693216.003.0004

8. "Sitting on Top of the World" by The Mississippi Sheiks
9. "Put the Blame on Mame" by Rita Hayworth
10. "I Wanna Be Your Dog" by Iggy and the Stooges

As I did this search, I had to dig into the catalogue of people who I know well: Led Zeppelin, Bob Dylan, and Iggy and the Stooges. However, I also had to examine the music or artists whom I knew very little about, but who upon reflection and consideration have very much influenced the sound of Jack White. Fascinating and enlightening. That's something that I can use in my classroom as I help people cover their favorite song. So can you!

WATER: "Seven Nation Army"

I have spent the past twenty years helping my students perform the song "Seven Nation Army" by The White Stripes (Jack White; see Figure 4.1). Here is the story of how the song was conceived:

> White stumbled upon the riff while warming up his hollowbody guitar. "I played the riff again and it sounded interesting," he said. White plugged in an octave pedal and wound his six-string down to a low twang. He had grand plans: "I thought if

Figure 4.1 Jack White, live in Tampa, Florida, 2022

I ever got asked to write the next James Bond theme, that would be the riff for it." He devised a storyline in which a protagonist discovers that his friends are talking about him behind his back. "He feels so bad he has to leave town, but you get so lonely you come back," said White. "The song's about gossip. It's about me, Meg and the people we're dating."

As is often the case with rock songs, it's hard to know exactly what these three verses are about without an explanation, which White has thankfully given to interviewers over the years. Much of the lyric, though, is still subject to interpretation. For instance, many have surmised that his Catholic background may have played a role in his writing the lines And I'm bleeding, and I'm bleeding, and I'm bleeding/Right before the Lord/All the words are gonna bleed from me/And I will sing no more/And the stains coming from my blood/Tell me go back home.

White recounted in greater detail to *Rolling Stone*'s David Fricke where the lyrics came from: "Seven Nation Army started out about two specific people I knew in Detroit. It was about gossip, the spreading of lies and the other person's reaction to it. It came from a frustration of watching my friends do this to each other. In the end, it started to become a metaphor for things I was going through. But I never set out to write an expose on myself. To me, the song was a blues at the beginning of the twenty-first century. The third verse ["I'm going to Wichita/Far from this opera forevermore"] could be something from a hundred years ago. It won a Grammy for Best Rock Song. [Laughs] Maybe it should have won for Best Paranoid Blues Song.[1]

Song lyrics come from our personal experience. The words that we choose quite often come from the words that we know and use in our everyday speech. Have your students do a search for the story of how their favorite song was conceived. The process of doing that will go a long way toward helping them understand their song, and will likely lead to a more informed performance.

Lesson Time

This lesson can take place in one 45-minute class. However, you will most likely have to extend it over multiple classes, especially if you work into the sequence them talking about why the song is their favorite or doing some research into how the song was written. You will need to allow time for this lesson to emerge organically from their interests. This is a seed of a lesson that will take you in many different directions if you allow it to. Their favorite song could lead into their favorite album, or you could decide as a class that they all love a particular album that you would like to take time to realize as a group over a number of class periods.

Lesson Instructions

This is very similar across cover song lessons. Check out the lesson on page 79 for a detailed breakdown.

Modifications for Learners

This is very similar across cover song lessons. Check out the lesson on page 81 for a detailed breakdown.

Learning Outcomes

- Choose a favorite song that you would like to cover. Share it with your peers.
- Work on the song either independently or within a peer group.
- Perform the song and accompany their voice with an instrument of their choosing, in front of their peers (or via a pre-recorded performance) for their peers (or not).
- Record the song performance.
- Engage in the process of understanding yourself better by covering your favorite song.

Assessment Considerations

This is very similar across lessons. Check out the lesson on page 82 for a detailed breakdown of both informal and formal assessment ideas. There is also a rubric that you can use there.

Further Reading/Resources

- Check out this article on the White Stripes and the value of simplicity: https://www.avclub.com/simplicity-gave-the-white-stripes-an-unlikely-sports-an-1798265982.
- Check out this article about what our favorite songs can tell us about ourselves: https://time.com/16129/what-the-music-you-love-says-about-you-and-how-it-can-improve-your-life/.
- Here is an article on why we love music: https://greatergood.berkeley.edu/article/item/why_we_love_music.
- Here is an article on why we listen to our favorite songs on repeat: https://www.mic.com/articles/99744/the-science-behind-why-you-listen-to-your-favorite-songs-obsessively.

- Here is a link to the music video for Weezer's "My Favorite Songs": https://www.youtube.com/watch?v=AGPdXYG1msg.

Songs That Drive Us Crazy

Materials

- See first cover song lesson (see page 77)

Context

There are some songs that completely drive us bonkers. We wonder sometimes, "Did they want to torture us when they wrote this one?" What is it about particular songs that make them incredibly annoying? Some of it has to do with how often they are played, and the conditions surrounding when we were introduced to them. As I write this book, the United States is in the middle of an election season, where political advertisements are being played over and over again. The very first milliseconds of these advertisements trigger a nauseous response from me and members of my family. There is a phenomenon known as misophonia, a chronic condition whereby particular sounds, specifically those produced by another person, trigger anger, impulsive reactions, and a number of other negative responses. It is a real thing that researchers have dedicated a lot of time to understand. Can you cover a song that drives you nuts? What might the process of covering that song do for your understanding of what drives you crazy about that song? Let's experiment and try it!

SUNLIGHT: Earworms

Certain songs have been earworms that seem to be reborn with every new generation. We might think of earworms scientifically as Receptiveness + (predictability-surprise) + (melodic potency) + (rhythmic repetition × 1.5) = earworm. Here are some of the most notable examples:

1. "Somebody That I Used to Know" by Gotye
2. "Moves Like Jagger" by Maroon 5
3. "California Gurls" by Katy Perry
4. "Poker Face" by Lady Gaga
5. "We Will Rock You" by Queen
6. "My Humps" by The Black Eyed Peas
7. "Beat It" by Michael Jackson

8. "Karma Chameleon" by Culture Club
9. "Shake It Off" by Taylor Swift
10. "Never Gonna Give You Up" by Rick Astley

Earworms aren't necessarily bad songs. In fact, I love almost all of the songs on this list. However, there's something about them that gets them caught in our brains to the point that we are unable to get them out. That makes them earworms. It takes some artistry to craft songs that can do that.

WATER: "My Humps"

This song, released in September 2005 by The Black Eyed Peas, is about a woman who uses her body to her own advantage. It features female vocalist Fergie in defiant sex-kitten mode, teasing the guys gawking her in the club and threatening to start some drama if they touch her "humps." Will.i.am plays the role of her enabler, asking what she's going to do with those humps of hers. The song stood out for its lyrical stupidity and proved that a good beat can overcome lyrics like "my hump, my hump, my lovely little lumps." This song can get lodged in your brain in a serious way. The song is perhaps the most divisive hit of the 2000s. To some, it's funny and catchy. Others think it has some of the worst lyrics in the history of popular music. Regardless, no one thought of the word "humps" the same way again after hearing it. Michael Scott used this as his ringtone in seasons 2 and 3 of *The Office*.

Lesson Time

This lesson can take place in one 45-minute class. However, you will most likely have to extend it over multiple classes, especially if you work into the sequence them talking about songs that annoy them. You will need to allow time for this lesson to emerge organically from their interests. This is a seed of a lesson that will take you in many different directions if you allow it to. Their most annoying songs could lead them to other "most annoying" aspects of songs that you would like to take time to unpack as a group over a number of class periods. Follow their interests. You can gain a lot positive energy for teaching and learning through a deeper understanding of the things that annoy us.

Lesson Instructions

This is very similar across cover song lessons. Check out the lesson on page 79 for a detailed breakdown.

Modifications for Learners

This is very similar across cover song lessons. Check out the lesson on page 81 for a detailed breakdown.

Learning Outcomes

- Choose an annoying song that you would like to cover. Share it with your peers.
- Work on the song either independently or within a peer group.
- Perform the song and accompany their voice with an instrument of their choosing, in front of their peers (or via a pre-recorded performance) for their peers (or not).
- Record the song performance.
- Engage in the process of understanding yourself better by covering an annoying song.

Assessment Considerations

This is very similar across lessons. Check out the lesson on page 82 for a detailed breakdown of both informal and formal assessments ideas. There is also a rubric that you can use there.

Further Reading/Resources

- Check out this article on how repetition can be good in some cases and annoying in others: https://www.reddit.com/r/LetsTalkMusic/comments/l43at3/what_makes_repetition_work_in_some_songs_and_be/.
- Here's a link to a take on the most annoying twenty songs ever written: https://www.mentalfloss.com/article/18894/most-annoying-songs-ever.
- Check out Felipe Trotta, *Annoying Music in Everyday Life* (New York: Bloomsbury Academic, 2020).
- Check out this book chapter on auditory preference and aesthetics in the book *Neuroscience of Preference and Choice*: https://www.sciencedirect.com/science/article/pii/B9780123814319000206.

5

Advanced Cover Song Seeds

Take the Song in Another Direction

Materials

- See first cover song lesson (see page 77)

Context

Some covers are more memorable than the original artist release of a song. In the history of music, there are a number of cases of this happening. Can you do a cover that channels something else, something special that will be of importance to an audience of your peers, class, community, or even your region? That is what you want your students to ask themselves when they attempt to move toward being advanced with their cover song prowess. We all must move through the various stages and learn from our process, as we move toward writing songs that are worth our time making and eventually hearing.

SUNLIGHT: Best Cover Songs of All Time

Here is a list of cover songs that are better than the originals. Take some time and listen to them in class. Can you hear why some people consider them to be better than the original versions?

1. "Hurt" by Johnny Cash (Nine Inch Nails)
2. "I Will Always Love You" by Whitney Houston (Dolly Parton)
3. "Nothing Compares 2 U" by Sinead O'Connor (Prince)
4. "All along the Watchtower" by The Jimi Hendrix Experience (Bob Dylan)
5. "Black Magic Woman" by Santana (Fleetwood Mac)
6. "Blinded by the Light" by Manfred Mann's Earth Band (Bruce Springsteen)
7. "I Love Rock 'n' Roll" by Joan Jett and the Blackhearts (The Arrows)
8. "The Man Who Sold the World" by Nirvana (David Bowie)
9. "Me and Bobby McGee" by Janis Joplin (Kris Kristofferson)
10. "Mr. Tambourine Man" by The Byrds (Bob Dylan)

Growing Songwriting. Clint Randles, Oxford University Press. © Oxford University Press 2024.
DOI: 10.1093/oso/9780197693216.003.0005

It is quite a task to take a song that is known by someone else and do it in a way that transcends the original. In some cases, these songs where lesser-known songs by the original artist until the person who covered them made them famous. In doing background work for writing this section of the book I discovered that "I Love Rock 'n' Roll" was NOT written by Joan Jett and The Blackhearts! That was news to me.

WATER: Johnny Cash and "Hurt"

Nine Inch Nails recorded the song "Hurt" for their 1994 album *The Downward Spiral*, a concept album that tells the story of someone's descent into darkness. The finale of the album is "Hurt," an emotional tour de force that begins "I hurt myself today / To see if I still feel." Producer Rick Rubin sent the song to Johnny Cash to preview and consider, but the veteran musician couldn't hear beyond the style that Nine Inch Nails did it in. "I think it was hard for him to hear it," Rubin told NPR.[1] "So, I sent him the lyrics. I said, 'Just read the lyrics. If you like the lyrics, then we'll find a way to do it that will suit you.' "

It took some convincing, but Cash was persuaded by Rubin's belief in the song and agreed to try recording it at the producer's home in L.A. Cash was suffering from autonomic neuropathy brought on by diabetes and by the time he recorded Hurt, his health was failing. "There were times when his voice sounded broken," said Rubin. "He tried to turn that into a positive in the selection of the music. It was a real struggle for him." Instead of being a song about a young individual on the downward spiral to self-destruction, Cash interpreted the lyrics as a man at the end of his life. The result is heartbreaking as the veteran musician sings in a quavering, emotional voice: "If I could start again / A million miles away / I would keep myself / I would find a way." Trent Reznor of Nine Inch Nails proclaims that after Cash sang the song, it really belonged to him. He owned it. That is quite an advanced way of covering a song.

Lesson Time

This lesson can take place in one 45-minute class. However, you will most likely have to extend it over multiple classes, especially if you break the creative process into searching for the perfect song that you can take in another direction. You will need to allow time for this lesson to emerge organically from the students' interests. This is a seed of a lesson that will take you in many different directions if you allow it to. Successfully taking a song in another direction based on how you personally own it might inspire you to do similarly with other such songs. Do you have a time when you owned a cover song like this? That could go a long way toward inspiring your class. Follow their interests. You can gain quite a lot of positive energy for teaching and learning through the sharing of individual student successes.

Lesson Instructions

This is very similar across cover song lessons. Check out the lesson on page 79 for a detailed breakdown.

Modifications for Learners

This is very similar across cover song lessons. Check out the lesson on page 81 for a detailed breakdown.

Learning Outcomes

- Choose a song that you take in a new direction. Share it with your peers.
- Work on the song either independently or within a peer group.
- Perform the song and accompany their voice with an instrument of their choosing, in front of their peers (or via a pre-recorded performance) for their peers (or not).
- Record the song performance.
- Engage in a process of understanding yourself better by covering a song that you take in a new direction based on your life experience.

Assessment Considerations

This is very similar across lessons. Check out the lesson on page 82 for a detailed breakdown of both informal and formal assessments ideas. There is also a rubric that you can use there.

Further Reading/Resources

- Check out this article on how to tap into your creativity: https://www.latimes.com/health/la-he-creativity-20170304-story.html.
- Gain some inspiration through the exploration of vulnerability in art making: https://www.milanartinstitute.com/blog/3-ways-to-express-vulnerability-in-your-art.
- Hear about how music can actually save lives: https://www.npr.org/sections/allsongs/2015/05/09/405250920/the-good-listener-can-a-song-really-save-your-life
- Perform an internet search on the phrase "how to mine life experience in your music" for some tips on improvisation to help you at any stage of your creative process.

Making a Mashup of at Least Two Songs

Materials

- See first cover song lesson (see page 77)

Context

I am sitting in a café as I write this book in the fall of 2022. On the radio is a song that features the artists Dua Lipa and Elton John, I hear a mashup of familiar songs within the song. I do a little digging and discover that the song is called "Cold Heart" (2021). It pays homage to John's career by expertly blending together four of his previously released singles: "Rocket Man" originally released in 1972, "Sacrifice" (1989), "Kiss the Bride" (1983), and "Where's the Shoorah?" (1976). Dua Lipa comes in singing the chorus of "Rocket Man." The song is an excellent example of how artists can weave together songs that weren't intended to be together but work out very well in the end. This idea is scalable in your classroom as a possible starting place for covering songs.

SUNLIGHT: Thinking about Theme and Structure

Here is a way that you might think about the structure of and story of a medley of songs:

1. Setting the theme
2. Song choices
3. Overarching structure
4. Song order
5. Writing transitions
6. Review

The first part of the process is thinking about the theme of the medley. The ua Lipa/Elton John song "Cold Heart" outlines a relationship that has taken turn for the worse. The theme is ultimately about breakup. So they chose the ur songs that we hear to help tell the story. Each songs adds another layer and rthers the narrative in some way. The order of the songs matters. Musical nsitions can become quite meaningful as well. What is the theme? How can order of the songs and musical choices accentuate the meta-narrative? Those the primary questions for your students as they put together a mashup of at t two songs.

WATER: The Beatles Cirque du Soleil Show

The soundtrack to the Cirque du Soleil show *Love* (2006) is a remix album produced by George Martin and his son Giles (Figure 5.1). The soundtrack contains thirty-seven named Beatles songs with musical fragments of many more. Producer George Martin called it the Da Vinci Code for Beatles fanatics: "I wanted to have a competition to see if anyone could spot everything we'd done in the right sequence.

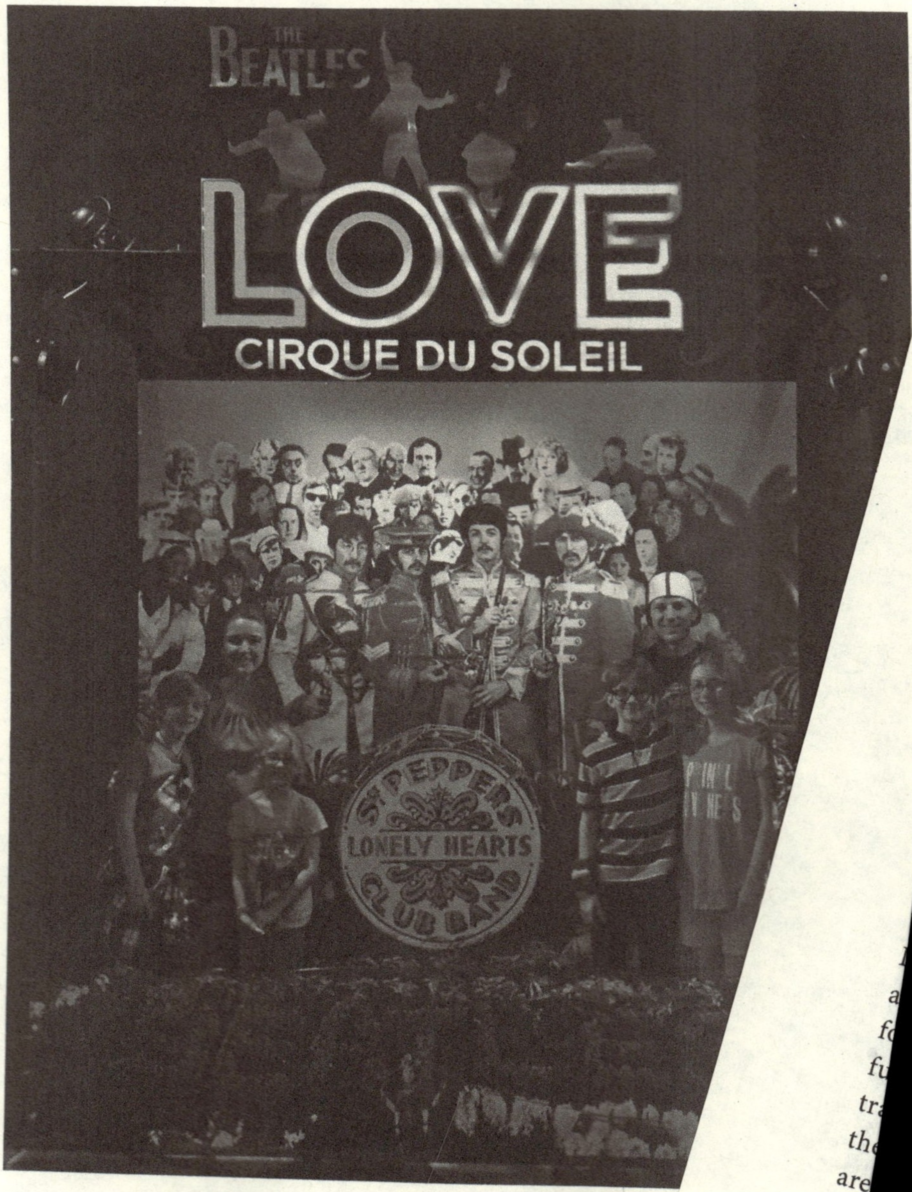

Figure 5.1 The Randles family at The Beatles Cirque Du Soleil ir

No one will be able to do it." The remix was a mashup combining elements from The Beatles' multitrack recordings from 1963 to 1969, fan club recordings, outtakes, and live crowd noises. The album won two Grammys at the 50th Awards ceremony on February 10, 2008, for Best Compilation Soundtrack Album and Best Surround Sound Album. Here is a list of all of the songs that were put together:

"Because"
"Get Back"
"Glass Onion"
"Eleanor Rigby"
"Julia" (Transition)
"I Am the Walrus"
"I Want to Hold Your Hand"
"Drive My Car"/"The Word"/"What You're Doing"
"Gnik Nus"
"Something"
"Blue Jay Way" (Transition)
"Being for the Benefit of Mr Kite!"/"I Want You (She's So Heavy)"/"Helter Skelter"
"Help!"
"Blackbird"/"Yesterday"
"Strawberry Fields Forever"
"Within You without You"/"Tomorrow Never Knows"
"Lucy in the Sky with Diamonds"
"Octopus's Garden"
"Lady Madonna"
"Here Comes the Sun"
"The Inner Light" (Transition)
"Come Together"/"Dear Prudence"
"Cry Baby Cry" (Transition)
"Revolution"
"Back in the USSR"
"While My Guitar Gently Weeps"
"A Day in the Life"
"Hey Jude"
"Sgt Pepper's Lonely Hearts Club Band (Reprise)"
"All You Need Is Love"

Take some time and listen to the songs that were mashed together. Sometimes tracks include the bass line of one song and the harmonic structure of another, over the melody of another. It helps to have really internalized the songs that are utilized. You could make the analyses of this album an assignment, a unit, or an interesting day of discovery.

Lesson Time

This lesson can take place in one 45-minute class. However, your creative and intuitive pedagogy might extend it over multiple class sessions. On the inspiration side of the equation, if your students are Beatles fans (the WATER segment in this lesson) then you might construct a whole unit. That particular band seems to have a massive amount of staying power over the decades that I have been teaching kids in schools! You will need to allow time for this lesson to emerge organically from their interests. This is a seed of a lesson that will take you in many different directions if you allow it to. What older songs or collection of songs can they put together to tell a story? What stories do they want to tell? How can you help them tell those stories?

Lesson Instructions

This is very similar across cover song lessons. Check out the lesson on page 79 for a detailed breakdown.

Modifications for Learners

This is very similar across cover song lessons. Check out the lesson on page 81 for a detailed breakdown.

Learning Outcomes

- Choose a collection of song fragments of different songs. Assemble them creatively. Share the work with their peers.
- Work on the song either independently or within a peer group.
- Perform the song and accompany their voice with an instrument of their choosing, in front of their peers (or via a pre-recorded performance) for their peers (or not).
- Record the song performance.
- Engage in a process of assembling songs that have personal musical meaning to tell a story.

Assessment Considerations

This is very similar across lessons. Check out the lesson on page 82 for a detailed breakdown of both informal and formal assessments ideas. There is also a rubric that you can use there.

Further Reading/Resources

- Check out this article on remixes and mashups: https://www.masterclass.com/articles/how-to-make-a-mashup.
- Check out how DJs create mashups: https://djcity.com.au/blog/how-to-mashup-songs-using-free-or-paid-daw-software/.
- On the art of the mashup: https://www.ableton.com/en/classroom/support/art-of-mashup/.
- Check out Paul Zala, *How to Make Great Music Mashups: The Start-to-Finish Guide to Making Mashups with Ableton Live* (London: Routledge, 2018).

PART II
THE MIDDLE GROUND

6
The Space Between

WATER: Dave Matthews Band

The song with the title "The Space Between" was released in 2001 by Dave Matthews Band. It's composed of the following lyrics that may or may not help us with understanding the middle ground between covering songs and writing our own original songs:

> You cannot quit me so quickly
> There's no hope in you for me
> No corner you could squeeze me
> But I got all the time for you love
>
> The space between
> The tears we cry
> Is the laughter that keeps us coming back for more
> The space between our wicked lies
> Is where we hope to keep safe from the pain

Matthews writes about the space between pain as what keeps hope for love alive. In this chapter I would like to get us to think about the common ground between the songs we cover and the ones that we write ourselves—the space between the familiar with the new-to-the-world. I'm not sure that anyone has dealt with this space in books on songwriting. So, I tread lightly and humbly here.

WATER: Michael Jackson's First Solo Album

Many might think of Michael Jackson's solo album as 1979's *Off the Wall*. However, in between the rise of the Jackson 5 and the television debut of the moonwalk in 1983, a thirteen-year-old Michael Jackson laid the foundation for the most storied career in American, if not global, pop culture history, by showing the world that he was a serious male vocalist with the 1972 release of his debut solo album, *Got to Be There*. "A carefully selected track list of rhythm and blues covers and originals gave the lead singer the opportunity to step beyond the shadow of the sibling package that collectively spawned Jackson 5 mania, which included a cartoon and tons of

Growing Songwriting. Clint Randles, Oxford University Press. © Oxford University Press 2024.
DOI: 10.1093/oso/9780197693216.003.0006

merchandise, and showcased the young MJ as a soulful man-child."[1] The album proved that he could excel at his own version of the grown folk music that he had rehearsed as a member of the Jackson family in Gary, Indiana.

From the opening track of *Got to Be There*, young Michael's confidence is staggering as he begins the album with the difficult task of delivering his own rendition of Bill Withers's "Ain't No Sunshine." Michael sets the tone of the album by owning the fact that his voice and vocal ability was maturing beyond the boyishness that everyone fell in love with when he first sang on "I Want You Back" alongside his older brothers, barely three years earlier. In this album, he is coming into his own. He's en route to becoming the King of Pop by covering the music of his heroes and finding his own voice by coming out of the shadow of his brothers. This chapter is all about making this part of the journey happen in the lives of your students.

Engaging the Process

When we think of the process of becoming a songwriter, we might think of starting with lyrics, melody, and rhythm and digging into the creative process straight off. However, as I have suggested here and other scholars in music education have proclaimed, the process really starts with covering the songs of our heroes. We learn best about how songs are constructed by studying the music of our favorite artists. So, covering songs is the place to start as you help your students create their own original songs. Before we get to writing our own songs, though, there is this strange yet interesting middle ground that can be filled in a number of different ways. This chapter is devoted to this middle ground and how we should think of it.

Remember, quite a lot of musicians never move from covering songs to writing their own original songs. In the town where I live there is a very active open mic scene. Many people who show up to perform at open mics spend most of their time creatively choosing cover songs and working through beginner, intermediate, and advanced ways of covering them. Getting better at covering songs can last a lifetime and is a personally meaningful pursuit where being musical is concerned. You don't have to and shouldn't feel like you need to shortcut this part of your students' journey toward becoming a songwriter. However, if we think of writing original songs as taking flight, there are some things that we can consider that will help us help some of them move into Part III of this book.

The organizational structure of this book breaks down a little when we think of the difference between advanced cover song lessons, middle ground lessons, and beginning songwriting lessons. I realize that the divisions are more imagined at times than real, and that some lessons could be moved around to different sections of the book based on your expertise and the flow of learning in your classroom. That is okay. Use anything and everything here how it makes the most sense for you to use it. We are partners in this. Nothing is sacred. I have your back as you have mine.

Middle Ground Thinking

So, you have used some of the lesson seeds in Part I and your students have done some performances and made some recordings as part of the process. They have been successful and people have started to take notice within your school and throughout your community. They will! It is inevitable. That's the power of music at work. Once you made the decision that you can and will use all the music in the world and that all the ways that people make music can and should be considered equally valid, you steered the musical lives of you and your students into some fertile soil. It's time to think about what it means to be a good gardener during the middle period as your students become songwriters.

Advice for Master Gardeners

Here are some strategies on how to keep your students engaged and learning through the space between covering songs and becoming a songwriter. I have borrowed this advice from master gardeners who desire to structure their vegetable gardens to produce vegetables year-round.[2] My comments follow advice from gardening professionals:

1. Extend the Growing Season

Use row covers and cold frames to provide additional warmth and shelter in spring and fall. Grow crops next to sheltered, sun-facing walls to help create a warm microclimate that can give plants a longer growing season. In the wall, sun-facing walls help cucumbers, peppers and other tender plants to continue to ripen.

We, of course, would love to extend our growing season—the time that our students spend writing, revising, performing, and recording their music. So, we take action to make sure that the environment (our classroom and school) is conducive to growing. Everything that you put in your classroom space could help in this area. Check out *Music Teacher as Music Producer* (Randles, 2022) for tips on how to transform your physical space for helping students do their best work.

2. Keep Crops Going over Winter

In colder climates, a cold frame or greenhouse is essential to keep crops going over winter. Space plants generously for good air circulation and to make the most of the weak winter sunlight. Pick salad crops and greens little and often so they have the energy to replace their harvested leaves.

In school settings, we would like our students to continue growing when they are not in school. So, giving them goals and ideas for recording projects when they are not with us is essential. We can encourage bands that form out of the class. A number of them will likely want to continue practicing when they are not in school—that was the goal all along!

3. Avoid the "Hungry Gap"

Plant broccoli, cabbage and late-season leeks in late summer to stand over winter and join the last of the winter-stored produce. Some perennial crops can also help plug the hungry gap, for instance, asparagus and rhubarb.

You want to always have goals for your students, so that they can imagine themselves doing projects without you. Once they have a taste of being a real musician—someone who can make their favorite music in the ways that they choose—they will constantly want to fill the gaps in their lives with more music-making. I have been in bands with engineers, microbiology professors, clock shop owners, and successful lawyers whose primary goals in life center on making the best music that they possibly can in bands. Music is a lifelong pursuit that always gives back to those who engage in it.

4. Get Ahead

Many seedlings can also be started off indoors under grow lights. Sow onions, chard, and peas into plug trays from late winter to transplant outdoors in spring. You can bring forward the sowing date for other early crops by a couple of weeks by pre-warming the soil. To do this, cover the soil with row covers or cloches a few weeks before you're ready to sow.

Try to always introduce new sounds and demonstrate new technologies to your students. Encourage them to be on the lookout themselves for new and inspiring timbres and tone-shaping devices. Music history is full of the adoption of new technologies. Check out *Music Teacher as Music Producer* (Randles, 2022) for more guitar-based effects than you ever wanted to know about. Use that as a place to start your own discovery of the world of tone and effects. You can transform even a low-budget instrument into a tool for new music creation with a few purchases on Reverb.com.

5. Spread Out Your Harvests

Sowing quick-maturing plants through spring and summer prepares your garden for a steady succession of harvests. Choose a mix of early-, mid-, and late-season varieties to really spread out your harvests so that, for instance, you can enjoy carrots from mid-spring to late winter, or strawberries from early summer through to fall.

As a music teacher as music producer, make sure that you have sufficient performance and recording goals to keep your students on the growing edge of their music-making. You should have both long-term and short-term assignments. Have them submit competencies, where they have to demonstrate skills in performance and recording along with performing and recording their cover and original songs. You need to plan for festivals as well as coffee shop performances to sustain the livelihood of your students.

6. Succession Plant

Set aside a dedicated "nursery" area in a greenhouse or cold frame, or in pots kept in a sheltered, sunny spot (or somewhere you can provide some shading if you experience hot summers). This way, you can raise crops from seed so they're ready to transplant the moment another crop is harvested.

In the business world, we might think of succession plants as disruptive technologies (a compliment to sustaining technologies) that are new, different, and promise to take the whole enterprise in new directions. These are plants that are prepared in advance to take over for the plants that will eventually grow, be harvested, and consumed. In your classroom you can think of succession plants as student leaders who will become the music teachers as music producers or the professional musicians of the future. You might also think of succession plants as music projects that run parallel to musical projects in the real world that push the limits in some way—recently, Lil Nas X's "Old Town Road" made its way into the country charts. That song is a succession plant!

Remember, my goal for this book is to give you some ideas for seeds of lessons, water (stories from the lives of professional songwriters), and sunlight (practical advice from the real world of helping people write their own songs) for growing the presence of songwriting in your curriculum.

Skill-Building Still Central to Daily Practice

The most important thing that you can do is make sure that the skills of your students are being nurtured daily. However, keep in mind that songwriting and creativities resist linear paths. We start with cover songs. We use preexisting forms and eventually write our own original lyrics. We use improvisation for motivation and inspiration, then follow our students' joy. We continue to make the following areas central to our daily operations:

1. discovering grooves
2. finding harmonic progressions
3. discovering melodies
4. writing lyrics

Revisit Chapter 1 on how to make these musical areas central to what your students do daily in the classroom. You might also peek at Chapter 10 where I discuss how to bring all those tasks together specifically to help you help your students write better songs.

In terms of the middle ground, what have you learned about your students as they practiced doing these four things at the onset of their journey? The middle ground is a place to consider what you might have missed and to think about what you might bring into students' daily experience in your classroom. If they are in groups, are the groups working out how they should be? Who is unhappy? Who is doing well? How are the ones who are doing well interacting with the ones who are not doing well? How might you make things better by bringing them together?

I cannot stress enough the importance of the four areas that I highlight here. You have to try to improve their experience in all of them. Only then will they have the best chance possible to find meaning through being and becoming a songwriter.

They will be working to set lyrics to music and to set music to lyrics very soon. Have you leveraged the power of understanding other peoples' music first, though? You could spend a lot of time, or not, in the middle ground. Remember that all of this is a marathon and not a sprint.

Making the Turn

Working up the songs of other people is absolutely still a creative task, full of possibility and potential for meaning-making and musical growth. In the middle ground between cover songs and writing original ones, we do things that songwriters do in conceiving of whole sections of music with transitions that tell some sort of story. The difference, though, is that we still use other people's lyrics and musical work—in both large and small amounts. It is a natural part of the progression of being and becoming a songwriter, this middle ground. We beg, borrow, and steal the music of our heroes, giving every ounce of credit where credit is due. Look at Elvis Presley! Examine the first two albums by Led Zeppelin! Some artists thrive in this middle ground. And, again, we could rightly question whether or not this middle ground even exists in the first place.

SUNLIGHT: Wisdom for Growing: Five Chinese Proverbs

Below are five Chinese proverbs with my commentary on how they apply to what you are doing to nurture the growth of your students as songwriters:

A flower cannot blossom without sunshine nor a garden without love.

They will need your guidance and inspiration. In the end, what will make the most impact on their well-being is knowing that you cared.

A book is like a garden carried in the pocket.

I hope with all my heart that this book is helpful to you as you grow songwriting in your classroom.

Pleasure for one hour, a bottle of wine. Pleasure for one year a marriage; but pleasure for a lifetime, a garden.

Pleasure is fleeting, but gardening is the gift that keeps on giving. Teaching is very much like gardening. We try to provide the ideal conditions for our students to grow. And we grow along with them, tending the same garden that we ourselves grow in. That is quite a responsibility.

If you would be happy for a week, take a wife; if you would be happy for a month, kill a pig; but if you would be happy all your life, plant a garden.

Growing songwriting in your classroom will transform the community in which you live. The effects can and should be long-lasting. Just as stories about being in the school band have been reflected upon by members of your community over the past eighty years, learning how to write, perform, and record songs in school will animate our collective stories of music education for decades to come.

Garden flowers larger, field flowers stronger.
We will start the growth of many plants in our classroom. However, the goal is to see them grow and thrive out in the wild.

SUNLIGHT: Advice about Staying Alert on Long Car Rides

Below is some advice for people driving on long car rides.[3] I suggest that there are things that a music teacher can learn about the journey of helping students become songwriters by viewing these bits of advice through the lens of a music teacher as music producer.

1. *Real food, not junk*
   Try to listen to the best possible music that you can as you navigate the long and winding roads of life.
2. *Plan for stops during long trips*
   Don't be afraid to stop your daily activity to ponder something that might seem unrelated but is highly inspirational.
3. *Plan for comfort*
   Songwriting is hard work. Be comfortable in your planning, with your deadlines, with your assessment of personal progress.
4. *Be mindful of your posture*
   Don't push too much or too little. You want continuous progress and you want to always avoid boredom.
5. *Don't drive drowsy*
   Get enough rest. Don't be afraid of falling behind. Be on the lookout for student fatigue and be ready to be a voice of reason and understanding.
6. *Reduce stress*
   Life is full of stress. The world is a hurricane of deadlines and judgment. Be on the lookout for ways that you can reduce stress in your classroom.

These tips go a long way to ensure that students, your passengers on the long trip that is learning in the school music environment that you proctor, enjoy and engage with the journey.

Do Your Homework

In this section I provide some suggestions for you as you seek to grow songwriting in your classroom. If we think of the process of your being and becoming a teacher who serves as a music producer to your students running parallel to their being and becoming songwriters, there are things that you are going to need to do to keep up the quality of your instruction. These things will help you grow. Consider them part of your professional development.

Practice What You Preach

You need to be doing all of the things yourself that you are teaching them to do. Time is precious. Yes, indeed. When I became a music teacher after receiving my undergraduate degree, especially my first three years, I didn't feel that I had time to be musical. But eventually I came to a place where I had enough time to attend rehearsals and rejoin the world of amateur and professional musicians. You are going to need to practice writing your own songs to able to best help them.

Remember that there are producers who are not actually musicians themselves. Rick Rubin is a shining example of someone who had a few guitar and songwriting lessons but never actually became a musician himself. He is one of the most influential producers of all time, founding Def Jam Recordings and helping usher in hip-hop music to the mainstream since 1981. He also has produced a number of top-selling artists from a variety of other genres including heavy metal (Danzig, Slayer, System of a Down), alternative rock (The Strokes, Red Hot Chili Peppers, Weezer, The Cult), and country (Johnny Cash, The Chicks). Rubin is definitely an anomaly, though. Practice the skills that you want to nurture in them.

This is time for you to practice performing and analyzing the music that most moves YOU. Have you always wanted to make beats? Now is the time for you to try it out. Have you always wanted to learn to put monotone lyrics together and create raps? Now is the time for you to try it out. Build yourself a classroom and/or home studio. Start with a computer and an audio interface (Randles, 2022). Start to build your DAW chops as you practice making your own music. The resources on YouTube right now for making your music sound better are encouraging. Many people built their own home studios during the COVID-19 pandemic. Countless musicians are sharing their stories of making music as well.

Consult the Sourcebooks

In Chapter 1 I mentioned the following books:

1. *Great Songwriting Techniques* by Jack Perricone (Oxford, 2018)
2. *Teaching Music through Composition* by Barbara Freedman (Oxford, 2013)
3. *Songwriting—a Complete Guide to the Craft* by Stephen Citron (Hal Leonard, 2008)

4. *Using Technology to Unlock Musical Creativity* by Scott Watson (Oxford, 2011)
5. *Electronic Music School: A Contemporary Approach to Teaching Musical Creativity* (Oxford, 2021)

You should internalize them as much as you do this book. I hope that you appreciate the friendly tone of this one as you dive deeper into these other books. I found inspiration in them. You will too. There are also a wealth of resources, including articles in *Music Educators Journal* on songwriting, out there for you to read and profit from. Become an assimilator of all things songwriting, producing, and performance/recording engineer. The world of music is vast. Tap into it. Dive deep into its waters. There are many treasures there to discover.

One of the strengths of the Perricone (2018) book is that it is separated by musical elements. Any one of these musical elements could easily produce a lesson seed. The chapters of the book are full of what I have called sunlight and water in this book. You just have to be a little more imaginative in drawing the connections. For those of you who read Western Classical music notation, he has a lot of examples where musical points come to life. Musical examples are taken from vastly different musical genres, and references to them are smartly made.

Freedman's (2013) book focuses on teaching music through technology. She centers her experiences on teaching in the curriculum in her book in her classroom. She places a high regard on making lessons align with the national content standards in the United States. Watson (2011) has been a pioneer of composing through technology in the context of large ensembles for over a decade. His work is admirable and important as we move into classrooms that address and provide opportunities to incorporate the diversity of creativities that occur in the world outside of school. Another excellent book is Will Kuhn and Ethan Hein, *Electronic Music School* (New York: Oxford University Press, 2021). It is essentially the curriculum of Lebanon High School, in Lebanon, OH, where the first author teaches classes that integrate and place musical creativities at the core. I highly recommend it.

The Citron (2008) book has been used in countless collegiate songwriting classes, in part because nothing else existed. In the past ten years, though, scholars inside and outside of music education have been working to remedy this shortcoming. In writing this book, I tried to design it for functionality in my own classroom, those of my master's students, and those of my undergraduate students soon to be teaching. Any book is going to be one (or two) author's experience with musical creativities in practice. Eventually, you will be able to write your own book as your students' work and successes will be able to fill the pages of new-to-the-world manuals on how to do this. That should inspire you! This is currently the cutting edge of music education. Lowell Mason and John Dewey would surely approve of what we are doing.

Keep a Journal and Save Student Work

Growing Songwriting is a movement. We are all on the same team, working to diversify and multiply the creativities found in the world of school and community music classrooms and beyond. Your journal entries could help us provide the next wave of support for the movement. Don't minimize your own contribution to this work. Keeping a journal will help you remember where you have come from, and also where you would like to go. See Figure 6.1 for a page from John Lennon's songwriting journal where he penned the lyrics to "In My Life" for inspiration. Your excellent efforts are proof that we are all not crazy, that progressive methods in collegiate music teacher programs are not in vain. We are making progress!

Your student work, and the stories that surround them, is gold for fueling this movement. In my own experience, the students who were in bands that I worked closely with twenty years ago are still making music. Some of them are music students at prestigious schools of music across the country, others are music pastors

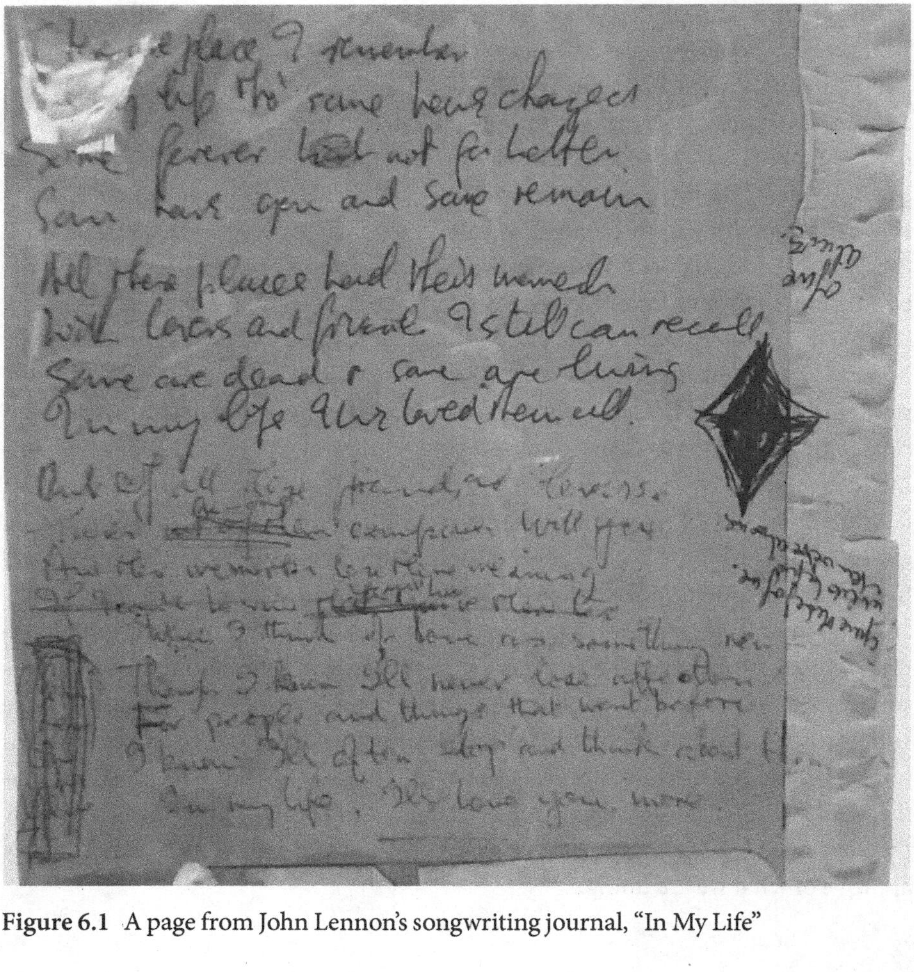

Figure 6.1 A page from John Lennon's songwriting journal, "In My Life"

at churches in the Midwest, while others are amateur/professional musicians making a living in part from the very things that I championed in music class so many years ago. It is one thing for me to share these stories, and quite another for all of us to unleash an avalanche of stories on the profession over the decades that will follow this publication. We need that avalanche. Music education will be better-off as a result of our efforts.

Their Best Work Is Just around the Corner

As you make the turn from covering songs, to the middle ground, to helping students write their own original music, stay focused on what matters most. You are connecting them with a well that will provide them with a lifetime of meaning and personal discovery. They will be able to keep going to it after they are finished with you. The goal is independence. There will come a day when they don't need your help at all. That is okay. It is to be expected. It is what you want. Cover songs and middle ground songs are necessary to get them to the point where they are confident that they have what it takes to be brave in the arena of lyrics and musical ideas. Everything that you have done thus far prepares them for what is next.

As you help them with middle ground work, remember where they came from and where you would like to take them next. Some of them will love the middle ground, while others will want to go back to cover songs, and still others will want to cut straight to original songs. You are not an advocate for one-size-fits-all music education. Actually, quite the opposite is true. You recognize that cover songs to the middle ground to songwriting is not a linear path. You and your students will make use of all of these ways of being musical at different times in life, while working in diverse settings. Make the most of your learning in each area and be open to where their excitement leads you.

Other Ways to Think about the Middle Ground

There are other ways of thinking about the nexus between cover and original songs. Quite a lot of new music, especially dance music, falls into a couple categories: mashups and remixes. A **mashup** is a song or composition created by blending two or more pre-recorded songs, usually by overlaying the vocal track of one song over the instrumental track of another. A **remix** is a pre-existing song that has been adapted, altered, and/or recombined with formerly existing musical materials to create something new. If we think of mashups and remixes as falling somewhere in between the cover song and original songs, then we can start looking for ways to grow this area. Some of your students will light up and only want to live in this area.

Have you ever created a mashup? If you haven't, it's time to start. Familiarize yourself with a DAW, and possibly a digital turntable, Maschine, or Abelton Push. These are some of the tools of the trade. Here is a flow chart for creating a mashup from the MasterClass series:[4]

1. Pick your songs. All song mashups feature two main audio files: an instrumental version of a track without vocals and an a cappella vocal track, which features the singer's voice without instrumentation. Instead of using an instrumental version of a song, you can sample an element from the original track—like the intro or a drum beat—and loop them together in your DJ software to create a new instrumental track.
2. Match the beats. Once you select your two main tracks, ensure their beats per minute (BPM) match up to keep them in time (a technique called beatmatching). Use your digital audio workstation (DAW) or DJ software to determine the BPM of each track, then utilize the warping or time-stretching functions to slow down or speed up each track so that the beats match.
3. Match the keys. In addition to beatmatching, the musical keys of each song should match in a mashup. Use the key-analyzing elements in your DAW or DJ software to help you match keys.
4. Line up the tracks. To mix the two tracks, play the instrumental version and line up the vocal track so both play in sync. Additional editing of the Waveform Audio File Format (WAV) files is sometimes necessary to ensure seamless transitions between vocal and instrumental tracks.
5. Add your final touches. Equalize (EQ) vocals to ensure they are the correct volume and balance with other frequencies in the track. Add effects—filters, additional samples, or reverb—to increase and broaden the mashup's sound palette.

So you need to figure out which songs that you'll be pulling from. Which songs would you like to bring together? Start playing around with the songs in your DAW, Maschine, or Abelton software. Listen to good examples of mashups and let your musical imagination guide you.

When it comes to remixes, your goal is to create an alternate version or reinterpretation of a preexisting song or instrumental arrangement. You first choose a song and then you start listening for the gaps. When you know where the gaps are, you can think about how you might fill those gaps or bring in new material. You start to think in terms of arrangement when you can identify where the major sections are and where there might be places to fill gaps musically. A lot of remixes that we hear on the radio are dance remixes, where the beat is intensified somehow to better facilitate movement on a dance floor. Of course, not all remixes do this. I am a big fan of the Brendan O'Brien remix of Pearl Jam's *Ten* album—not a dance album, but beautifully done remixes of classic songs.

WATER: Daniel Kim

Vancouver-based musician Daniel Kim is a master of the mashup. One of his most memorable works is "Pop Danthology 2014", where he brings together Meghan Trainor's "All about That Bass" with Tiësto's "Red Lights," Katy Perry's "Birthday," and Jessie J's "Bang Bang," among many other songs. While Daniel didn't write any of these songs, and he isn't covering the song in the sense that he sings and plays an instrument for a performance or recording, he is creating something completely new to the world—a reconfiguring of multiple songs into one new-to-the-the-world musical work. The artistic merit of such work can be found in the listening. It takes a lot of understanding of music across genres to understand how pieces that don't go together might go together well with a little encouragement. Don't take my word for it. Check it out for yourself. Follow him on Instagram @canadankim and YouTube: https://www.youtube.com/channel/UCKhEl5o5IzgBGaX2Oxd_GMw.

SUNLIGHT: The Best Remixes of All Time

As you think about creating a place for mashups and remixes in your curriculum, it is a good idea to start listening to some of the best. You might also create lessons around some of these songs as you teach them about remixes. Here is a list of the top ten by Spotify:[5]

1. Marvin Gaye—"Sexual Healing" (Kygo Remix)
2. Tracy Chapman—"Fast Car" (Jonas Blue feat. Dakota Remix)
3. Elton John—"Cold Heart" (Pnau Remix)
4. The Doors—"Riders on the Storm" (Infected Mushroom Remix)
5. Ella Fitzgerald—"Blue Skies" (Maya Jane Coles Remix)
6. Aerosmith—"Dream On" (GRiZ Remix)
7. Nancy Sinatra—"Bang Bang (My Baby Shot Me Down)" (David Guetta feat. Skylar Grey Remix)
8. Madonna—"Frozen" (Sickick Remix)
9. Nina Simone—"I Put a Spell on You" (Pretty Lights Remix)
10. AC/DC—"Thunderstruck" (Crookers Remix)

So what makes these remixes so catchy? How do artists bring seemingly unrelated musics together in ways that are appealing to us as listeners?

Technology in the Middle Ground

There is a lot to know about both (1) live remixing and (2) creating remixes in DAW environments. These two worlds interact with one another and can be where many of your students land as their primary modes of engaging with creativities in music. Here is some terminology that you are going to need to start internalizing and practicing. There is gear that is specific to this world. Software interacts with hardware devices. There are skills that you will need to practice and some websites that I will provide you with for exploration and discovery.

Stems

Songs can be broken into stems that consist of:

1. Vocals
2. Drums
3. Bass
4. Synth or Other (guitars, etc.)

When you isolate and are able to manipulate songs based on these song voices, astounding things can emerge as any one of those pieces of songs can be used to build other songs either in DAW environments in cover song and/or original songwriting contexts, or in live performance. It is also possible that you can creatively arrange music in live contexts with DJ hardware/software instruments and record them in studio applications for covering song and songwriting recordings. As always, live performance and recording worlds work together.

Stems can be purchased or created by using online services or apps. Here are some of the online and app-based stem-creating services that I have come across in my daily interactions:

1. Songtostems.com
2. Ezstems.com
3. XTrax Stems: https://audionamix.com/xtrax-stems/
4. RipX DeepRemix: https://hitnmix.com/remix-software/
5. Spectralayers Pro 8: https://www.steinberg.net/spectralayers/
6. RX 10: https://www.izotope.com/en/products/rx.html

I use XTrax Stems. It costs me $45 per year to use. You can upload unlimited songs for stem extraction.

Traktor Pro 3 comes with bundles of stems for you to add to your music for instant remix capability. You can isolate stems to just the drums, bass, vocals, or other musical elements and mix them into the song that you're playing live. Of course, you can also isolate these tracks and add them into your DAW environment as you write songs. Apps like Tunelf help you convert Apple Music files to MP3 files that you can use in your DJing. The middle ground is full of begging, borrowing, and stealing music for use in your new musical creativities. I have more to say about the world of hip-hop and sampling in a section to come.

DJ Hardware/Software

While *Music Teacher as Music Producer* (Randles, 2022) dealt a lot with various music technologies in both live and recording settings, I did not address DJ hardware/software in that publication. I hope to do a separate project on just hip-hop live performance and recording in a future book project. For the time being, here are some of the most important DJ hardware devices in the market now to get you started in this world:

1. Pioneer DJ DDJ-200 2-deck Rekordbox DJ Controller (used with Serato software)
2. Native Instruments Traktor Kontrol S2 MK3 2-channel DJ Controller (used with Traktor Pro3). You can see that hardware and software work hand in hand. You have Pioneer hardware with Serato software and Native Instruments hardware that is used with Native Instruments software. Both of these working pairs are commonly used (see Figure 6.2).

These Pioneer and Native Instruments hardware devices work with the following software packages:

1. Serato DJ Pro $249 (free version Serato DJ Lite)
2. Traktor Pro 3$49 (free version Traktor DJ 2)

Native Instruments Traktor Kontrol S2 MK3
2-channel DJ Controller

Pioneer DJ DDJ-200 2-deck Rekordbox
DJ Controller

Figure 6.2 Pioneer and native instruments hardware for DJing

Both of these software packages come with a free version and a trial period for the professional version. You should think of these hardware/software pairings as instruments like a guitar or a keyboard (Randles, 2013; Williams, 2014). You will go to them just as you would another instrument that could accompany your voice. They are live performance instruments in the same league as those other instruments. You go to them for inspiration as you engage with the creative process. Of course, you can also get lots of gigs as a professional DJ at parties and other civic functions! In the middle ground, you will use the music of other people as a starting place to fuel your own projects where musical creativities are concerned.

WATER: Artist "Kittens" and Her Gear

When you think about musical creativities in practice, you have to think about the world of music technology as it affords and constrains our creative pursuits.

Enter Kittens, aka Lauren Abedini, a Pioneer Turntable and Serato Pro artist. While Abedini grew as a dancer, she was eventually drawn to DJing through exposure to Los Angeles's underground beat scene. While sneaking out to be a part of Low End Theory nights as a teenager, in L Abedini soon transitioned to turntables. She has found her creative outlet in the middle ground.[6]

While she identified with the music, Abedini was struck by the total absence of women in the DJ world and resolved to be a part of the solution. Abedini has made significant contributions to the world of DJ/producers—working with Kid Cudi and Usher. She has released remixes for Fool's Gold, and currently produces alongside Falcons, Hoodboi, and Promnite as the Athletixx crew. She has been an outspoken feminist both in and outside of the music industry and hosts regular female-only DJ workshops! Besides all of that, she is a dope DJ and selector of musical examples. Check out her music!

SUNLIGHT: A Step-by-Step Introduction to Digital DJing

Here is the process that one goes through to DJ with a digital DJing rig from the experts at Digital DJ Tips, The Global DJ School:[7]

1. Find and load the next tune—Get the tune you want to play next on to an unused deck, making sure that deck is not live (i.e., its faders are closed). Route that tune's audio to your headphones by pressing its "Pre-fader listen," "Headphones," or "Cue" button.
2. Prepare the tune for playing—That means setting the channel gain so the tune isn't too quiet, or distorting; checking its EQ (to make sure there's not too much or too little bass, and it doesn't sound too muddy or harsh, for example); getting its tempo right; and picking the place you want to play it from, cueing

it up at that point (usually a downbeat or what I call a "one beat," which just means the first significant beat of a section).

3. Test the transition—This is like a dress rehearsal for the transition you'll be doing for real soon enough. Waiting until a good place in the current track, you get the tune playing. Then, with one ear listening to the speakers or booth monitors (that are playing the current tune out loud), and the other ear listening to your headphones (that are playing the new tune privately—hence the DJ look with a hand holding a single headphone cup to a single ear), you make any small adjustments to tempo, while at the same time deciding for sure if you've made the right choice of tune. If not, you go back to step one and try again with something else.
4. Begin the transition—Returning the tune to your chosen "in" or "cue" point, you start it playing over the top of the current tune, effectively repeating step 3, but for the final "real" time.
5. Make the new tune live—This means turning its levels up so your audience can finally hear it too. This could be at exactly the same time as the previous stage, or it could be a few beats, bars, or a whole musical phrase or two later, with you monitoring in your headphones in the meantime.
6. Perform the transition—Depending on the type of transition you're doing, here's where you manage the two tunes as they play together, using the levels and tone controls of one or both of them to move your audience's attention from one tune to the next. When beatmixing, this stage can go on for several musical phrases; with many types of mixes, it is very short, and for one type of mix, it is nonexistent (when you cut straight from one tune to the next).
7. Stop the outgoing tune playing—When the transition is totally over, you stop the old tune playing. Its deck is now the unused deck.
8. Return to step 1.

I admittedly have a lot to learn in this arena, but I am progressing. Maybe you can work to develop your skills as well.

Hip-Hop and Sampling

In the same vein as remixes and mashups is the way that hip-hop artists sample previously existing songs and tracks for just the right musical material to build hype and to provide hooks for their songs. Sampling began in its modern form in the 1970s. Major labels have interpreted it as stealing. For beginner and even very experienced hip-hop producers attempting to emulate Grandmaster Flash, sampling has been a quick, easy, and inexpensive way of making beats. The appropriation of samples in music might be considered a middle ground kind of task. Do some musicians' use of samples transcend the origins of the original songs that they stem from with regard to their level of artistry? Is the process of tastefully using samples in music a complex and valuable form of musical artistry? I think that in most cases we can agree emphatically that "yes they do" and "yes it is." So what do we do with this knowledge?

As music teachers striving to be on the cutting edge of our field, we must not ignore the power of hip-hop music as an American musical art form of the highest caliber built upon the uniquely American experience. We should encourage hip-hop music-making in our classrooms and allow sampling of any and all varieties to emerge as part of the musical growth of our students. We should be aware of the laws as far as sampling is concerned. We can point our students to specific court cases and how they were decided regarding artists' appropriation of other artists' work.

Calling sampling a part of what we might think of as the middle ground shouldn't dissuade anyone from holding it in the highest regard. Remember, a person could live completely and exclusively in the realm of covering songs for performance and recording and find a seemingly endless source of meaning making in and through music. The progression of song covers to middle ground to songwriting is a natural one that occurs regularly in the real world of community music-making. So embrace your students' use of samples in their songs. Provide lots of examples of how artists masterfully use sampling in their work.

WATER: Paul's Boutique

Perhaps the height of seeing how far you as an artist can utilize sampling and get away with it is the 1989 Beastie Boys album *Paul's Boutique*. Some have called it the "Sgt. Pepper of Hip-hop."[8] One hundred five songs are sampled in *Paul's Boutique*, including twenty-four songs sampled on the last track of the album alone. Michael "Mike D" Diamond (vocals, drums), Adam "MCA" Yauch (vocals, bass), and Adam "Ad-Rock" Horovitz (vocals, guitar, programming) spent two years on the project, recording most of it in record producer Mike Dike's apartment in Los Angeles. Audio engineer/producers "The Dust Brothers" wanted the album to be sonically different and for multilayered sampling to be viewed as an art in and of itself. While sales of *Paul's Boutique* didn't reach that of the hugely successful *License to Ill*, it did land and stay as one of the crowning achievements of the band, consistently making lists of the greatest hip-hop albums of all time.[9]

Middle Ground Workgroups

Just as I reviewed covering songs in groups, and as I will discuss creating songwriting workgroups, I would like to present a middle ground workgroup concept here that I believe is practical for use in your classroom. There are various stages of the creative process that contain specific roles that each of the students in a group of four or five could perform. Here they are:

1. Song(s) Choice
2a. Groove Production
3a. Listeners' Feedback
4. Recording Musicians
3b. Listeners' Feedback
5. Production/Engineering
3c. Listeners' Feedback
6. Performers
3d. Listeners' Feedback

1. Song(s) Choice

If you choose to utilize the workgroup concept of class organization in your daily creative process, then you will start with choosing the song or songs that you will remix. This is of course an essential and seminal part of the process. It affects everything that comes after in the process. What music do they gravitate toward? If you look at the top remixes of all time that I shared earlier in this chapter, you will notice that most of the music that is remixed share common themes. First, the songs were previously big hits. Second, the songs contain universal and timeless themes of love, crossing thresholds, and dreaming big. Sometimes the focus is lost love. Sometimes the focus is the pursuit of life goals that are hugs and seemingly unobtainable. You can really help them at this stage if they are struggling to find songs that contain these types of themes. Use your knowledge of the greater world of music over the decades that you have been alive to perhaps put songs in front of them that they might not have ever heard or thought of. Let their desires guide your assistance at all times.

2. Groove Production

You need people in each group who can create tantalizing grooves. These people are usually good at working within DAW environments. Remember, beats and grooves can come from a variety of places. They can be sampled, created within DAW environments, performed live, produced via turntables, ripped from YouTube clips, and so on. The sky is the limit. For certain, though, the grooves that you produce need to somehow make their way into a DAW eventually. You can help them get that musical information to a DAW environment or put them in contact with someone in your room who can (if you are new and learning yourself). Give them ample time to play around in the world of groove. You will know when they find something that they really like by the excitement on their faces. At this time, you need to have the class listen to give them feedback.

3a. Listeners' Feedback

We work with sonic yumminess in the world of music. In order to know whether or not the auditorily digested food that we make tastes good, we need to have other people listen. That is where you should have each group listen and provide feedback along the way, and why at particular times during the creative process you should have the entire class listen to the unfolding musical products. More tasters means more diverse feedback. Remember that songwriter/producer Max Martin would always take his mixes to a club and try them out on a room full of dancers to figure out what worked and what did not work. You should do the same.

4. Recording Musicians

You will need some musicians to record the musical parts of the songs that are created in your room. They will likely be musicians from within the small workgroups. You might consider doing things differently, though. Maybe there are some musicians who record certain parts for every group. Each workgroup might decide that they want a particular person to record all the bass lines. Individuals and workgroups should be given creative liberty to handle the process. You are there for support, in the ways that are described in detail in *Music Teacher as Music Producer* (2022). Sometimes they will want you to play parts with them. As I write this, I am preparing to play guitar for a student group next Thursday for a performance in class that we will record. They came to me and asked if I could play a lead guitar part. I agreed. They were in the driver's seat. At that point, I am simply a musician in the room whom they trust to play a part, NOT the person that the university has hired to be in charge. My primary job is to help them realize their vision for the song. You might do this as well. Do they need a turntableist? Do they need a Maschine player? Could you do that for them? If the answer is "no" to any of those questions, then you have some practicing to do.

3b. Listeners' Feedback

Again, you will need feedback from within the workgroup and from without. Have the groups perform their work for each other regularly to achieve this important part of the process. As they work up their arrangements, it is helpful to have them give each other feedback about how it is going. Their feedback for each other is very valuable. Research suggests that it might be the most important form of feedback (Randles, 2009b). So provide time for it to occur in the regular workings of your class. After preliminary arranging in small groups, it would be a good time to get some constructive feedback form the group. Remember than in the middle ground we focus on remixes and mashups, so you will need to test your music out on a moving audience. That is why Max Martin took his to the dance floor.

5. Production/Engineering

After their songs have been worked on substantially, they will need someone to realize the final form within a DAW environment. It is probable that all the work thus far in the middle ground happened within a DAW environment since here you are taking preexisting songs and adding parts—samples, vocals, instrumental parts, and the like—to them. That is the nature of a remix. Someone in every workgroup is going to need to specialize in this who has the technical know-how to make individual tracks and the whole sound better. These are the people who know exactly how to create stem tracks of songs so that you can creatively assemble parts and pieces that will make your remix magnificent to dance to. Of course, in most cases you will have to be the one who teaches them how to do all of these things, and you will be able to do it because you yourself have been working to create music this way in your daily practice. Relax, though, and remember that all of this is a marathon and not a sprint. Take it one day at a time. Try to constantly learn and add to your production skillset. Check out the feedback that I provided in *Music Teacher as Music Producer* (Randles, 2022) for tips on how to grow your skill set. Look for *Sound Production for the Emerging Music Teacher Producer* (Randles, Aponte, & Johnson, forthcoming).

3c. Listeners' Feedback

Back to listening and listener feedback. There is no substitution for having other ears listen. Listener feedback might also happen well in some of the online music-sharing communities like Spotify's Marquee, SoundCloud, Free Music Archive, ccMixter, Indaba Music, Bandcamp, Jamendo, OpSound, Tribe of Noise, and others. These online communities are global and filled with discussion boards and built-in communication platforms. You might also consider asking community members to provide support for this. I have a friend who used to work in radio who is an excellent source of feedback for what sounds good. Remember, some of the best producers of all time (e.g., Rick Rubin) are people who listen well and have a highly developed taste for what sounds good. Seek out those people as sounding boards for the music of your students.

6. Performers

Who will perform the music? Of course, when I say that in the context of remixes—who will play the music primarily from a computer and a DJ console in front of people? That could be anyone in the group. Maybe it will be the entire group in some shape or form. Let them decide. It is possible that when these remixes are performed, some members of the group perform along to a click track (the original song in some form) while the added tracks come from live musicians. The sky is the limit. Look at examples of how others do this. Commonplace at the time of writing this book is for there to be few musicians on stage and one or two people behind a computer and turntable setup. That is fine. However, they (you) might decide that more performers should be added and that a more band form with computer backing is required. Have fun making these decisions with them.

3d. Listeners' Feedback

This is the part of the process where you take your student work to the community. That means performing for parents and other community members, livestreaming to an online audience, and sharing recordings/performances within online music communities. Take the music of your students to the ends of the earth. Here is a website of one of my students from a few years ago: www.DJnightmixer.com. I taught her how to use an iPad to compose music for her animation. I also shared with her how to make music using a computer, which she took to the world of professional DJing. Her dad built her a recording studio in their house and she began sharing her music with a global audience. She has created multiple albums and wants to make a career out of her original music creation. Music can change lives. That is what happened to Michaela. I am so happy that I could play a part in it.

Resources Worth Exploring

Source	Expertise	URL
Biggie: I Got a Story to Tell	Chronicles the Story of The Notorious B.I.G. and his life in hip-hop	www.netflix.com
Hip-Hop Evolution	This is a series that started in 2016 that stories the history of hip-hop	www.netflix.com
Wu-Tang Clan: Of Mics and Men	Documents well the history of Wu-Tang Clan	www.sho.com
Making Beats: The Art of Sample-Based Hip-Hop	This is a well-written book on working in sample-based hip-hop	https://www.amazon.com/Making-Beats-Sample-Based-Hip-Hop-Culture/dp/0819574813/
FutureDJs—How to DJ: A Guide to DJ-ing and Electronic Music	This book provides the reader with quite a lot to think about around being and becoming someone who understands the musical needs to listeners	https://www.imdb.com/title/tt4229236/
Pete Tong's Online DJ Academy	Learn the ins and outs of remixing from a team of knowledgeable experts	https://petetong-djacademy.com/

SEEDS FOR MIDDLE GROUND LESSONS

7
Beginner Middle Ground Seeds

Your First Remix

Materials

- You can use a digital audio workstation (DAW) with various keyboard and pad controllers.
- Consider using DJing hardware/software (Serato/Pioneer or Traktor/Native Instruments).
- Access to the information universe via phones, tablets, computers.
- Audio recording software like GarageBand/Logic, FL Studio, Audacity, Soundtrap, Abelton Live, ProTools, and so forth on a computer/tablet/phone.
- Computer connected to a video projector.
- Optional: Computer connected to audio interface with a pair of condenser microphones to capture live audio.
- Sound system that contains speakers to amplify your computer's sound.
- Optional: Video camera to capture live student performances.

Context

The purpose of this section of middle ground lessons is to get you thinking about ways to allow your students to remix songs and to start using samples in their cover and original songs. This first lesson seed is provided to get the ball rolling for you. You are going to need to take some time and remix some songs yourself as you prepare to make these experiences a possibility for your students. Of course, it is okay and completely acceptable to not have it all figured out as you start this work. You can learn alongside your students. They will teach you as much as you teach them.

WATER: The Story of Sickick's Remix of Madonna's "Frozen"

Sometimes remixes that start out as bootlegs are officially released with the blessing of the artist. That happened after Canadian producer Sickick reworked Madonna's 1998 hit "Frozen" in 2021. The new version exploded on TikTok and so Madonna

Growing Songwriting. Clint Randles, Oxford University Press. © Oxford University Press 2024.
DOI: 10.1093/oso/9780197693216.003.0007

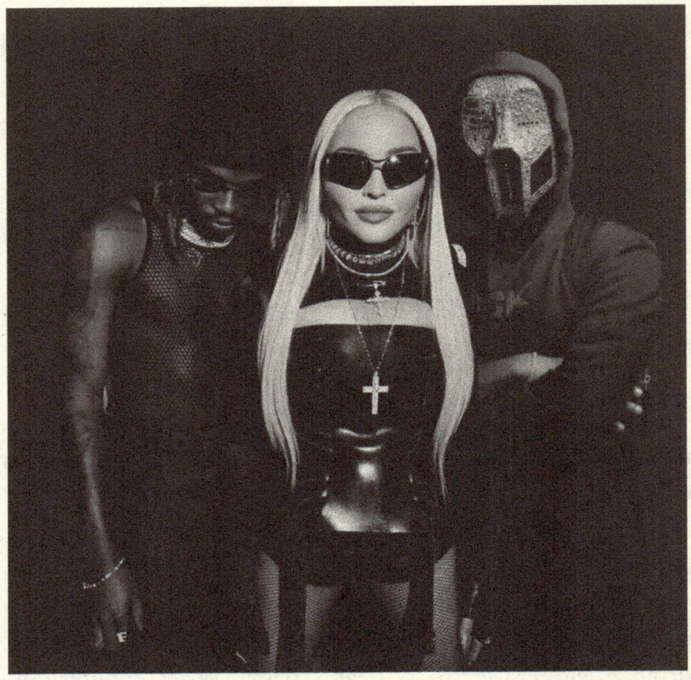

Figure 7.1 Madonna, Sickick, and Fireboy DML

cosigned his version and gave it an official release in December of that year. Then the creative process continued as Nigerian singer Fireboy DML joined the duo for a second remix of the song (Figure 7.1).[1] The new track features Fireboy floating naturally above Sickick's version of Madonna's original vocal. The progression of original song to remix to the incorporation of a new vocalist with new lyrical content is a great example of multiple overlapping musical creativities occurring in the greater world of music (Burnard, 2012). You can make your classroom a microcosm of that world. Your students can remix each other's music. They can create alternate versions of their own songs and their own covers. The middle ground can be an exciting place from a curricular perspective. It is not a lesser space than songwriting or covering songs. Each of the three categories exists as pathways to lifelong music-making. It is an exciting new world of music education.

SUNLIGHT: New Skills to Practice

Stems is an open file format that allows DJs to play, layer, and rearrange independent parts of a track. A stem file contains a track split into four musical elements, like drums, bass, melody (synth), and voice. DJs manipulate and layer the bass line of one track, the vocals from another, and the leads from a third. As I said in Chapter 6, you are going to need to familiarize yourself with some new tools. I have been using

Traktor Pro 3 to work on my live remixes. In the context of a classroom as recording studio, you should think of a computer with software as an instrument. Sound leaves the instrument via an 1/8-inch headphone cable and goes into your mixer. It becomes just like any other electronic instrument (acoustic/electric guitar, electric guitar, bass, keyboard, iPad, etc.). Madonna's "Frozen" is originally in an A♭ major keyality. When Sickick slows it down, it changes to a D♭ major keyality. Part of his creative process must have been creating a bassline and/or other melodic content as the master track and then adding "Frozen" as a synch track. Who knows. I would have to ask him. Maybe he slowed her voice down and then found the new material to come up with what we hear on the track.

You are going to have to take a deep dive into new instruments, new processes, and new conceptions of what making good in performance might mean. In *Music Teacher as Music Producer* (Randles, 2022) I discuss diversifying performance in chapter 7. The Madonna example of the multigenerational coming together of Madonna, Sickick, and Fireboy DML is an example of making good in performance because the music-making exchange brought together people who would not have come together had it not been for music. We need to be sensitive to what forms that making good could take in music classrooms. We need to be vigilant to promote alternate forms of making good that are not necessarily perfectly executed or spotless performances.

Lesson Time

This lesson will take multiple classes to take on a complete form. You will need to allow time for your students' learning to grow. It is a seed that will take you in many different directions if you allow it to. Remember that this is the goal of the book—to give you many places to start a creative lesson that centers on songwriting (covering songs, the middle ground, and writing originals). You could make this an individual lesson or you could have them self-select their own remixing workgroup. If you have the ability to put them in small bands with differing instrumentation, that might be amazing.

Lesson Instructions

Preparation (10 minutes)

Gather the class and give them a short lesson on remixes. Start with some of the best of all time that I shared in Chapter 6. Talk about how these songs were created. Tell them a bit about what you know about the artist and the remixer. Demonstrate how you go about finding the original and remixed keys online. Show them how some searches give songs with chords that say "capo" for a guitar while other songs give you tablature ("tab"), a short form of musical notation for guitar players. Teach them how to transpose the key of a song if a capo is used. You might demonstrate using a digital turntable—one of the two varieties that I mention in Chapter 6.

Choose the Song (10–15 minutes or longer)
Give them some time to search for a song to remix. They will have to agree on which one that they want to do. This could take a lot of time or not, depending upon the group and their dynamics (if they are working in a workgroup). Help them only when they need your help; otherwise, stay out of the way. They come to you with diverse opinions and highly developed tastes for what they like. Let them lead the way. You will sometimes have to move them away from music with explicit content. You know your school culture and what is allowed/tolerated. Monitor the activity in the room carefully to make sure that it stays productive.

Work on the Song (30 minutes or most likely much more)
Allow them time to work on the song. This can be complicated if they are working in workgroups. If they are working on the song individually, you will have a different series of considerations. Most of your students will likely be self-conscious about their singing abilities. You will have to create a safe place to not be perfect all of the time. You will have to discuss the role of feedback and what is acceptable. Positivity needs to be the mantra in your classroom for students to feel safe singing in front of each other. Also, it is a great idea for you to model singing in front of them. It is okay for your performances to not be perfect as well. Performing in front of them goes a long way to establish a positive and supportive culture in your classroom.

Perform (Another Class Period)
Depending on how many groups/individuals you want to perform in class, you will have to leave time for all students who want to perform. You will have students with severe performance anxiety. For them you will have to create alternate performance opportunities. They could record their performances and submit them electronically to you from home. During the pandemic, this is how we made music together. You could make the band collaborate that way as well, adding their parts to the recording video/audio. If you have a small performance stage in your class, this would be an excellent opportunity to utilize it. This is meant to be a beginner exercise, so these performances will likely be rough. You need to celebrate their success, be positive, and provide them with a clear path to what they will need to improve—basically, they will need to continue practicing the process. Let their student peers be the first to provide feedback. Provide guidelines for the feedback: for example, give one positive comment and a comment that they could use to improve by.

Record (Another class period or multiple class periods)
It is nearly always worth your time and effort to record the songs/performances of your students. They learn by engaging in practice and reflection upon their practice. There is not a better way of self-assessment for musicians than critically listening

to our performances. You can be meticulous and professional about recording or not depending upon your expertise with recording arts. An audio interface with a XY-configured microphone pattern would capture the sound of a room well. If you have a computer at each station that your small groups are in you could multitrack-record their performance and engineer the audio for matching with your video. You could simply use your phone or tablet to record the performances with the built-in microphone. All of these options are available to you. You have to choose a path that makes sense for your setting and work life.

Modifications for Learners

Recording at Home Modification

For those of your students with performance anxiety, allow them to record their performances at home on their phones or with their computers with DAWs. Many times their desire to make use of this modification has nothing to do with their interest in your class or the lesson, but everything to do with their anxiety about performing in front of their peers. Allow them to record at home. Doing so still means that they are developing a connection to the real world of people making music in the world. They could come around to the possibility of performing in front of their peers when they develop a bit more confidence. You should encourage them to share their videos with the class as a way of encouraging their live performance prowess.

You Perform with Them Modification

If performing the accompaniment is too difficult a task for them, you can always sit in and perform an accompaniment for their singing. This is a widely used accommodation by me when I am working with younger students. It is not easy to play an instrument and sing at the same time. Remember, though, as you are working on developing this skill in your students that singing and playing together is wrapped up in quite a lot of cultural capital. They will gain skills that can last a lifetime with these abilities.

Learning Outcomes

- Choose a song chorus that makes them happy. Share it with their peers.
- Work on the song either independently or within a peer group.
- Perform a song chorus of a song of their choice and accompany their voice with an instrument of their choosing.
- Perform the song in front of their peers (or via a pre-recorded performance) for their peers (or not).
- Record the song performance.

- Learn what it feels like to engage in a process of covering a song that makes you happy.

Assessment Considerations

Informal Assessment. You will assess their learning for this lesson by the extent to which they engaged with the process. Are they sitting on the side and not talking? Are they leading the group? Are they taking notes on their phone? Are they smiling? Are they messing around? It is difficult to know exactly what they are getting out of a particular experience. In some cases it may seem that they are not engaged when they actually are quite engaged. You will need to have a loose set of criteria for assessing their learning. Think of assessment in this case as part performance quality assessment, part mechanics of performing their accompaniment, part mechanics of singing, part creativity of the song choice, part creativity of the performance, and part intangibles that are difficult to describe. Your assessments should be additive in nature and should avoid reduction. In other words, there should be multiple ways for them to do well on the assignment, and fewer ways that they can bury themselves in a low performance score. Failure to do any of the parts that I have outlined here could cause that. Remember, though, that learning in this setting is non-linear and that most of all you need to celebrate successes, even minor ones, to help ensure that future learning takes place.

Formal Assessment. Here is a rubric that you might use for this exercise. Rubrics like this one encourage your students to look for specific things as they grow their skills. Along with formal assessments like this, it is a good idea to give worthwhile qualitative feedback that helps your students grow in each area that you would like to see them grow.

Criteria	**Ratings**					**Pts**
This criterion is linked to a Learning Outcome "Recording"	**4 to >3.0 pts** **Expert** I love that your recording is approaching professional quality	**3 to >2.0 pts** **Practitioner** I like that you demonstrated very good recording technique (including balance)	**2 to >1.0 pts** **Apprentice** I'm concerned that the recording isn't very good	**1 to >0.0 pts** **Novice** What's up? Your recording is really difficult to listen to	**0 pts** **No Marks**	4 pts
This criterion is linked to a Learning Outcome "Musicianship"	**4 to >3.0 pts** **Expert** I love that you displayed almost professional levels of musicianship	**3 to >2.0 pts** **Practitioner** I like the level of musicianship you displayed in your performance—it's very good	**2 to >1.0 pts** **Apprentice** I'm concerned with how many errors showed up in your performance	**1 to >0.0 pts** **Novice** What's up? Your performance seems lacking in musicianship quality	**0 pts** **No Marks**	4 pts

Criteria	Ratings					Pts
This criterion is linked to a Learning Outcome "Creativity"	**4 to >3.0 pts** **Expert** I love that the creativity you displayed could end up on a recording	**3 to >2.0 pts** **Practitioner** I like that you displayed a very good sense of creativity	**2 to >1.0 pts** **Apprentice** I'm concerned that your performance did not display very much creativity	**1 to >0.0 pts** **Novice** What's up? There was really no sense of creativity in your music	**0 pts** **No Marks**	4 pts
Total Points: 12						

Further Reading/Resources

- Check out Prince Charles Alexander, *Hip-Hop Production: Inside the Beats* (Boston: Berklee Press, 2022).
- Check out "11 Seriously Useful Sampling Tips": https://www.musicradar.com/tuition/tech/11-seriously-useful-sampling-tips-604107.
- Check out Nate Patrin, *Bring That Beat Back: How Sampling Built Hip-Hop* (Minneapolis: University of Minnesota Press, 2020).
- Check out DJ City's "A Complete Guide to Sampling": https://djcity.com.au/blog/how-to-sample-a-song-a-complete-guide/#:~:text=The%20general%20approach%20to%20sampling,new%20sound%20for%20your%20song.
- Check out Mark Ronson's TED talk on how sampling changed music: https://youtu.be/H3TF-hI7zKc.

8

Intermediate Middle Ground Seeds

Doing Some Sampling

Materials

- You can use a digital audio workstation (DAW) with various keyboard and pad controllers.
- Consider using DJing hardware/software (Serato/Pioneer or Traktor/Native Instruments).
- Access to the information universe via phones, tablets, computers.
- Audio recording software like GarageBand/Logic, FL Studio, Audacity, Soundtrap, Abelton Live, ProTools, and so forth on a computer/tablet/phone.
- Computer connected to a video projector.
- Optional: Computer connected to audio interface with a pair of condenser microphones to capture live audio.
- Sound system that contains speakers to amplify your computer's sound.
- Optional: Video camera to capture live student performances.

Context

The purpose of this lesson seed is to get your students into sampling music for the purpose of making a meaningful socially charged point. This first lesson seed is provided to get the ball rolling. You are going to need to take some time to do some sampling yourself as you prepare to make these experiences a possibility for your students. Of course, it is okay and completely acceptable to not have it all figured out as you start this work. You can learn alongside your students. They will teach you as much as you teach them.

WATER: A Lesson from Kanye West

Kanye West samples Billie Holliday's "Strange Fruit" in his song "Blood on the Leaves" and reuses power that comes from the original song (see Figure 8.1). Here is what MTV.com had to say about the mashup:[1]

Growing Songwriting. Clint Randles, Oxford University Press. © Oxford University Press 2024.
DOI: 10.1093/oso/9780197693216.003.0008

Kanye West's album *Yeezus* is controversial for so many reasons: its noisy, industrial sound, the title, the lack of packaging lyrics that have raised eyebrows and the bizarre promotional film, among others.

The track "Blood On the Leaves" manages to encompass many of those controversies in one. It see-saws from a plaintive cover of the jazz classic "Strange Fruit," to Kanye's Auto-Tuned vocals about the perils of fame and molly, while layering in a skittering, blown-out horn riff, the sounds of an animal's growl and a sung interpolation of an iconic No Limit street anthem.

It's a lot to take in, but the haunting refrain that rises above the din is the sound of Nina Simone singing about "bodies swinging in the Southern breeze."

That line comes from Billie Holiday's original 1939 recording of "Strange Fruit," which was a simmering shot across the bow of racism in America. West tapped the 1965 cover of the ballad by Simone as the dramatic centerpiece sample on the song, in which he takes words originally written by teacher/songwriter Abel Meeropol for the Marxist magazine "The New Masses" and twists them into a modern fable about race, identity and materialism.

Holiday's version, with moving vocals that brought the story of lynchings of black Americans to a startling poignancy, remains one of the most towering, important songs of the 20th century. In West's re-telling, the Simone version of the song opens the track with the lines, "Strange fruit hanging from the poplar trees/ Blood on the leaves," before West turns it into a churning anthem about conspicuous consumption and a drug-fueled hook-up.

It's that apparent dichotomy that makes the song a powerful example of West's signature melding of the sacred and the Profane according to Craig Werner, professor of Afro-American Studies at the University of Wisconsin-Madison and

Figure 8.1 Kanye West sampled Billie Holliday's "Strange Fruit" by way of Nina Simone's vocals in his song "Blood on the Leaves"

author of "A Change is Gonna Come: Music, Race & the Soul of America" and "Playing the Changes From Afro-Modernism to the Jazz Impulse."

Kanye West brilliantly wove together a sample from a song that makes a socially conscious point about the ugliness and brutality of racism in America in 1965 (1939) to get the attention of listeners about other social ugliness.

SUNLIGHT: Most Iconic Samples of All Time

Here is a list of some of the most iconic samples of all time as published by NME:[2]

1. M.I.A.—"Paper Planes" (2008)—Samples The Clash—"Straight to Hell' (1982)
2. Sugar Hill Gang—"Rapper's Delight" (1979)—Samples Chic—"Good Times" (1978)
3. A Tribe Called Quest—"Can I Kick It?" (1990)—Samples Lou Reed—"Walk on the Wild Side" (1972)
4. Beyoncé—"Crazy in Love" (2003)—Samples The Chi-Lites—"Are You My Woman (Tell Me So)" (1970)
5. The Notorious B.I.G.—"Mo Money Mo Problems" (1997)—Samples Diana Ross—"I'm Coming Out" (1980)
6. N.W.A.—"Express Yourself" (1988)—Samples Charles Wright & the Watts 103rd Street Rhythm Band—"Express Yourself" (1970)
7. Kanye West—"Blood on the Leaves" (2013)—Samples Nina Simone's version of Billie Holiday's "Strange Fruit" (1965)
8. Black Box—"Ride on Time" (1989)—Samples Loleatta Holloway—"Love Sensation" (1980)
9. Madonna—"Hung Up" (2005)—Samples ABBA—"Gimme! Gimme! Gimme! (A Man after Midnight)" (1979)
10. Beastie Boys—"Rhymin & Stealin" (1986)—Samples Led Zeppelin—"When the Levee Breaks" (1971); Black Sabbath—"Sweet Leaf" (1971); The Clash—"I Fought the Law" (1977)

Use these samples in your teaching as demonstrations of how artists have used samples historically for maximum effect in their music.

Lesson Time

This lesson will take multiple classes to take on a complete form. You will need to allow time for your students' learning to grow. It is a seed that will take you in many different directions if you allow it to. Remember that this is the goal of the book—to give you many places to start a creative lesson that centers on songwriting (covering songs, the middle ground, and writing originals). You could make this an individual lesson or you could have them self-select their own sampling workgroup. Your technology setup might very well dictate how these workgroups could function. Do you have headphone hub environments? Do you have a computer for every student? Answers to these questions will guide your structure of the lesson time.

Lesson Instructions

Preparation (10 minutes)

Gather the class and give them a short lesson on samples and sampling. Start with some of the best of all time that I shared in the SUNLIGHT section. Talk about how these songs were created. Tell them a bit about what you know about the artists doing the sampling and the original artist who created the music being sampled. Demonstrate how you go about finding music to sample. Show them how to listen to music for catchy and/or potentially impactful musical or lyrical material. Show them how to create a stem track from a song by using the app Xtrax Stems. Use a DAW to organize song elements. Add musical materials from loops or other readymade music to demonstrate how a sample can add so much to a song.

Choose the Song (10–15 minutes or longer)

Give them some time to search for a song to sample. They will have to agree on which one that they want to do. This could take a lot of time or not, depending upon the group and their dynamics (if they are working in a workgroup). Help them only when they need your help; otherwise, stay out of the way. They will come to you with diverse opinions and highly developed taste for what they like. Let them lead the way. You will sometimes have to move them away from music with explicit content. You know your school culture and what is allowed/tolerated. Monitor the activity in the room carefully to make sure that it stays productive.

Work on the Song (30 minutes or most likely much more)

Allow them time to work on the song. Since this is a middle ground lesson, it may be that they are using a sample to add support to a previously existing song (cover) or that they are using it to add support to a new song that they are working on. This can be complicated if they are working in workgroups. If they are working on the song individually, you will have a different series of considerations. Most of your students will likely be self-conscious about various musical abilities. You will have to create a safe place to not be perfect all of the time. You will have to discuss the role of feedback and what is acceptable. Positivity needs to be the mantra in your classroom for students to feel safe sharing with one another. Also, it is a great idea for you to model all aspects of the creative process in front of them when you can. It is okay for your performances to not be perfect. Performing in front of them goes a long way to establish a positive and supportive culture.

Perform (Another Class Period)
Depending on how many groups/individuals you want to share in class, you will have to make a plan for how everyone can share. You will have students with severe performance anxiety. For them you will have to create alternate sharing opportunities. They could record their performances and submit them electronically to you from home. During the pandemic, this is how we made music together. You could make the band collaborate that way as well, adding their parts to the recording video/audio. If you have a small performance stage in your class, this would be an excellent opportunity to utilize it. Play their music from computers on the stage. Celebrate their success, be positive, and provide them with a clear path to what they will need to improve—basically, they will need to continue practicing the process. Let their student peers be the first to provide feedback. Provide guidelines for the feedback: for example, give one positive comment and a comment that they could use to improve by.

Record (Another class period or multiple class periods)
It is nearly always worth your time and effort to record the songs/performances of your students. They learn by engaging in practice and reflection upon their practice. There is not a better way of self-assessment for musicians than critically listening to our performances. You can be meticulous and professional about recording or not depending upon your expertise with recording arts. An audio interface with a XY-configured microphone pattern would capture the sound of a room well. If you have a computer at each headphone hub station that your small groups are in you could multitrack-record their performance and engineer the audio for matching with your video. You could simply use your phone or tablet to record the performances (sharing sessions) with the built-in microphone, capturing students' responses to each other's work. All of these options are available to you. Choose a path that makes sense for your setting.

Modifications for Learners

Recording at Home Modification
For those of your students with performance anxiety, allow them to record their performances at home on their phones or with their computers with DAWs. Many times their desire to make use of this modification has nothing to do with their interest in your class or the lesson but everything to do with their anxiety about performing in front of their peers. Allow them to record at home. Doing so still means that they are developing a connection to the real world of people making music in the world. They could come around to the possibility of performing in front of

their peers when they develop a bit more confidence. You should encourage them to share their videos with the class as a way of encouraging their live performance prowess.

You Perform with Them Modification

If performing the accompaniment is too difficult a task for them, you can always play their work from your computer. This is a widely used accommodation by me when I am working with younger students. Sometimes it's easier when someone else shares your work. Remember, though, as you are working on developing this ability in your students that sharing your music is wrapped up in quite a lot of cultural capital. They will gain important life skills that can last a lifetime by engaging in creative processes that end with sharing and explaining the steps of their work.

Learning Outcomes

- Choose a sample to use in a cover or original song.
- Work on the song either independently or within a peer group that utilizes that sample.
- Share how the sample adds to the narrative of the song.
- Share the song in front of their peers (or via a pre-recorded performance) for their peers (or not).
- Engage in a creative process with the song that involves producing within a DAW environment.

Assessment Considerations

Informal Assessment. You will assess their learning for this lesson by the extent to which they engaged with the process. Are they sitting on the side and not talking? Are they leading the group? Are they taking notes on their phone? Are they smiling? Are they messing around? Ask them what they are getting out of the experience at various points along the way. In some cases it may seem that they are not engaged when they actually are quite engaged. You will need to have a loose set of criteria for assessing their learning. Think of assessment in this case as part performance quality assessment, part mechanics of performing their accompaniment, part mechanics of singing, part creativity of the song choice, part creativity of the performance, and part intangibles that are difficult to describe. Your assessments should be additive in nature and should avoid reduction. In other words, there should be multiple ways for them to do well on the assignment, and fewer ways that they can bury themselves in a low performance score. Failure to do any of the parts that I have outlined here could cause that. Remember, though, that learning in this setting is non-linear and that most of all you need to celebrate successes, even minor ones, to help ensure that future learning takes place.

Formal Assessment. Here is a rubric that you might use for this exercise. Rubrics like this one encourage your students to look for specific things as they grow their skills. Along with formal assessments like this, it is a good idea to give worthwhile qualitative feedback that helps your students grow in each area that you would like to see them grow.

Criteria	Ratings					Pts
This criterion is linked to a Learning Outcome "Recording"	**4 to >3.0 pts Expert** I love that your recording is approaching professional quality	**3 to >2.0 pts Practitioner** I like that you demonstrated very good recording technique (including balance)	**2 to >1.0 pts Apprentice** I'm concerned that the recording isn't very good	**1 to >0.0 pts Novice** What's up? Your recording is really difficult to listen to	**0 pts No Marks**	4 pts
This criterion is linked to a Learning Outcome "Musicianship"	**4 to >3.0 pts Expert** I love that you displayed almost professional levels of musicianship	**3 to >2.0 pts Practitioner** I like the level of musicianship you displayed in your performance—it's very good	**2 to >1.0 pts Apprentice** I'm concerned with how many errors showed up in your performance	**1 to >0.0 pts Novice** What's up? Your performance seems lacking in musicianship quality	**0 pts No Marks**	4 pts
This criterion is linked to a Learning Outcome "Creativity"	**4 to >3.0 pts Expert** I love that the creativity you displayed could end up on a recording	**3 to >2.0 pts Practitioner** I like that you displayed a very good sense of creativity	**2 to >1.0 pts Apprentice** I'm concerned that your performance did not display very much creativity	**1 to >0.0 pts Novice** What's up? There was really no sense of creativity in your music	**0 pts No Marks**	4 pts
Total Points: 12						

Further Reading/Resources

- Check out Amy Schwartz, *100 Things That Make Me Happy* (New York: Abrams Appleseed, 2015).
- Check out this TED talk by Dan Gilbert titled "The Surprising Science of Happiness": https://www.ted.com/talks/dan_gilbert_the_surprising_science_of_happiness.
- Check out Clint Randles, *To Create: Imagining the Good Life through Music* (Chicago: GIA Publications, 2020).

- Check out Gretchen Rubin, *The Happiness Project* (New York: Harper, 2009).
- Check out Dalai Lama, Desmond Tutu, and Douglas Carlton Abrams, *Book of Joy: Lasting Happiness in a Changing World* (New York: Avery, 2016).
- Check out Taylor Swift's song "Happiness": https://www.youtube.com/watch?v=tP4TTgt4nb0.

9

Advanced Middle Ground Seeds

Next-Level Thievery

Materials

- You can use a digital audio workstation (DAW) with various keyboard, pad controllers, and turntables.
- Consider using DJing hardware/software (Serato/Pioneer or Traktor/Native Instruments).
- Consider using Maschine (Native Instruments) or Ableton Push (Ableton) software.
- Access to the information universe via phones, tablets, computers.
- DAW environment such as GarageBand/Logic, FL Studio, Audacity, Soundtrap, Abelton Live, ProTools, and so forth on a computer/tablet/phone.
- Computer connected to a video projector to demonstrate the creative process.
- Optional: Computer connected to audio interface with a pair of condenser microphones to capture live audio.
- Sound system that contains speakers to amplify your computer's sound.
- Optional: Video camera to capture live student performances.

Context

The purpose of this lesson seed is to get your students further into sampling music for the purpose of making a meaningful socially charged point or other artistic statement. This next lesson seed is provided to take your students' sampling into new and interesting territories. You should use examples of prior student success and other musical examples to fuel the work that they do as they work through this lesson seed.

WATER: The Weekend's "Out of Time" Sampled a Popular Japanese Song

As you enter the world of sampling, DJ culture, remixing, and other forms of musical appropriation, consider looking outside of your part of the world to

Growing Songwriting. Clint Randles, Oxford University Press. © Oxford University Press 2024.
DOI: 10.1093/oso/9780197693216.003.0009

find inspiration. "Out of Time," a song by artist The Weekend on the *Dawn FM* album (2022), for example, sounds like a classic '80s R&B song. The song samples "Midnight Pretenders" (1983), a song written by Japanese composers Tomoko Aran and Tetsurō Oda, and originally performed by Aran. Quite a number of songs sample music from Asia as a way of piquing musical interest. Here are a few noteworthy examples that you can use in your classroom:

1. GZA feat. Ghostface Killah, Killah Priest & RZA—"4th Chamber" (1995), Samples Kalyanji-Anandji—"Dharmatma Theme Music (Sad)"
2. Company Flow feat. Breeze Brewin & J-Treds—"The Fire in Which You Burn" (1997), Samples Ravi Shankar (see Figure 9.1)—"Raga Puriya Dhanashri"
3. Erick Sermon feat. Redman—"React" (2002), Samples Asha Bhosle, Manna Dey, Meena Kapoor, and Mohammed Rafi—"Chandi Ka Badan"
4. Truth Hurts feat. Rakim—"Addictive" (2002), Samples Lata Mangeshkar—"Thoda Resham Lagta Hai"
5. Jay-Z feat. Kanye West—"The Bounce" (2002), Samples Alka Yagnik & Ila Arun—"Choli Ke Peeche Kya Hai"
6. Jaylib—"Survival Test" (2003), Samples Lata Mangeshkar—"Poorab Disa Se Pardesi Aya"
7. The Game—"Put You on the Game" (2005), Samples Lata Mangeshkar & Mohammed Rafi—"Baghon Mein Bahar Hai"
8. The Black Eyed Peas—"Don't Phunk with My Heart" (2005), Samples Asha Bhosle—"Aye Naujawan Sab Kuchh Yahan" and "Yeh Mera Dil Pyar Ka Deewana"

Listen outside of your comfort zone for ideas for music to sample. Have your students do the same.

Figure 9.1 Changing the pitch of a sample in Logic Pro X

SUNLIGHT: You Can Change the Key and Tempo of Samples

DAW environments allow you to change the key and tempo of samples. Procedures for how to do this are specific to your DAW. Here is the process for Logic Pro X. Do a quick search for "how to change the key and tempo of my sample" for your specific DAW and you will be ready to start playing with key and tempo. Keep in mind that most DJ software allows you to do this quite easily. Start looking at Pioneer turntables (Serato software) and Traktor controllers (Traktor Pro 3 with Native Instruments software) and dropping songs into the software. You can create a master track (maintains key and tempo values) and a synch track (adjusts key and tempo to the master track).

Here are the steps to change the key of samples in Logic Pro X:

1. Select a region in the Tracks area.
2. Click the Inspector button in the control bar, or press I on your keyboard.
3. In the Inspector, if necessary click the disclosure triangle icon next to Region to view region parameters. Or, press Option–R to open the Region inspector in a separate window.
4. Do either to transpose or fine-tune an audio region:
   - To choose a preset value, click the Transpose or Fine Tune pop-up menu and choose a pre-set value.
   - To set a custom value, click-and-drag in the Transpose or Fine Tune field.

Here are the steps to change the tempo of a sample:

1. In the Logic Pro Tracks area, select the audio region to which you want to match the project tempo.
2. Control-click the Cycle button in the control bar, and make sure the Auto Set Locators by Region Selection option is *not* selected.
3. Set the left and right locator positions in the ruler. The locator range should closely match the length of the region—usually to the nearest bar.
4. Choose Edit Tempo Adjust Tempo using Region Length and Locators.
   A dialog asks if you want to change the tempo of the entire project, or create a tempo change for the section of the project occupied by the selected region.
5. Do one of the following:
   - *To adjust the tempo of the complete project to the audio region:* Click Globally.
   - *To create a tempo change that spans the length of the audio region:* Click Create.

Lesson Time

This lesson will take multiple classes to take on a complete form. You will need to allow time for your students' learning to grow. It is a seed that will take you in many different directions if you allow it to. Remember that this is the goal of the book—to give you many places to start a creative lesson that centers on songwriting (covering songs, the middle ground, and writing originals). You could make this an individual lesson or you could have them self-select their own sampling workgroup. Your technology setup might very well dictate how these workgroups could function. Do you have headphone hub environments? Do you have a computer for every student? Answers to these questions will guide your structure of the lesson time.

Lesson Instructions

Preparation (10 minutes)

Gather the class and give them a short lesson on samples and sampling. Start with some of the best of all time that I shared in the SUNLIGHT section. Talk about how these songs were created. Tell them a bit about what you know about the artists doing the sampling and the original artist who created the music being sampled. Demonstrate how you go about finding music to sample. Show them how to listen to music for catchy and/or potentially impactful musical or lyrical material. Show them how to create a stem track from a song by using the app Xtrax Stems. Use a DAW to organize song elements. Add musical materials from loops or other readymade music to demonstrate how a sample can add so much to a song.

Choose the Song (10–15 minutes or longer)

Give them some time to search for a song to sample. They will have to agree on which one that they want to do. This could take a lot of time or not, depending upon the group and their dynamics (if they are working in a workgroup). Help them only when they need your help; otherwise, stay out of the way. They will come to you with diverse opinions and highly developed tastes for what they like. Let them lead the way. You will sometimes have to move them away from music with explicit content. You know your school culture and what is allowed/tolerated. Monitor the activity in the room carefully to make sure that it stays productive.

Work on the Song (30 minutes or most likely much more)

Allow them time to work on the song. Since this is a middle ground lesson, it may be that they are using a sample to add support to a previously existing song (cover) or that they are using it to add support to a new song that they are working on. This can be complicated if they are working in workgroups. If they are working on the song individually you will have a different series of considerations. Most of your students will likely be self-conscious about various musical abilities. You will have to create a safe place to not be perfect all of the time. You will have to discuss the role of feedback and what is acceptable. Positivity needs to be the mantra in your classroom for students to feel safe sharing with one another. Also, it is a great idea for you to model all aspects of the creative process in front of them when you can. It is okay for your performances to not be perfect. Performing in front of them goes a long way to establish a positive and supportive culture.

Perform (Another Class Period)

Depending on how many groups/individuals you want to share in class, you will have to make a plan for how everyone can share. You will have students with severe performance anxiety. For them you will have to create alternate sharing opportunities. They could record their performances and submit them electronically to you from home. During the pandemic, this is how we made music together. You could make the band collaborate that way as well, adding their parts to the recording video/audio. If you have a small performance stage in your class, this would be an excellent opportunity to utilize it. Play their music from computers on the stage. Celebrate their success, be positive, and provide them with a clear path to what they will need to improve—basically they will need to continue practicing the process. Let their student peers be the first to provide feedback. Provide guidelines for the feedback: for example, give one positive comment and a comment that they could use to improve by.

Record (Another class period or multiple class periods)

It is nearly always worth your time and effort to record the songs/performances of your students. They learn by engaging in practice and reflection upon their practice. There is not a better way of self-assessment for musicians than critically listening to our performances. You can be meticulous and professional about recording or not depending upon your expertise with recording arts. An audio interface with a XY-configured microphone pattern would capture the sound of a room well. If you have a computer at each headphone hub station that your small groups are in you could multitrack-record their performance and engineer the audio for matching with your video. You could simply use your phone or tablet to record the performances (sharing sessions) with the built-in microphone, capturing students responses to each other's work. All of these options are available to you. Choose a path that makes sense for your setting.

Modifications for Learners

Recording at Home Modification

For those of your students with performance anxiety, allow them to record their performances at home on their phones or with their computers with DAWs. Many times their desire to make use of this modification has nothing to do with their interest in your class or the lesson, but everything to do with their anxiety about performing in front of their peers. Allow them to record at home. Doing so still means that they are developing a connection to the real world of people making music in the world. They could come around to the possibility of performing in front of their peers when they develop a bit more confidence. You should encourage them to share their videos with the class as a way of encouraging their live performance prowess.

You Perform with Them Modification

If performing the accompaniment is too difficult a task for them, you can always play their work from your computer. This is a widely used accommodation by me when I am working with younger students. Sometimes it's easier when someone else shares your work. Remember, though, as you are working on developing this ability in your students that sharing your music is wrapped up in quite a lot of cultural capital. They will gain important life skills that can last a lifetime by engaging in creative processes that end with sharing and explaining the steps of their work.

Learning Outcomes

- Choose a sample to use in a cover or original song.
- Work on the song either independently or within a peer group that utilizes that sample.
- Share how the sample adds to the narrative of the song.
- Share the song in front of their peers (or via a pre-recorded performance) for their peers (or not).
- Engage in a creative process with the song that involves producing within a DAW environment.

Assessment Considerations

Informal Assessment. You will assess their learning for this lesson by the extent to which they engaged with the process. Are they sitting on the side and not talking? Are they leading the group? Are they taking notes on their phone? Are they smiling? Are they messing around? Ask them what they are getting out of the experience at various points along the way. In some cases it may seem that they are not engaged when they actually are quite engaged. You will need to have a loose set of criteria for assessing their learning. Think of assessment in this case as part performance quality assessment, part mechanics of performing their accompaniment, part mechanics of singing, part creativity of the song choice, part creativity of the performance, and part intangibles that are difficult to describe. Your assessments should be additive in nature and should avoid reduction. In other words, there should be multiple ways for them to do well on the assignment, and fewer ways that they can bury themselves in a low performance score. Failure to do any of the parts that I have outlined here could cause that. Remember, though, that learning in this setting is non-linear and that most of all you need to celebrate successes, even minor ones, to help ensure that future learning takes place.

Formal Assessment. Here is a rubric that you might use for this exercise. Rubrics like this one encourage your students to look for specific things as they grow their skills. Along with formal assessments like this, it is a good idea to give worthwhile qualitative feedback that helps your students grow in each area that you would like to see them grow.

Criteria	Ratings					Pts
This criterion is linked to a Learning Outcome "Recording"	**4 to >3.0 pts** **Expert** I love that your recording is approaching professional quality	**3 to >2.0 pts** **Practitioner** I like that you demonstrated very good recording technique (including balance)	**2 to >1.0 pts** **Apprentice** I'm concerned that the recording isn't very good	**1 to >0.0 pts** **Novice** What's up? Your recording is really difficult to listen to	**0 pts** **No Marks**	4 pts
This criterion is linked to a Learning Outcome "Musicianship"	**4 to >3.0 pts** **Expert** I love that you displayed almost professional levels of musicianship	**3 to >2.0 pts** **Practitioner** I like the level of musicianship you displayed in your performance—it's very good	**2 to >1.0 pts** **Apprentice** I'm concerned with how many errors showed up in your performance	**1 to >0.0 pts** **Novice** What's up? Your performance seems lacking in musicianship quality	**0 pts** **No Marks**	4 pts
This criterion is linked to a Learning Outcome "Creativity"	**4 to >3.0 pts** **Expert** I love that the creativity you displayed could end up on a recording	**3 to >2.0 pts** **Practitioner** I like that you displayed a very good sense of creativity	**2 to >1.0 pts** **Apprentice** I'm concerned that your performance did not display very much creativity	**1 to >0.0 pts** **Novice** What's up? There was really no sense of creativity in your music	**0 pts** **No Marks**	4 pts
Total Points: 12						

Further Reading/Resources

- Check out Amy Schwartz, *100 Things That Make Me Happy* (New York: Abrams Appleseed, 2015).
- Check out this TED talk by Dan Gilbert titled "The Surprising Science of Happiness": https://www.ted.com/talks/dan_gilbert_the_surprising_science_of_happiness.
- Check out Clint Randles, *To Create: Imagining the Good Life through Music* (Chicago: GIA Publications, 2020).

- Check out Gretchen Rubin, *The Happiness Project* (New York: Harper, 2009).
- Check out Dalai Lama, Desmond Tutu, and Douglas Carlton Abrams, *Book of Joy: Lasting Happiness in a Changing World* (New York: Avery, 2016).
- Check out Taylor Swift's song "Happiness": https://www.youtube.com/watch?v=tP4TTgt4nb0.

PART III
SONGWRITING

10

Developing an Artistic Voice

WATER: Rick Rubin

Sylvia Massey in Recording Unhinged (2016) calls Rick Rubin the "fan" producer (p. 199) because he loves consuming music. When he starts working with an artist, he'll ask them to write 300 songs so that he can pick the best twenty-five to record. He enjoys putting music that people would normally not put together in the same place to see what will happen. In so doing he has helped create some of the most memorable songs of all time. Artists that he has worked with include: Beastie Boys, LL Cool J, Public Enemy, Geto Boys, Run-DMC, Red Hot Chili Peppers, Kanye West, Rage Against the Machine, Adele, Tom Petty, Slayer, and Johnny Cash. That is quite an eclectic list!

The takeaway for music teachers is that in order for your students to write songs that they are proud of, they are going to need to write many more than they end up using. That is key. Make it a part of daily practice to implement the lesson plan seeds in this book as a way of filling the pages of their songwriting journals. In order to find your own voice as a songwriter, you have to put in the hours required of anyone to be good. That means writing way more songs than you ever record, way more not-so-good songs than good ones. That will ensure that you have some songs that you are really proud of in the end.

SUNLIGHT: Plans and Happy Accidents

Both things listed in this section's title are necessary and important. We make plans where nurturing musical creativities are concerned. But those plans should be abandoned in a heartbeat if something better and more productive for students presents itself. Those are words that other music education leaders might not tell you, but that doesn't scare me from saying it. You need to explore unexpected outcomes, AND you need to allow time for unexpected things to happen. When you serve as a music producer in your classroom, you constantly look for magic in the less compressed moments.

Some of the most memorable musical outcomes in the songwriting process happen first as accidents. You didn't intend to come in a measure early, but you did and it was pretty cool. Keep it. You didn't intend to not use a bass player in a song, but the day when your bass player was absent and it sounded better moved you

Growing Songwriting. Clint Randles, Oxford University Press. © Oxford University Press 2024.
DOI: 10.1093/oso/9780197693216.003.0010

to change and take a different course. A slipped word choice, a fumbled finger, a cymbal accidentally crashing to the floor can produce an unintended outcome that ends up being pure magic. We are in the business in classrooms where creativities are valued to embrace happy accidents.

There is not a single more potent form of music education than engaging in the process of songwriting. The process contains within it lyrical composition, musical composition, production, performance, recording, and publication. It is a process that you can do independently (many artists across time have performed all the parts to their own songs, produced, recorded, and released their music to the world) or in a group. Songwriters are passionate about their music, constantly looking for ways to improve their craft. Writing songs is a lifelong musical pursuit. The time is now for growing songwriting in school and community music settings!

As you know, this book is laid out in three main sections: Covering Songs, the Middle Ground, and Songwriting. The sections before this one and all the lessons and experience that come with implementing them in practice have prepared you and your students for songwriting. Remember that the real world does not function linearly. Some of your students may have skipped right to songwriting without working through covering songs and doing middle ground work. That's okay! You are completely free to move around based on what each of them needs at any particular time. Your primary goal is to develop their platform for self-expression through the craft of songwriting. In reality, we all get to that place differently.

The lesson seeds that follow fall primarily into two categories: lyrical starting places and musical starting places. To be success as a songwriter, you need both. So my goal with this chapter and the lesson seeds that follow is to give you places to start in both of those arenas. Most songwriting texts focus on helping you do aspects of those two areas better. You can and should use those other texts in addition to this book. I come to you from a music education perspective. I want to help YOU the teacher become a better songwriter so that you can demonstrate the skills that I reference here in this book. You don't have to be perfect when you start teaching songwriting. However, your goal should be to get better at all these skills as you practice your craft of both songwriting and teaching songwriting. There is a symbiotic relationship between songwriting and teaching songwriting. Doing one will make you better at doing the other.

Songwriting Journals Are Essential

As I wrote in Chapter 1, keeping a songwriting journal is the most important thing that budding songwriters can do (Errico, 2022). It is their life blood as a songwriter. You sketch all kinds of ideas, object write, pair words, collect metaphors, and write prose, poetry, and some nonsense in your songwriting journal. It is essential. [emphasis] Start one yourself and have each of your students start one. There is no substitution for doing this. There are endless stories of songwriters getting inspired and writing lyrics on the backs of letters, on bathroom stalls, and recording voice memos on their phones. However, the organizational utility of having your best ideas in one place that you can easily page through and jump around within is something not to be overlooked.

Here is some wisdom from Ewer (2016) on the value of keeping a songwriting journal:[1]

> If you play a musical instrument, it's a no-brainer that you'll spend a good deal of time practicing. But as a songwriter, you may not consider practicing to be a big part of improving your abilities. But practicing your songwriting is important. It doesn't just hone skills, it helps keep writer's block at bay by giving you smaller tasks that are easier to complete, and completion of a task makes you feel successful.

He likens keeping a songwriting journal and recording your writing exercising like the daily task of practicing your instrument:

> A songwriting journal can be anything you want or need it to be, so first and foremost, it needs to be something from which you'll get fairly immediate benefit, or you'll quickly lose interest in keeping one.

Here are some ideas on how to use your journal:[2]

1. Make a list of main songwriting topics. This list should include Lyrics, Melodies and Chord Progressions. In addition to having a section called "Lyrics," you might want to be more specific; within that section, write "Imagery," or "Rhyming," or some other such aspect.
2. Include other items on the list that are of particular musical interest to you. This might include: Instrumentation Ideas, Songwriters, and anything else in the world of songwriting that interests you.
3. Create categories for your journal. Transfer the list of topics you've created to your journal, so that you now have a multi-sectional journal that's ready to use. In addition to the topics that make it to your own list, include a category called "Listening." This will be a list of songs (and observations about those songs) that you've listened to, enjoyed, and feel that you can learn from.

Ewer (2016) suggests that your songwriting journal can function both as a scrapbook and as a workbook. You will want to keep anything that you find interesting and potentially useful when it comes time to writing songs in your journal. While functioning as a scrapbook, it will naturally become very useful as a workbook as you labor through the process of writing. It is of course one of the most meaningful kinds of labor (Randles, 2020).

WATER: Eddie Vedder's Notebooks

Eddie Vedder is the lead singer of one of my favorite bands of all time—Pearl Jam. He is known to have a cheap coil-ringed notebook under his arm with the words "NOT YOURS" written on the front. In his notebooks are "thoughts, observations, doodles, and ideas that will eventually be transformed into Pearl Jam songs."[3] When he completes a notebook, he files it away on a shelf with all of the other notebooks that he has kept through the years. They remain a constant source of ideas and inspiration for songs that have not yet been written.

He is protective of his notebooks and still remembers a time when two of his notebooks were stolen backstage while Pearl Jam was playing the Melody Club in Stockholm, Sweden. He has never fully recovered from that. It almost felt as though he had lost a family member. Can you imagine what songs that those journals might have produced?! What a profound loss for us all. Keep a journal and keep it safe. Create space for your students to keep a journal as well.

Lyrical Beginnings

To help with writing lyrics, you are going to need to focus on daily exercises that get your students to stretch out how they think about using language. I am going to provide you with ways that professional songwriters go about the hard work of generating lyric ideas for their songs. There are no shortcuts to the process of doing this better. The truth is that some of your students might be gifted at creative writing. Maybe they have written poems. Perhaps they are even good at it. Their process might center more on musical beginnings that attach themselves to their written poetry. Great! One size will not fit all. You are going to have to think diversely and embrace multiplicity in your pedagogical approaches. That is part of what makes teaching in classrooms that focus on creating pathways for multiple creativities to grow an exciting place to be for both students and teachers alike.

Object Writing

As I wrote in Chapter 1, one of the best tools that I know of to help jump-start the creative process is to engage your students in object writing sessions where they free write around a topic, idea, sentiment, person, place, thing, action, and so forth. Set the timer for five minutes. That is generally enough time for them to come up with interesting talking points, but not too long that they start to find more interesting things to do with their time. [smile] The idea is to generate ideas, to think outside normal logical stream of consciousness, and to break down our tendency to immediately organize thought content.

The process of coming up with interesting descriptions of the objects being studied is what matters most. Object writing precedes any notion of rhyming scheme or overall theme. Your students will look to the results of your object-writing sessions to help you create rhyming schemes that are new and compelling. Object writing is too easily skipped by songwriters who think that they have to hurry up and go straight to rhyming phrases. My undergraduate students are guilty of this. Make sure to have your students choose the topics of your object-writing sessions. It always ends up being good fun. Talking about ideas generated is illuminating and inspiring, as the combination of all ideational activity is always much more than any of their individual thought paths. This is why collaboration is so important!

Nouns and Verbs Ladders

Tweedy (2020) writes about songwriting exercises that, like object-writing sessions, center on getting us out of our normal ideational patterns in language. Happy accidents and non-linear pathways to fruitful endings are the goal. This could be the exact opposite of how music teachers are prepared. We tend to focus on activity that is linear and sequential, centered on notions of efficiency. So by nature, the work of music teacher producers (Randles, 2022) must embrace more diverse philosophical beliefs about both pedagogy and practice.

I present lesson seeds that make use of nouns and verbs ladders in the next chapter. I suggest that you practice this exercise yourself before you try it out with a class. If you are anything like me, you will find the process of practicing this exercise challenging and rewarding. Record this practice activity in your songwriting journal. You will keep coming back to it as you work on your songs. If you are fortunate to teach multiple classes during your school day where students write their own songs, you will find that your journal will become full of ideas rather quickly!

Musical Beginnings

Along with lyrical beginnings, many times we start the songwriting process with musical beginnings. Melody, harmony, rhythm, meter, dynamics, and so forth become the building blocks by which you can structure exercises that will fill the pages of your students' songwriting journals. They go to those journals to gather ideas that they will use to write their songs. Perricone (2018) has a lot to teach us about starting with musical ideas. What follows is some of the best ideas that I have gleaned from primarily his work, but also that of hosts of others.

Melody

Melody is the pitch and rhythm of the main musical line of songs. Melodies are typically sung by the lead vocalist and sometimes passed around to other instruments in the ensemble. Melodies usually emerge from our musical sense of the movement of the harmonies. Jeff Weedy has said that he typically starts with musical beginnings—harmonic progressions—that he hums improvised musical lines over until he finds a melody that he likes. He then consults his songwriting journal for lyrical ideas at any stage of being developed.

The movement of our melodies should enhance the meaning in some way of the songs that we write. They move both by pitch and by rhythm. In a perfect reality, melody and lyrical content would be born at the same time. That is not, however, how it happens most of the time. One tends to build off whatever comes first, lyrics or melody. We need practice composing both ways. You will need to provide opportunities for your students to start with either lyrics or melody.

WATER: Elton John and Bernie Taupin

Elton John teams up with Bernie Taupin in a songwriting team, with Elton creating the music and Bernie the lyrics. The two work completely independently. Elton realizes that this is a somewhat strange working relationship, but has decided not to question the approach as it has worked so well thus far. "I just go to the studio and there's 24 lyrics waiting for me and I look through them and see which one I want to start with, and then I try to write a song. I never, ever know what the lyrics are gonna be up front," he told US talk show host Jimmy Kimmel.[4] Perhaps this model is something that we as music teachers can try out in our classrooms.

"When I first started working with Bernie it was exactly the same as it is now; I would get a lyric, I would go away and write the melody and play it to him. That's never changed. It's the same thing now and it's as exciting now as it was then. So if I write a song on this album and I've finished it I go and bring him in and say, 'Listen, this is the song,' and then the band come in and learn it and we put it down. There must be some people who write like that but (I don't know them). We've been writing 49 years together, this year, and I don't try to analyze it. It's strange but it works." The pair does talk about what they would like to do beforehand, which Elton both consider vital to the process.

Chord Progressions

Songwriters utilize chords in songs by giving them an implied directionality or motion. It matters to your song how the chords progress. Like melody, chord motion or progression adds to your storytelling ability, as there is so much emotion and meaning wrapped up in them. Each chord within (or without) a particular key reveals melodic potential. Chords, like melody, move by pitch (different voicings and inversions) and by rhythm. The order of the chords in your progressions does a lot to enhance the drama of your story. Here are some words of wisdom from an interview with Joni Mitchell on the point of drama and harmony:[5]

> Throughout the interview, Mitchell described her vocal craft by using the language of theater, just as she explained her sense of harmony in terms of painting. Metaphorically, these art forms make a lot of sense together: The chord movement is the painting of the stage scenery—the context and structure of the music—and in the vocal parts, she steps onto the stage to act out the part she has scripted for herself. Mitchell's goal as a singer, like that of a good actor, is to embody the words and rise above what she called the "emotional fakery" of pop music.

So when we design how our chord progression is going to play out, we prepare the setting that our drama will grow within. We then become the actors on the stage and the song our narrative.

I think of harmonic structure as closely related to the form of a song. Perricone (2018) calls harmony "the great organizer" (p. 261). We hang the lyrical content with melody on the framework of chord progressions and form: verse/chorus/bridge/instrumental sections. I realize though that one might think about chord progressions differently. I do a lot of performance from lead sheets in my professional musician work, where the value of chord progressions is paramount. Songs take shape in this environment primarily through our interpretation of how chord progressions move through songs. Groove and playing by feel are the primary techniques by which this movement occurs. Use your chord progressions as an extension of form to help you organize your songs. Teach your students to think about harmony as a way to build their songs.

SUNLIGHT: "Musician on a Mission"—New Zealand

One of my favorite YouTubers on songwriting and music production is "Musician on a Mission," otherwise known as Rob Mayzes. He's from one of my favorite countries on the planet—New Zealand. He has this to say about chord progressions and the songwriting process:

> A chord progression is the order chords are played, one after another, in a song or a piece of music. The chords you use, and the order you play them in make up the harmony of a song. Like most of music, chords and their progressions come in patterns. A chord progression is just that—the pattern of chords in songs you play or write. Songwriters want to put chords together that sound good.

More importantly they want chords that feel good . . . or sad . . . or angry, tense, moody, sexy, whatever! As songwriters, the chords you use and the way they're put together is important. It can help create the melody or give context to how the melody makes us feel. You can have as many chords as you like or work with just two—a progression has to have at least two. But a song can work with even a single chord. So being able to use a chordal instrument, like a guitar or piano, is a powerful songwriting tool. Because here's the thing—there aren't many instruments that actually play chords (i.e., two or more notes at once).

Check out musicianonamission.com for lots of ways to augment your skills as a songwriter, music producer, and audio engineer. Also, check out Mastering.com for the most recent work from Rob and his ideas regarding teaching the songwriting process as a "Reverse Engineer." Then, practice, practice, practice. That is what we musicians and music teachers do best!

Riffs and Tracks

Riffs are melodic phrases of musical interest that work in conjunction with the vocal melodic lines. We can think of a riff as a hook—that is, a musical idea or phrase used in popular music to catch the ear of the listener. Riffs are essentially hooks. When we write/perform/record riffs, we employ compositional strategies of counterpoint. The main idea is that we compose multiple lines of music that serve as (1) independently interesting musical statements and (2) complementary musical players on the "team" of musical sounds. Riff-based composition is all over popular music and is something that producers employ regularly when they work with artists. Here are some guidelines for how counterpoint works:

1. When one voice is active, the other voice is not active or less active.
2. Entrances and exits are key places to bring particular voices out in the mix.
3. The motion or direction of each voice is important in establishing independence of voice and for creating interest.

Here are four types of motion in music when thinking about how riffs interact with the rest of the music:

1. Contrary motion
2. Oblique motion
3. Similar motion
4. Parallel motion

Riffs can employ all these different compositional movements.

Tonal Cues

The tonal environment that you choose for your songs is an essential toolkit for developing both melodic and harmonic content. You can employ both major and minor tonal environments and switch it up even within songs. You can employ blues, rock, R&B, and modal environments in your songs. There is no substitution for listening broadly and outside of your normal patterns when considering tonal landscapes. All things are possible. Explore and keep an open mind.

Developmental Techniques

There are a number of strategies that composers and songwriters alike have used to develop both the lyrical and musical sides of songwriting (Randles and Sullivan, 2013). I will share some of those ideas for you here in hopes that you will use them to help your students write their songs. I have borrowed many of these ideas from composer Alan Belkin's *A Practical Guide to Music Composition* (2008).

Musical Flow

Each musical event must arise convincingly from the previous one. We owe it to our ears to make this true. We can create surprises, but they must be limited in their degree of contrast, to avoid incoherence. Our music generally proceeds in such a way as to maintain our listener's sense of flow. We want them to follow our story, so we make it as easy as we can to do this.

Contrast

We need to provide enough contrast to make our songs interesting to listen to, but not too much contrast as to lose our listeners along the way. Good stories shift and take us new places. Stories that we can remember and enjoy keep us engaged from beginning to end. However, there is nothing more annoying than stories that jump off the deep end suddenly and/or are hard to follow because the writer/director hasn't prepared us for the changes.

Suspense

We as listeners like to be kept on the edge of our seats. We are engaged in that way when there are interesting things going on in the music. Songwriters think of that as they engage with the creative process that, as we have said throughout this book, involves quite a lot of music production along the way.

Points of Reference

To help the listener make sense of your song, it is important to provide recognizable signposts. We might think of these as reference points that help to tie the work together. If our music goes on for a long time without a clear reference to something well defined and familiar, the listener can feel lost. Motives and themes often fulfill this function. Make use of them to help hold things together.

Climax

Think of climax as the punchline. Not only must the continuation carry the previously presented ideas further along in a coherent flow, but that flow must develop in intensity. This process of intensification helps create momentum and direction. Climax represents the fulfillment of that momentum. It was the goal all along. We went through all of the trouble early on in creating a story worth telling. The climax is where we learn what ultimately happens to our characters, the honest voices behind our melodies. Take the listener somewhere along the way and make the ending a worthwhile part of the journey.

Organization: Song Maps

One of the most helpful resources for teaching songwriting is Hawkins's (2016) *Song Maps*. Each of the seven maps can serve as a seed for songwriting lessons that start with lyrical beginnings. I have provided a seed that utilizes each here in the following chapters. It would be great if you could also pick up the Hawkins text along the way. But if you don't, you'll have a lot to get you started with the ideas that I have presented here. To review, here are the seven maps with a brief explanation. Check back to Chapter 1 for an introductory treatment of each. Here I provide a primer to what you will see in the lesson seeds:

1. Tension/Response
2. Problem/Declaration
3. Timezones
4. Places
5. Roles
6. Twist
7. Literal/Figurative

Tension/Response

With this song map our lyrical content introduces some sort of tension that is addressed in particular ways during the choruses and/or bridge. To make this song map work in practice, you need to have some tension/response ideas. You are in luck . . . as life is full of tension and drama! So start making a list of the tensions that you experience every day, as THOSE are what you should focus your writing attention on. You will find that writing about your tension helps you to process it. Songwriting can function as a form of therapy for the drama that can at times rule our lives. Purge the drama and the negative hold that it can have on you by writing it out of your system. Maybe you can help someone else process their drama by engaging with your song.

Problem/Declaration

With this map, you state a particular problem in Verse 1 and follow it with some sort of declaration in the Chorus. In Verse 2, you write in a response to the problem and follow it with a declaration—Chorus. Then, you write about what it all means in the Bridge and follow it with the Chorus. To distill all of that into something that might make more sense, your song makes a declaration based on your response to a problem and what that means for you. So, like tension/response songs, this type of song starts with a problem (result of tension). I don't know about you, but my life is a collection of problems. We all have plenty of inspiration! Make a list. Consult it. Use your best problems that are appropriate for the ages of students that you work with as places to start.

Timezones

This type of song leverages our basic human need to think of things chronologically. Life happens over time. Music unfolds over time. That's no small consideration/ connection. You start the story in Verse 1 in some significant well-chosen point in the life of your character(s), and you follow up with a chorus that is your title in musical form. In Verse 2, your story continues. Follow that up with another presentation of your title in musical form—Chorus. Then you give the listener the payoff in the form of a Bridge and follow that up with another Chorus. This song map is all about telling a story by utilizing points in time in the lives of your characters.

Places

In this song type, you take the listener to different places in each verse. The Chorus is basically once again your title in musical form. The bridge ends up being your payoff again or the main point of the story. Each place introduced in subsequent verses moves the story along purposefully. When you write this type of song, it might be best to start with the Title/Chorus and then use the places idea to help you craft/frame the narrative. You move the listener through the story by putting your characters in particular places. It might be equally productive to think of the payoff first—the Bridge—and then work backward.

Roles

This type of song map starts with understanding particular roles that a character or characters can assume. Each verse then centers on an individual role to provide a narrative organizational frame for the song. There is a declaration that occurs with every Chorus that usually is directly related to the title of your song. Like "Places" songs, "Roles" songs feature some sort of payoff in the Bridge. Who are your characters? What will be the primary sentiment in your song (payoff)? What title sums up what your characters will feel over the course of the song? Focus on the roles that each character assumes as you tell their story over the course of the narrative.

Twist

This type of song centers on the Bridge that functions here as it does in a number of the other song maps as the payoff. From a storytelling perspective you might best start with considering what the twist might be. You are going to lead with telling the story a particular way with the knowledge that during the Bridge you are going to turn the main idea on its side. That means that you are going to surprise the listener in some way by concealing a vital part of the story until then. Each verse tells more of the story. Each chorus is the title in musical form that cheekily plays on the title in musical form without giving away the payoff until it is time. This song map is carefully executed trickery that will delight your listener. Check out "A Boy Named Sue" by Johnny Cash.

Literal/Figural

This type of song plays on our ability to flip back and forth between literal and figurative. A few things help us get started with this type of song. What is the title that will keep coming up in the choruses? What will the payoff be? You start with these ideas in place. Then, you consider how you might play on using a literal/figural progression across the verses of the song. Like all of these song maps, you still are confronted with the guiding principle of determining what your song is about. Who is your audience? What is your song about? What good do you hope to achieve with it?

Using a DAW during the Creative Process

A digital audio workstation (DAW) is our number one technological tool as we are engaged in the songwriting process. While I have been persuaded by some of my colleagues in countries where technology is more difficult to come by to find ways to do the things that I do without technology or with very little technology, you would do well to start building your skills using a DAW. There are many to choose from; the most noteworthy for me and my students are Logic Pro X (for Apple computers) and FL Studio (for Windows computers). You can use Pro Tools, GarageBand, Audacity, Soundation, and hosts of other software programs as a DAW to assist you in the creative process.

A DAW allows you to record pieces of the musical aspects of your song as you go. These might not be the final versions of your work, but they very well could be. There are things to know and learn about the technology associated with a DAW that I treat much more comprehensively in *Music Teacher as Music Producer* (Randles, 2022). You will need an audio interface to convert your musical/sound information into digital information. It matters what kind of audio interface that you purchase. How many channels will you need? There are some really great-sounding preamps in some of the more pricey audio interfaces. Is that something that you are interested in?

Practically speaking, you use your DAW to layout your song. How long is your introduction? How many bars is your verse, pre-chorus, and chorus? What harmonic progressions are you going to use for each of those sections? What instruments are you going to use to fill in the groove of your song once you know what the harmonic progressions for each section are going to be? Are you going to use hooks? Of course, you are! What are they going to be? You try out ideas by using the loop function in your DAW. You use the DAW in every step of creating your song.

Flow Chart for Writing a Song Using a DAW

Here is a basic flow chart for writing a song using a DAW during the creative process:

1. Establish your tempo and key.
2. Find a drum loop or build a drum groove that fits the style of music that you are working on.

3. Use an accompaniment instrument like a bass or guitar to play along with the drum groove and rough in the harmonic progression of the introduction, verse, or chorus of the song.
4. Go to your songwriting journal and find some lyrical material that you would like to use for this song. Chances are that you have thought about what this song is going to be about before now, but you might not have, and that's okay. Your song will need some lyrics. Go to the place where you have been developing your lyrical ideas for a place to start.
5. As you listen to the section that you started with—many times it is the chorus, but not always—look at your lyrical material and see if anything fits or jumps out at you.
6. If you started with your chorus and you were able to come up with some sort of musical and lyrical idea, consider what your song might be about. What is the story? Who are the characters? Who is your audience? What would you like to achieve with your song?
6. When you have sufficiently answered the previous questions, or when you think that you might have enough answers to get started, rough in either the lyrical or musical section of the verse. I usually start by roughing in the music (with bass or guitar or keys; any accompaniment instrument will do) and retrofit the lyrics, but I know people who work in the opposite order. If you start with music, you can capture your work in your DAW. You can then, as you did with the chorus, loop the verse section and try out your lyrical ideas as you listen.
7. At this point, you might want to consider looking at the song maps for ideas about how your verses might hang together. The best thing that song maps can help with is giving you an idea about how you might best tell a story over multiple verse sections, how you might build a "payoff" section into the storyline.
8. Write each section of your song this way. Use your DAW to help you organize the structure of your work. The nice thing about starting with a tempo and key is that you can copy and paste sections of your song around in the DAW as you would in a word processor. The drum and accompaniment instrument lines can be copied and pasted into the verse section of Verses 2 and 3 as soon as you know what Verse 1 is going to look and sound like. You can always make changes to these forms later, but having a visual placeholder on your computer screen helps you think about your song in totality.
9. Work in production aspects of your song as you go, or wait until all the sections are there, when you know more precisely what it is going to be about, and fill them in. The biggest thing to think about as you fill in the musical portions of your song is that you want something musically interesting happening the whole time. You should plan out where you want the peaks and valleys of the song to be.
10. Perform the parts in yourself, or, better yet, get some of your friends involved in the creative process. We are better together. The sum total of all of

our creative energy in a group is more powerful than the individual parts. Remember that and lean into group collaborative creativities. You won't be disappointed that you did.

Old Thinking and New Technology

The creative process of songwriting has been assisted through the use of DAW technology. The DAW acts as the recording studio console and tape machine of days gone by. People used to have to splice tape together to copy and paste. That took time. Engineers, producers, and musicians thought as they did this work, and that thinking was probably really great for their creative process. We probably do our thinking now with DAWs at different stages of the process. Some musicians like to record music in old ways to try to achieve some of the excellent musical products that we have come to know and love.

One of the pioneers of old ways of thinking about recording is Jack White. His Third Man Records studio in Nashville, TN, is equipped with a sound-on-acetate-record recording device so that artists can be recorded right on to vinyl. The vinyl format itself is an old way of thinking about listening to music that has come back in style. There is something about sitting down and dropping a needle—committing to being there as the needle is dragged across the grooves of a record—that is illuminating in a different way than streaming. Recording to vinyl or tape, listening to music on records, forces us to think and act in old ways. We can take those old ways of thinking and use new technology to break new (sometimes old) ground.

SUNLIGHT: *Song Exploder*

There is a series on Netflix called *Song Exploder*[6] that you should check out as you augment your skills in songwriting and its teaching. The main story in each episode is how a song emerges from the working life of an artist. It chronicles the collaboration that occurs around each song. It peels back each layer of the creative process that surrounds the birthing of songs that we have always heard but never truly understood until we take this 30-minute journey into the creative lives of artists. The host uses the song stems to break down where songs started, progressed, and finished. The series is truly inspiring.

Songwriting Workgroups

A way forward for songwriting in the classroom might be borrowing some idea from our friends in Sweden regarding taking apart the songwriting process and spreading it across members of our classroom communities. Of course, the idea didn't start in Sweden: the Brill Building in New York housed the writers and performers of Tin Pan Alley of the late nineteenth and early twentieth centuries, Berry Gordy employed it at Motown in Detroit in the 1960s, and Capitol Records did it throughout the 1960s and 1970s with the Wrecking Crew in Los Angeles. We have examples of compartmentalizing the creative process where songwriting is concerned. So why don't we try it out in our classrooms?

We can have some students specialize on particular aspects of the songwriting process and hand their work on to other members of the community for their input in collaboration. We can create a microcosm of the real world of songwriting. You, as the teacher in this type of classroom songwriting environment, might start with the tasks that need to be completed before a song can be birthed, recorded, produced, and performed. Here is a breakdown of some of the specific tasks that need to be completed before songs can be completed, followed by how you might think of making each a specific task to be completed by particular students on a songwriting team. It will take imagination on your part to be able to fit each of your students within specific teams.

1. Idea generation
2a. Lyric Writing
2b. Musical Writing
3a. Listeners' Feedback
4. Recording Musicians
3b. Listeners' Feedback
5. Production/Engineering
3c. Listeners' Feedback
6. Performers
3d. Listeners' Feedback

WATER: Motown

When Berry Gordy put up the sign "Hitsville U.S.A." on his house in 1959 and turned his garage into a studio, his newly started label had yet to have any actual hits (see Figure 10.1). However, his experience at the Ford factory served him well, and he was convinced that he could create a musical equivalent to the assembly line. It turned out to be a lesson in collaboration. Every day began with a 9:00 A.M. "quality control" meeting, where songwriters and producers would listen to each other's songs and critique them. Then they'd vote. Only the highest votes made it. Everything else went in the vault. If you arrived at 9:01 A.M., you wouldn't get in, says Smokey Robinson, who had to wait until the next meeting

Figure 10.1 Hitsville U.S.A., Detroit

to get a chance to share many of his songs. As the house band, the Funk Brothers were paid by the day. The primary goal was to record as many songs as possible each day. This wasn't a problem for Marvin Gaye, as the vocals on many of his biggest hits are first takes. As we listened to the vocal track of "How Sweet It Is" (a first take), we could even hear him turn the pages of the sheet music. The track's producer, Lamont Dozier (one of the great Motown songwriters), says that Gaye had complained that the key was too high. "I knew he would do that," Dozier said. "Singers tend to be lazy. But I also knew that when he had to reach for the notes, that's when he produced the best vocals." That phenomenon is quite common in music. If singers have to push for the high notes they come out with an urgency and better tone. If you don't believe this, try it out for yourself. Berry Gordy gave us all a model of how we can do songwriting in our classrooms, borrowed from the world of automotive manufacturing, in the greatest state and city in the United States. [smile]

1. Idea Generation

Task a group of your students to think of topics for songs. This group should focus almost entirely on object writing, noun-verb associations, and ideation. Their work should be purely imaginative and generative, short of coming up with musical lines that rhyme. A theme such as "tough relationships" will fill pages upon pages of thoughts on the topic. They should develop pages and pages of thoughts on specific themes—love, God, peace, joy, patience, school, heroes, anxiety, politics (well, maybe), and so on. The more ideas for songs and creative writing that leads to idea generation, the better.

To prepare for using the workgroup idea in your classroom, you might start with idea generation with the entire class. You can then produce quite a mass of ideas that could be sifted through by the lyric writing group. In any case it will take time for this first group to come up with ideas. You will have to plan for that to occur somehow. With a well of ideas to draw from, your lyric writing team will be off to the races.

SUNLIGHT: Suspend Judgment

When you are in idea generation mode you can be your worst enemy by being overcritical. Idea generation is just that—coming up with ideas. Selecting the best of the ideas for purposes of bringing about lyric ideas will come later. What you need to do initially is come up with a lot of ideas. Here are some guiding principles to help you make sense of idea generation. These can help you when you guide your students through object writing lessons:

1. **Fluency**—You want to come up with as many ideas as you can. Quantity is central to this concept.
2. **Flexibility**—You want to come up with different kinds of ideas. So your ideas can come from different aspects of the thing or concept that you're generating ideas about.
3. **Originality**—You want to come up with novel, sometimes strange, and even sometimes strangely novel ideas as part of the collection that you turn out during your idea generation session.

You want to focus on each of these concepts: (1) coming up with many ideas that can be (2) organized into diverse categories, and that (3) are sometimes highly original and spark thought and reflection on your part. If you hit on all of these features of idea generation you will be sure to come up with enough interesting ideas to help you with your lyric development. The whole point of idea generation is to cast a net into your imagination and collect as many different and interesting thoughts surrounding a topic. Stay loose, fluent, flexible, and original.

2a. Lyric Writing
So much good work in the idea generation group has brought the task of coming up with original lyrics that much more approachable. The lyric writing team has some things to think about, in no specific order:

- What is the song going to be about, based on one of the themes and collection of ideas that the idea generation group has come up with?
- How are you going to tell the story within the song structure? Which song map will you use?
- How can you artistically grab and assemble from the idea bag a coherent song lyric that follows a narrative that: (1) speaks to a specific audience and (2) has something meaningful to say?

The lyric writing group might be a collection of duos or a bigger group of four or five. It will take a lot of versions to be able to select from among them which songs will be suitable for actually recording/performing. All the groups should work to have their songs be the ones to be used, but also should be ready to accept the chance that their song could be tabled for a bit. There is nothing requiring that any student could take the lyrics and finish the song on their own. That sort of thing should be encouraged by you.

2b. Music Writing
Happening at the same time as the lyric writing group is the music writing group. With the collection of themes and ideas from the idea generation group in hand, the music writing group messes around with musical ideas, chorus and verse chord progressions, riffs, and musical transitions. They work to develop the feel of how songs might go. This group is keen to use all of the performance and effects technologies presented in *Music Teacher as Music Producer* (Randles, 2022) and found elsewhere. It is all about the impression that the music makes on listeners. Particular effects can do particular things for us.

At some point, when a critical mass of ideas have been developed in both the lyric writing group as well as the music writing group, you will need to bring them together. Have each group share their best material. Both groups will have ideas about what might fit with what. Let each voice be heard from each group. Ideas for combining the work of both groups will be proposed. Write everything down. Develop a plan for combining that work for a preliminary performance for the whole class.

WATER: Cheiron Studios

Cheiron Studios was a recording studio in Stockholm, Sweden, founded by Denniz PoP and Tom Talomaa in the early 1990s. It was famous for being the place where

Backstreet Boys, Boyzone, Robyn, NSYNC, Britney Spears, and Westlife produced many of their greatest hits in the late 1990s and early 2000s. Like Motown in Detroit in the 1960s, Cheiron employed some of the most talented songwriters, engineers, and producers in Sweden. They worked in teams just as they did at Motown. They had fun and did great work. The Swedish aspect of their writing can be traced backed to the popular group ABBA in the 1970s. They wrote with tasteful hooks and many times would get listeners' feedback by taking the songs into clubs and trying them out on the dance floor. After playing the song in the clubs they would go back to studio and improve it, adding hype to flat sections and adding more dramatic impact when necessary.

3a. Listeners' Feedback
Have a performance for the class of new songs. Individual students can do this, or you along with them. The goal here is to present preliminary versions of songs to the class. Performances at this stage might actually be worked up in DAW environments. That is how I like to do it. What you want at this stage is for everyone to freewheel ideas for how they might approach the final version of the song. Harmony ideas? Hooks? Instrumentation? Performance ideas? Your classroom is a collection of musicians with different strengths. Try to get them all involved. The better job you do of that, the better the overall quality of your final projects. *Everyone* has *something* to offer the group creative process. How you handle the tone and quality of feedback will go a long way to determining the quality and culture of your classroom.

SUNLIGHT: John Kratus

John Kratus wrote an excellent groundbreaking article for *Music Educators Journal* in 2016 that you should stop right now and check out.[7] Here is what he had to say there about the nature of feedback as you teach songwriting:

1. **Supportive**. Early in a songwriting course, students are likely to give each other positive but not very specific feedback. "That was good." "That's really cool." "I really liked it." In a songwriting class, the students know that they will have their turn in the front of the room, and they usually treat each other as they hope they will be treated when it is their turn. Supportive feedback is worthwhile at the beginning of a songwriting class because it provides the students with a sense of security and increases their trust in other class members and the instructor. But it does not offer the songwriter much in the way of focused guidance. The teacher's role during this phase in the course is to ask students to tell the songwriter specifically what they liked in the song. Was it the singer's expressive voice? Or was it the way the lyrics described her hometown?

2. **Descriptive.** In the second phase, descriptive feedback, the instructor asks the class questions about the musical and lyrical characteristics of the song just performed. For example, "What unexpected incident happened to the man in the last verse?" or "What melodic hook was used to unify the song?" These are the same kind of questions that the teacher would ask when leading guided listening activities in the teacher-led portion of the class. The purposes of descriptive feedback are (a) to highlight those unique aspects of the song that other class members might want to employ in their own songs and (b) to provide the songwriter with the knowledge that his or her song is worthy of analysis. In effect, the class is saying, yes, we really did notice that you changed the strumming pattern in the last verse.
3. **Prescriptive.** Prescriptive feedback provides the songwriter with suggestions for improvement. At this point, it is possible to have the songwriter try out some of the suggestions in front of the class. When the class reaches the prescriptive level of feedback, it has become a type of master class for songwriters. Unlike most master classes, however, in which the "master" musician makes all the suggestions, the prescriptive form of master class allows for all class members to comment and make suggestions. Essentially, the students in the class become each other's teachers. It is not advisable to move to the prescriptive level too soon. Regardless of how accomplished or experienced a songwriter may be, it is necessary for the student to develop sufficient confidence in his or her own abilities and trust in the teacher and peers. This does not come quickly.

The work of John Kratus at Michigan State University in East Lansing as a pioneer in the growth of songwriting in music education should not be underestimated (2007, 2016, 2019). Professor Kratus changed my life and gave credence to so many things that I had believed about music education but couldn't say until I met him. My time with him from 2003 to 2010 at MSU set the course for this book and all of its contents (see Figure 10.2).

4. Recordings

Now is the time to record tracks. Use your best musicians and your own skills at times to make this happen. You should also discover the people in your class that you might train to be engineers and recordists. The structure of your facility will determine how you proceed with recording. If you are able to utilize play-in-headphone environments in your classroom, then use them to record all of the material that doesn't require silence during the recording process. If you can set up a vocal booth as part of your room setup for recording vocals, that would be amazing. These make the quality of your vocal tracks that much more professional sounding.

Please check out *Music Teacher as Music Performer* (Randles, 2022) for a rationale for and brief history of recording arts. This is a wide-open frontier for music education currently. We should be making recorded music in music classes half of

Figure 10.2 John Kratus and the author presenting at the First International Music Education Conference in Cairo, Egypt, in 2010

the time and performing the other half. Performing and recording should go hand in hand as a part of a foundational music education for all human beings. Assemble a team of your students to handle recording. You will need at least one of the following people, depending on what you do yourself:

1. **DAW Handler (software).** Someone needs to sit at the computer and press record and manage the creation of new tracks within the DAW environment. This person needs to be competent in using the software (Logic Pro X, GarageBand, ProTools, FL Studio, etc.). Most of the time this will be you. However, be on the lookout for people who are interested in learning this well. You could change someone's life with training in this area. You should be working to give all of your students opportunities to work within DAW environments. That being said, maybe some of them have the potential and interest to make doing this their career. Give them time behind the computer in your classroom.
2. **Mixer/Audio Interface Handler (hardware).** Someone needs to be responsible for the hardware side of sound collection. This person makes sure that the person at the DAW station gets a proper strong signal for of the channels that you are using. This person makes sure that all of the settings on the mixer/interface are working satisfactorily. If your studio setup involves tube preamps or other EQ devices pre-interface, then this person is also in charge of that. There is a signal chain of effects that can be utilized before sound meets the digital side of things, before it is turned into chains of 0s and 1s. You need someone to manage this. Many times this will be you. Again, though, turn things over to the students when you can.

WATER: The Engineers of Abbey Road Studios

Oasis, Pink Floyd, Radiohead, Ed Sheeran, The Hollies, Adele, Ella Fitzgerald, and of course The Beatles have recorded their most iconic music at Abbey Road Studios (formerly EMI Studios) in the St. John's Wood section of London. Furthermore, some of the most incredible cinematic soundtracks have been conducted and recorded there, including *Harry Potter*, *Star Wars*, *Lord of the Rings*, and *Indiana Jones*. It is a sacred space: hallowed ground for music lovers. Let me introduce you to some of the most iconic engineers of Abbey Road Studios.

Geoff Emerick

Geoff Emerick began his career at age fifteen when he joined Abbey Road Studios, and as fate would have it on his second day be began working on The Beatles' first-ever recording session on September, 4, 1962. In April 1966, when he was twenty, Emerick was promoted to engineer on the first session for *Revolver*. Emerick took over for Norman Smith, who had worked with The Beatles previously.[8] "Tomorrow Never Knows" was the first track recorded for the sessions and the first that he worked on. It was Emerick's suggestion to record John Lennon's vocal through a Leslie speaker on the song, to get the ethereal sound Lennon wanted, and to close-mic Ringo's drums, formerly a prohibited practice at EMI Studios.[9] How important would that trick be in the history of recording drums?!

In 1967, he engineered "Being for the Benefit of Mr. Kite!," one of the most musically interesting songs on *Sgt. Pepper's Lonely Hearts Club Band*. Lennon told Martin he wanted to re-create the "carnival atmosphere" of the Pablo Fanque circus poster that inspired the song. For the middle eight bars, Emerick spliced together multiple recordings of fairground organs and calliope in an attempt to create a unique sonic world. After a great deal of unsuccessful experimentation, Martin instructed Emerick to chop the tape into pieces with scissors, throw them up in the air, and re-assemble them at random. It worked very well. Emerick received Grammy Awards for the engineering of *Sgt. Pepper's Lonely Hearts Club Band* and *Abbey Road*. Emerick's youthful age and willingness to experiment with recording techniques aligned perfectly with The Beatles' quests for new sounds. He is a role model for our young student engineers to aspire to.

Alan Parsons

A nineteen-year-old Alan Parsons began his first professional gig as a tape operator for The Beatles' *Abbey Road* album sessions.[10] After his experiences working with The Beatles, Alan took that knowledge and continued as an engineer at Abbey Road. Alan soon refocused on rock music, engineering for The Hollies, Roy Harper,

Wings, and Pink Floyd, for the last of which most notably a little album called *The Dark Side of the Moon*.

Dark Side of the Moon was recorded by only Alan and the members of Pink Floyd. Imagine the five of them messing around with cash registers and coins to get the sounds for "Money." There's a story of how the clock sounds from "Time" were discovered. Sent off to capture another sample, Alan visited a clock repair shop in St John's Wood and helped record the chiming and ticking later to be heard on "Time."[11] Many of the other sounds were ready and waiting in the famous "Abbey Road effects cupboard," including the airport announcement heard on "On the Run."[12]

Glyn Johns

Producer and sound engineer Glyn Johns has worked on classic albums for such stars as the Rolling Stones, Eric Clapton, The Eagles, The Who, The Beatles, and The Clash.[13] As a recording technician, he has captured some of the most exciting and dramatic performances in music history, including The Who's "My Generation," The Rolling Stones' "Gimme Shelter," and Led Zeppelin's "Dazed and Confused."[14]

As a producer, he's worked his subtle magic on the first three albums by The Eagles, *Who's Next* by The Who, *A Nod Is as Good as a Wink . . . to a Blind Horse* by The Faces, and Slowhand by Eric Clapton, among many others. Of Johns's work, Pete Townshend has said, "We were just getting astounded at the sounds he was producing." He was the go-to guy for bands who wanted to sound like the best versions of themselves. That is quite an important position to assume. You should constantly be on the lookout for the Glyn Johnses among your students.

3b. Listeners' Feedback

Once again, have a performance for the class of new songs. Share the latest of the greatest of the work. Times like these in the flow of your class will build confidence and be a source of celebration. They will also serve as a sounding board for improvement. Remember the volatility of creative work and heed the words of John Kratus on how feedback might best proceed in your class. Lean on the supportive and descriptive at first. You will know when they are ready for prescriptive feedback. Songwriting, recording, and performing is a marathon and not a sprint. Embrace the long-haul approach to it all. Your goal is for them to see in your daily process something that they could continue doing for a lifetime. Never ever lose sight of that.

WATER: Dr. Dre's Musical Magicians

Dr. Dre (Andre Romelle Young) has empowered and helped launch numerous musicians including Eminem, 2Pac, Snoop Dogg, T.I., 50 Cent, and Mary J. Blige.

His Aftermath Entertainment is a development machine for incredibly talented engineers. Here are some of his most trusted:

Lola Romero—KeepItOnTheLo

Lola Romero is best known as KeepItOnTheLo. She is a Grammy Award–winning engineer. Her stage name derived from a play on words using her actual name, which transformed into a way of life. Keeping it on the "Lo" represents a combination of her unique work ethic and humility. From the Bay to L.A., Lola has managed to make an astounding name for herself with only six years in the game. She has worked with Dr. Dre & Snoop Dogg, the infamous Kanye West, Golden Globe winner Andra Day, as well as Grammy Award winners Lalah Hathaway and Anderson .Paak.[15]

Her overall love for music, and her unique style to bring out the beauties and intricacies within it through her mixing abilities, inspired her to become an engineer and keep her steadily going. With an open outlook to discover what each day holds—a mantra that carries her throughout her personal and professional life—Lola's spiritual background and belief in God serve as a foundation for her success and overall life.[16]

Quentin Gilkey

As Aftermath Entertainment's chief engineer, Quentin Gilkey (Dr. Dre, Kendrick Lamar, and Earl Sweatshirt) believes that people perform at their best when they're challenged. For Gilkey, music has been the driving force for everything in his life. He grew up playing classical piano before transitioning over to jazz, and music performance remained his primary focus until his junior year at college. "Every night I performed at concerts or played jazz at local cafes, weddings, and other events. It was all I knew. I never questioned how a record was actually made."[17]

After a while, he and his friends wanted to start making beats and writing rhymes for fun. So he purchased some basic recording equipment, including a small Shure mic, Pro Tools, and a pair of speakers and began a new journey into the recording process. He told me about a school in Phoenix, Arizona, called The Conservatory of Recording Arts. "After extensive research on the program, I knew audio engineering was what I needed to pursue." His journey from an assistant to full-time engineer afforded him the opportunity to work with a number of unique artists in several studios and try out different recording techniques. Fast forward to today and, after being in the right place at the right time, he's currently chief engineer at Dr. Dre's famed Aftermath Entertainment, a division of Universal Music.[18]

Paul Montes

Paul Montes is the director of studio operations for Dr. Dre's Aftermath Entertainment, where he maintains all aspects of the recording studio facilities from top to bottom. Paul has had the opportunity to work with the biggest names in modern hip-hop, including Dr. Dre, Kendrick Lamar, Anderson Paak, Snoop Dogg, Eminem, and many more. Before securing his role at Aftermath Entertainment, he worked as an audio engineer for various A-list movies and TV releases at the post-production studio Mi Casa Multimedia and as a studio supervisor for Interscope/IGA Studios. In addition to managing studio operations, Paul is also a partner/consultant for the brand KeepItOnTheLo, owned by Grammy-winning audio engineer/mixer Lola Romero, and is working on consulting and mentoring for up-and-coming audio engineers looking to further their careers in the entertainment industry under the moniker "Raised by Wolf."[19]

5. Production/Engineering

A good bit of production/engineering has had to have happened before this point, but after performing and getting feedback twice in class, you are ready to kick the production up a notch. Here is where everything that you have been able to glean from online resources like Mastering.com (formerly Musician on a Mission) and others on how to make tracks sound better comes into use. Also, the book *Sound Design for the Emerging Music Teacher Producer* (Randles, Aponte, and Johnson, forthcoming) is an excellent resource to help you in your production/engineering efforts.

You want to think whole/part/whole about the process of making your tracks sound better. The whole while you are listening to the whole song and then soloing individual tracks to see how they dance with the entire song. You will spend a lot of time working on EQ and gain/compression to make sure that everything is being heard. Then, depending on your style and sound aesthetic, you may work to simplify your arrangement. What really needs to be heard? And when? Consider the main points of *The Addiction Formula* (Findeisen, 2015) mentioned in Chapter 1. You want to think about the narrative of the song and the major impact points as you tell the story.

3c. Listeners' Feedback

You got it, you need to have another performance/sharing session with people who have a vested interest in the song(s). You have worked in your Music Teacher as Music Producer classroom to build a sense of community. You have modeled supportive, descriptive, and prescriptive feedback that has at its core a sense of camaraderie and brother/sisterhood—everyone who works on developing their creativities in this classroom will be supported in every way that they desire until their song(s) are successfully completed. It is a way of life that you have nurtured above all else.

6. Performers

Who will perform the song(s)? You need to have established this all along, really. Will it be the songwriter? In most cases it will be. However, be open to its being someone else. There is no good reason that I see for someone besides the songwriter performing and recording the song. The decision should rest ultimately with the songwriter. Perhaps you are recording a cover version of a song written and performed previously by someone in your classroom. How great would that be?! Let the songwriter guide whom you enlist to play for them. They really should call the shots. You are there for support and logistics. In some cases you arrange things for other performers or enlist arrangers from among the broader school music community that you have been working with colleagues (hopefully, you have other music teacher collaborators to work with) in developing.

WATER: The Wrecking Crew

Hal Blaine, Plas Johnson, Carol Kaye, Earl Palmer, Don Randi, and Tommy Tedesco played on hundreds of pop songs and albums, working with everyone from Frank Sinatra to The Beach Boys, Herb Albert to The Byrds, Phil Spector's girl groups to Elvis and The Righteous Brothers. If you've seen *Love and Mercy*, the drama about Brian Wilson, they're the band recording the tracks for "Pet Sounds." And they almost never received credit for their contributions, which meant that only the artists and engineers knew their legacy. At least until a few years ago.[20]

Danny Tedesco (son of the late Tommy Tedesco) started recording interviews with these musicians and others (Glen Campbell and Leon Russell were members of the rotating lineup that broke through to solo success) more than a decade ago. These artists and others, including Cher, Nancy Sinatra, Mickey Dolenz, Herb Alpert, and Dick Clark, sketch out the culture of the recording industry in the 1960s and 1970s, a life that had these musicians working day and night, getting called into a session at all hours of the day and putting down tracks within minutes of learning the parts. They created the West Coast sound, and just as fast as they rose to the top of the profession, most of them slipped into obscurity when the era of the studio musician gave way to rock groups of the 1970s that insisted on playing their own sessions.[21]

Every school could have their own Wrecking Crew of musicians, who might play on numerous tracks and albums within a school music culture. Can you imagine it? I can. I have seen it to some extent, and that is where my imagination takes off. This could be such an exciting development in the history of music education practice. We would model the real world of music-making and be a conduit for thousands of musicians who might continue on to work in the music industry. This is a music education that would capture the imagination of the masses. Please, please, please . . . Can someone make a movie on the life of Carol Kaye, bass player in the Wrecking Crew?! The world deserves to hear her story exclusively.

3d. Listeners' Feedback
This stage of listening should be at the end before you work to get the work out there. Getting student work out into the world could mean getting the ASCAP or BMI royalties set up and releasing the songs via your school record label. It might also be doing the royalty work—I suggest that you always do this to protect your students—and then releasing the songs in one or more formats. Files are easy to pass around and circulate, but you might also want to make a vinyl record or compact disc. Maybe some of you will also want to release a cassette tape! Nearly every format out there that has existed has purists running a campaign to maintain the integrity of the medium.

In Conclusion

The songwriting workgroups idea that I have presented here leverages the power of collaboration and mirrors the reality of the real world of the music business. People rarely work in isolation, doing every step of the process themselves. Of course, some people do and that is pretty amazing. However, most of the time, music that we love to listen to over and over is made in teams. So setting up your classroom in a way that leverages the power of teamwork is a good idea.

How could this idea be grown and extended? Do you have your own ideas that I have not mentioned? I hope that my dreaming in front of you in these pages has given you some places to start in leveraging the unique power that engaging in the process of making tracks and records can have on the musical life of the communities that we find ourselves as teachers serving. All you need is one idea to spark a whole series of change initiatives with the capability of overhauling your music learning and making scene. Start by imagining what might be possible by gaining inspiration from stories of the professional studio world.

Take a field trip to a music studio in your area. Here in Tampa we have Morrisound Studio. Tom and Jim Morris are brothers who have worked in the music industry for a very long time. They have worked with diverse artists from Warrant and the Tran Siberian Orchestra to Destiny's Child. They are incredibly knowledgeable about everything gear and creative process where recording studios are concerned. People like them are all around us. The Morris brothers set up shop in a 1920s-era bank, where they record musicians. Start looking around for people like them where you are.

Resources Worth Exploring

Source	Expertise	URL
Berklee Online's Free Songwriting Handbook	You can download a PDF of tips for songwriting by *Berklee Online*'s staff	https://cloud.info.berklee.edu/bol-songwriting
Master Writer Software	Here is a software application created to help you organize your songwriting process	https://masterwriter.com/songwriters/
Songwriters Resource Network	This is a comprehensive list of songwriters resources	https://songwritersresourcenetwork.com/resource-links.php
Taxi.com	Helps independent songwriters, artists, and composers get their music to record labels, film & TV music supervisors, music libraries, music publishers, music licensing companies, ad agencies, and video game companies	https://www.taxi.com/songwriter/
Songs Alive	A grassroots, philanthropic, volunteer-managed charity organization run by songwriters for songwriters and is dedicated to nurturing, support, education, and promotion of songwriters	https://www.songsalive.org/
ASCAP/BMI	You will need to join ASCAP or BMI to get your music copyrighted	https://www.ascap.com/

SEEDS FOR SONGWRITING LESSONS

11

Beginner Songwriting Seeds

Object Writing as a Place to Start: "Right Now"

WATER: Red Hot Mojo Rising

The album *Blood Sugar Sex Magik* was recorded by the Red Hot Chili Peppers (RHCP) at a four-bedroom house owned by producer Rick Rubin in Los Angeles over a period of seven weeks in 1991. The album was RHCP's first with Rubin. It birthed four major hits: "Give It Away," "Under the Bridge," "Breaking the Girl," and "Suck My Kiss." It also reached number 3 on the Billboard 200; it would go on to sell over 13 million copies worldwide, 7 million of them in the United States. It is an example of a very effective, very innovative creative process. Here are some facts about the album taken from a *Rolling Stone* magazine article:[1]

1. The band was initially reluctant to work with Rick Rubin.
2. *Blood Sugar Sex Magik* was the first album ever recorded at the Mansion, Rick Rubin's massive Laurel Canyon estate.
3. One RHCP member was turned off by the Mansion's haunted reputation, while another was totally turned on.
4. Kim Gordon inspired Flea to simplify his bass playing.
5. All of John Frusciante's guitar solos are first or second takes.
6. "Give It Away" may be the only song in history inspired by both River Phoenix and Nina Hagen.
7. Anthony Kiedis wrote the words for "Under the Bridge" as a poem, never intending to use them in a RHCP song.
8. Kiedis wrote "I Could Have Lied" about his short-lived relationship with Sinéad O'Connor.
9. *Blood Sugar Sex Magik* was originally supposed to be a double-CD set.
10. The band only played "Breaking the Girl" once on the entire *Blood Sugar Sex Magik* tour (see Figure 11.1).

The album is a funk-rock masterpiece that proved to be one of the most memorable of all time for RHCP. Rubin struck gold with the band, in his home studio, in a period of only seven weeks. The same sort of thing can happen in as much time in a school classroom.

Growing Songwriting. Clint Randles, Oxford University Press. © Oxford University Press 2024.
DOI: 10.1093/oso/9780197693216.003.0011

Figure 11.1 Red Hot Chili Peppers live in 2022

SUNLIGHT: The Power of Collaboration

The magic of playing in a band is discovering what possibilities can emerge from creative synthesis. Ashley (2022) writes about the power of collaboration in the songwriting process. Here are some of his main points:

1. **Listen to the truth**. Listen to what other people tell you about the musical aspects of your songs.
2. **Check your ego at the door**. The person most likely to come between you improving as a songwriter is you.
3. **Different minds bring fresh perspectives**. When you bring collaborators into your songwriting process, you bring the wealth of life experience that each other person brings.
4. **Variation opens up new melodic and harmonic possibilities**. When you collaborate with people who are into different music, who write in different keys, and specialize on different instruments, you open up the door to new possibilities.
5. **Two heads are really better than one**. This saying is not at all superficial. The more ideas on the table, the more of a chance that you have to come up with work that is really good.

When students in your room combine their creative efforts in small groups, chemical reactions of sorts occur where the results are greater than the sum of the individual parts. It really is like magic in a way. One of the primary strengths of a Music Teacher as Music Producer classroom is the focus on small group creativities, where collaboration is central to daily music-making.

Materials

- A room full of accompaniment instruments including but not limited to guitar, keyboard, bass guitar, drum kit, drum sequencer, ukulele, and so forth. You can use a digital audio workstation (DAW) with various keyboard and pad controllers as instruments as well. You can also use homemade instruments and/or body percussion.
- A playlist full of songs of diverse style and orchestration.
- Examples of prior object writing exercises.

Context

This is a beginning songwriting lesson that in my experience has always led to good results with classes of students. It centers on their ability to generate ideas around a topic. You use the tip that I gave in Chapter 1 on object writing. Go back and review what I wrote there. Here is a summary:

Object Writing. One of the best tools that I know of to help jump-start the creative process around songwriting is to engage your students in object writing sessions where they free write around a topic, an idea, a sentiment, a person, a place, a thing, an action, and so forth for a timed duration. I set the timer for five minutes when I object write with students, and ten minutes when I do it myself in practice. Five minutes is generally enough time for them to come up with interesting talking points, but not too long that they start to find more interesting things to do with the time.

Lesson Time

This lesson can take place in one 45-minute class. However, you will most likely have to extend it over multiple classes depending on what you would like to do with the song—special recording or performance. You will start with the object writing session (see Box 11.1). Set a timer and ask them to think of as many different things about a particular topic as they can in five minutes. Have them write them down, type them into their phones, write them in their journals. I like the journal option

Box 11.1 A sample object writing session

"I Need a Break"

Paul

Chorus maybe
I'm gonna break . . . myself out
I'm gonna run away . . . to my momma's house

Stuck inside tryin to break away . . . from my house, from my room, from my bored

"Drivin Around on a nature trip" "Im getting a break of inspiration"

I need a vacation
From society
I need a vacation
for my sanity

Sam

Getting a break of inspiration. Finding ways to recharge. Making things fresh

Break from routine

Daniel

Talk about things we need a break from. Homework projects, work at any other jobs we have.
A break from everything happening in the world today maybe also

David

Im tired and I'm bored, and I don't know what's in store.
But I know at my core there is no mistake, I need a break

Lydia

Breaking the law just to feel something

Evan

I need a break
my muscles ache
feeling fine
but I'm a fake
pile leaves
I need a rake

Carson
You know when you need. A break when you break a chair because you need a break

Asher
From expectations

Nina
Maybe tomorrow
the idea of wanting to push things/ procrastinate

Maerosa
Escaping the pressures
of my day to day

the best. This lesson will play out into your writing a song together. Exercises like this will inspire them because they will be able to see a creative process from beginning to end. I had each of my students object write around the topic "I Need a Break." It was the day before spring break on this particular day. After giving them time to brainstorm individually, I asked if anyone would be willing to share what they wrote. Below is what they gave me.

Lesson Instructions

Preparation (10 minutes)

Gather the class and give them a short lesson on object writing. Share with them the results of prior object writing sessions. If you don't have other examples (i.e., this is the first time that you have ever tried this) use the example "I Need a Break" that I have provided here. Talk about how everyone comes up with ideas that you can share as you come up with ideas for a song together. Demonstrate how the results of object writing sessions are used to produce lyrics later. Talk about how you are not looking for rhyming lyrics at this point, only ideas that you will later use to come up with other ideas. Share some songs that were written using this strategy.

Object Writing (5 minutes or longer)

This is the part of the lesson where you give them time to write. Make sure that this time is quiet and focused.

Pull Together Ideas (10 minutes or most likely much more)

This is where you will need to tap into your skills of inspiration, imagination, and creativity. All the time that you spend making music yourself will help you do this part well. You field their ideas and copy them into one central location that you will later draw from to come up with lyrics that pull everything together.

Box 11.2 Lyrics for "Right Now," what started as "I Need a Break"

"Right Now"

Verse 1
I need a break so bad
my muscles ache
Feeling oh so fine
but a rest? I won't hesitate
Piling on, so many leaves
I need a rake
Make no mistake

I need a vaca
From society
I need a vaca
for my sanity
From all my projects in a row
From Zoom and all the things I know

Pre-Chorus
Taking some time for inspiration.
Finding out ways to recharge.

Chorus
I'm gonna break myself out
Gonna run away to somewhere else
I'm Gonna hitch a train to destinations unknown
This I know . . . I've got to get away right now

Verse 2
5 minutes of work
5 hours of play
Escaping pressures
of my day to day
Perhaps tomorrow
Maybe today
I've got all week
So I'll take in the Rays

Figuring it out
Is oh so good
As I sit right here

in the middle of my neighborhood
Doing some writing
Reading some books
But only when I want to

Pre-Chorus

Chorus

Outro
(Instrumental)

Write Lyrics to a Verse and/or Chorus (Another class period)
When coming up with lyrics, I like to have some sort of musical idea or musical fragment to build around. I like to start with a beat (or sometimes a bass line) that encapsulates the feel of the song. Another way I have done this lesson is to start with a chord progression on the guitar or piano. In the performance of the progression is the feel of the verse or chorus that helps provide the backdrop for how the lyrics should sound. So it matters how you perform it. You can have a student who has a progression perform it at this point. Ultimately, you just want to demonstrate a creative process that started with object writing and led to the writing of a song.

Record (Another class period or multiple class periods)
I suggest that you record the song along the way, as you write it. As soon as you know the overall structure, establish a tempo and lay out the various sections in a DAW. Rather than thinking of production elements later—as an afterthought—include them up front as ideas come. You can think of what Findeisen (2015) has to say in *The Addiction Formula* from the beginning. You are wielding energy en route to telling the most impactful story as you come up with your song. Recording can and should come before performance in most cases.

Perform (Another class period or multiple class periods)
It is time to perform the song. This might come in increments before the song exists in a recorded form. Depending on how long it has been since you did the object writing, it might be a good idea for you to show them the initial object writing session so that they can remember where you started. From beginning to end, especially for this first object writing seed, try to have the entire shell of the song written in two class sessions or less. I have written an entire song in one day with classes. This can be very inspirational for them, especially if the song has catchy or memorable elements.

Modifications for Learners

Let Them Work in Pairs

Some of the best object writing sessions of all time happened with John Lennon and Paul McCartney trying to outwit one another and pushing the overall quality of their combined work to new heights.

Object Write in Private

Some students will have severe apprehension for sharing their object writing brainstorming with their classmates. Allow them to take their work home and share it with only you. Try to encourage them to open up. Remember, though, that a lifetime of songwriting is a marathon and not a sprint. Growth is what you are about. You can see growth in private as much as you can in public.

Have Them Write for Others in the Class

It is entirely possible and probable that you will have students who have a knack for songwriting but who are not at all about performing. Perhaps you can let them be great at what they are great at and encourage performance, but not hang their success or failure on it. Think of the Swedish music culture, or Motown, where people specialize in particular aspects of the music-making enterprise.

Learning Outcomes

- Complete an object writing session.
- Translate object writing lesson work into lyrics of a song (verse, chorus, and/or bridge).
- Work out a creative arrangement, either solo or within a group setting.
- Identify and internalize the conventions of song structure.
- Perform and record your original song for yourself and/or peers.

Assessment Considerations

Informal Assessment. How did they respond to the lesson? Were there any gains that are difficult to categorize in a rubric? Sometimes lessons don't look like a success on paper, but when you gauge the interest and enthusiasm in the room, accomplishment and student achievement can clearly be seen. The success of an object writing lesson as a starting point for songwriting is seeing the value of generating ideas around a topic that does not initially have to be tied to lyrics.

There are times when I have taught a lesson that didn't work very well with a class as a whole, but one student made such massive gains that inspired the rest of the class to up their game in some way. Be careful with how you wield the assessment hammer. Your primary goal is that when your students leave your care, they continue writing, recording, and performing their songs. Your assessments should be formative and fair enough that they want to continue practicing their craft. These are tricky waters to navigate. Be careful.

Formal Assessment. Here is a rubric that you might adapt and use as a way of helping your students develop their songwriting craft:

Criteria	Ratings					Pts
This criterion is linked to a Learning Outcome Lyric Writing	**4 to >3.0 pts Expert** I love that your lyricism is approaching professional quality	**3 to >2.0 pts Practitioner** I like that you demonstrated very good lyric writing technique (including many strategies discussed in class)	**2 to >1.0 pts Apprentice** I'm concerned that your lyric writing isn't very good	**1 to >0.0 pts Novice** What's up? Your lyric writing is really difficult to follow	**0 pts No Marks**	4 pts
This criterion is linked to a Learning Outcome Musical Interest	**4 to >3.0 pts Expert** I love that you displayed almost professional levels of musical interest	**3 to >2.0 pts Practitioner** I like the level of musical interest that you conveyed in your song—it's very good	**2 to >1.0 pts Apprentice** I'm concerned with how many errors showed up in your song	**1 to >0.0 pts Novice** What's up? Your song seems lacking in musical interest quality	**0 pts No Marks**	4 pts
This criterion is linked to a Learning Outcome Creativity	**4 to >3.0 pts Expert** I love that the creativity you displayed could end up on a recording	**3 to >2.0 pts Practitioner** I like that you displayed a very good sense of creativity	**2 to >1.0 pts Apprentice** I'm concerned that your performance did not display very much creativity	**1 to >0.0 pts Novice** What's up? There was really no sense of creativity in your music	**0 pts No Marks**	4 pts
Total Points: 12						

While I have focused this rubric on lyric writing, musical interest, and creativity, you might focus this lesson on any number of musical qualities and characteristics. Everything is on the table for you as an artist teacher to utilize. If you are a teacher in North America and you want these rubric focal points to be specific National Content Standard areas, you can make that happen. The same thing is true if you are working within the Australian Curriculum and you want to align these assessments with your national assessment areas.

Further Reading/Resources

- Jeff Tweedy, *How to Write One Song* (New York: Dutton, 2020).
- *Rolling Stone* magazine article/video on how Jeff Tweedy writes a song: https://www.rollingstone.com/music/music-features/jeff-tweedy-songwriting-book-excerpt-1070889/.
- Broken Records Masterclass with Jeff Tweedy on songwriting: https://www.youtube.com/watch?v=s0f45VBPTFs.
- Wilco, Live on KEXP: https://www.youtube.com/watch?v=Z8U4zw84gyE.

Start with Word Ladders: Nouns and Verbs

WATER: "It's Tricky"

"It's Tricky" is the fourth single released from Run-DMC's third album, *Raising Hell* (1986). We find the trio from Hollis, Queens, New York, at its best on this album, particularly with this song. In 1998, American producer Jason Nevins remixed the song under the amended title "(It's) Tricky," and that version was very successful. They masterfully weave together wit and style. Check out the lyrics for nouns and verbs:

> In New York the people talk and try to make us rhyme
> They really (hawk) but we just (walk) because we have no time
> And in the city it's a pity cos we just can't hide
> Tinted windows don't mean nothin', they know who's inside
> When I wake up people take up mostly all of my time
> I'm not singin', phone keep ringin' cos I make up a rhyme
> I'm not braggin', people naggin' cos they think I'm a star
> Always tearin' what I'm wearin', I think they're goin' too far
> A girl named Carol follows Daryll every gig we play
> Then D dissed her and dismissed her, now she's jockin' Jay
> I ain't lyin', girls be cryin' cos I'm on TV
> They even bother my poor father cos he's down with me

Study how Run-DMC crafts their lyrics. The story of what the song says is always the most important aspect. You can see that when you look at all of the lyrics in their entirety. They talk about rocking and rhyming in the chorus—how difficult (tricky) it is to do that. Of course, you won't worry about that at first when you have them do this nouns and verbs exercise to get things started.

SUNLIGHT: Beatles Tips for Mixing Things Up

You know by now that I am a Beatles nerd of the highest order. Here are some tips on how they changed up songs to add interest:[2]

1. Change up your chorus. Try putting the chorus first, not after an instrumental introduction and first verse the way we typically do.
2. Add blues to your melody. Try experimenting with blue notes in your melodies.
3. Delay the root chord. You don't have to start on the topic chord. Try starting on something else to delay the sound of tonic.
4. Utilize the outside chord and use non-diatonic chords and secondary dominants. Out of 188 Beatles songs, only 22 remained solidly in one key. Add interest by using chords outside of the key.
5. Restate your lyrics. Reuse some of your memorable lyrics to bridge the various sections of your song. The Beatles did it in the verses of "A Day in the Life":

    I read the news today, oh boy
    And though the news was rather sad/holes were rather small
    Found my way downstairs/coat/way upstairs
    I just had to laugh/look

6. Take risks. Try some harmonic progressions that don't make analytical sense. Put together chords that sound good together but don't necessarily make sense from a numbering system perspective. Put some chords on pieces of paper and put them in a hat. Pull them out one at a time and record the order. Build a song based on that order.
7. Change of keys from minor to major. If you start in minor, do the chorus in major. Try using parallel majors and minor instead of relative majors and minors. The result is pretty striking.

There is so much in the creative processes of The Beatles that we can learn from. A book that I have loved over the years is *Revolution in the Head* (2005) by Ian MacDonald. It provides a background story for all (188) of The Beatles songs. This band provides an endless source of inspiration.

Materials

- A room full of accompaniment instruments including but not limited to: guitar, keyboard, bass guitar, drum kit, drum sequencer, ukulele, and so forth. You can use a digital audio workstation (DAW) with various keyboard and pad controllers as instruments as well. You can also use homemade instruments and/or body percussion.

Guide	Cup
Mentor	Car
Instruct	Computer
Assist	Phone
Listen	Glasses
Hear	Book
Interpret	Bag
Feel	Bush
Care	Cupcake
Hope	Cactus

Nouns and Verbs Ladder

Figure 11.2 Sample nouns and verbs list

- A playlist full of songs that contain unique pairings of nouns and verbs.
- Examples of prior nouns and verbs starting points.
- Some way of displaying your nouns and verbs ladders (digital or otherwise).
- Songwriting journals for every student.

Context

This is a beginning songwriting lesson that I have borrowed from Jeff Tweedy. It is a smart way of what he calls "loosening up the habitual way we use language." It functions a lot like object writing in that when you complete the exercise, it gives you places to grab lyrical ideas for your songs. By keeping a journal with the results of all of your word ladder exercises (as well as other exercises that I will share with you in this book), you will be able to generate lyrical ideas when you have musical ideas that need lyrics.

Word Ladders: Nouns and Verbs. Make a list of ten verbs that are associated with a teacher. Then make another list of ten words that are in your field of vision. Then, take a pencil and connect the words in both of the columns that you think work nicely together. Follow up this exercise by writing a poem that makes use of these connections.

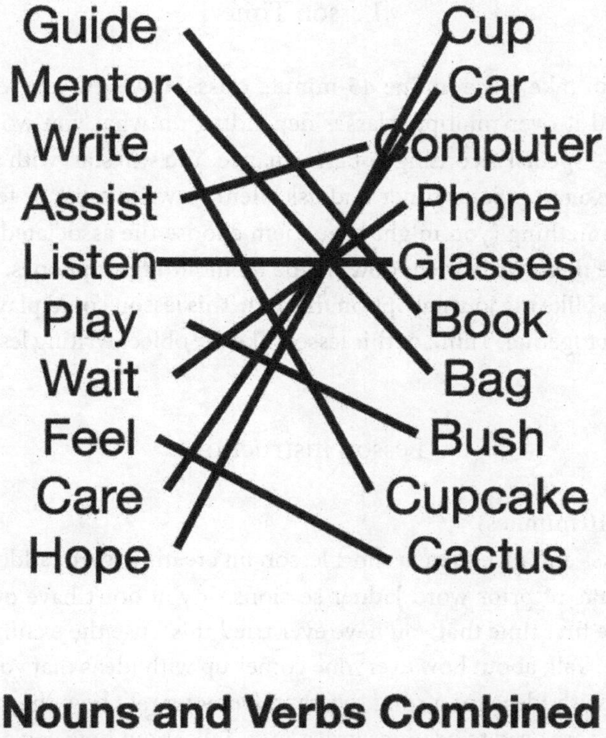

Figure 11.3 Nouns and verbs combined list

The cactus feels today
I drink a cup of hope
While my phone waits
Computer assisted
My glasses they listen
But does your car care?
Sounds of Bush blaring
Write a cupcake on my chest
When this guide book's written
In your bag's a mentor

Sample Poem

Figure 11.4 Sample poem from nouns and verbs combination

Lesson Time

This lesson can take place in one 45-minute class. However, you will most likely have to extend it over multiple classes depending on what you would like to do with the song—special recording or performance. You will start with the nouns and verbs ladder exercise. Set a timer and ask them to write a list of ten verbs associated with something (you might have them choose the associated thing) in five minutes. Have them write them down, type them into their phones, write them in their journals. I like the journal option the best. This lesson could play out into your writing a song together. Think of this lesson like the object writing lesson.

Lesson Instructions

Preparation (10 minutes)

Gather the class and give them a short lesson on creating word ladders. Share with them the results of prior word ladder sessions. If you don't have other examples (i.e., this is the first time that you have ever tried this), use the example that I have provided here. Talk about how everyone comes up with ideas that you can share as you come up with ideas for a song together. Demonstrate how the results of word ladder sessions are used to produce lyrics later. Talk about how you are not looking for rhyming lyrics at this point, only ideas that you will later use to come up with other ideas. Share some songs that were written using this strategy. I have provided you with the song "Right Now" just in case this is the first time that you are trying out this strategy.

Word Ladders (5 minutes or longer)

This is the part of the lesson where you give them time to write. Make sure that this time is quiet and focused.

Pull Together Ideas (10 minutes or most likely much more)

This is where you will need to tap into your skills of inspiration, imagination, and creativity. All the time that you spend making music yourself will help you do this part well. You field their ideas and copy them into one central location that you will later draw from to come up with lyrics that pull everything together.

Write Lyrics to a Verse and/or Chorus (Another class period)

When coming up with lyrics, I like to have some sort of musical idea or musical fragment to build around. I like to start with a beat (or sometimes a bass line) that encapsulates the feel of the song. Another way I have done this lesson is to start with a chord progression on the guitar or piano. In the performance of the progression is the feel of the verse or chorus that helps provide the backdrop for how the lyrics should sound. So it matters how you perform it. You can have a student who has a progression perform it at this point. Ultimately, you just want to demonstrate a creative process that started with word ladders and led to the writing of a song.

Record (Another class period or multiple class periods)
I suggest that you record the song along the way, as you write it. As soon as you know the overall structure, establish a tempo and lay out the various sections in a DAW. Rather than thinking of production elements later—as an afterthought—include them up front as ideas come. You can think of what Findeisen (2015) has to say in *The Addiction Formula* from the beginning. You are wielding energy en route to telling the most impactful story as you come up with your song. Recording can and should come before performance in most cases.

Perform (Another class period or multiple class periods)
It is time to perform the song. This might come in increments before the song exists in a recorded form. Depending on how long it has been since you did the word ladders, it might be a good idea for you to show them the initial word ladders session so that they can remember where you started. From beginning to end, especially for this first word ladders seed, try to have the entire shell of the song written in two class sessions or less. I have written an entire song in one day with classes. This can be very inspirational for them, especially if the song has catchy or memorable elements.

Modifications for Learners

Let Them Work in Pairs

Some of the best word ladders sessions of all time happened with John Lennon and Paul McCartney trying to outwit one another and pushing the overall quality of their combined work to new heights.

Word Ladders in Private

Some students will have severe apprehension for sharing their word ladder brainstorming with their classmates. Allow them to take their work home and share it with only you. Try to encourage them to open up. Remember, though, that a lifetime of songwriting is a marathon and not a sprint. Growth is what you are about. You can see growth in private as much as you can in public.

Have Them Write for Others in the Class

It is entirely possible and probable that you will have students who have a knack for songwriting but who are not at all about performing. Perhaps you can let them be great at what they are great at and encourage performance, but not hang their success or failure on it. Think of the Swedish music culture, or Motown, where people specialize in particular aspects of the music-making enterprise.

Learning Outcomes

- Complete a word ladder writing session.
- Translate word ladder lesson work into lyrics of a song (verse, chorus, and/or bridge).
- Work out a creative arrangement, either solo or within a group setting.
- Identify and internalize the conventions of song structure.
- Perform and record your original song for yourself and/or peers.

Assessment Considerations

Informal Assessment. How did they respond to the lesson? Were there any gains that are difficult to categorize in a rubric? Sometimes lessons don't look like a success on paper, but when you gauge the interest and enthusiasm in the room, accomplishment and student achievement can clearly be seen. The success of a word ladder lesson as a starting point for songwriting is seeing the value of generating ideas around a topic that does not initially have to be tied to lyrics.

There are times when I have taught a lesson that didn't work very well with a class as a whole, but one student made such massive gains that inspired the rest of the class to up their game in some way. Be careful with how you wield the assessment hammer. Your primary goal is that when your students leave your care, they continue writing, recording, and performing their songs. Your assessments should be formative and fair enough that they want to continue practicing their craft. These are tricky waters to navigate. Be careful.

Formal Assessment. Here is a rubric that you might adapt and use as a way of helping your students develop their songwriting craft:

Criteria	Ratings					Pts
This criterion is linked to a Learning Outcome Lyric Writing	**4 to >3.0 pts Expert** I love that your lyricism is approaching professional quality	**3 to >2.0 pts Practitioner** I like that you demonstrated very good lyric writing technique (including many strategies discussed in class)	**2 to >1.0 pts Apprentice** I'm concerned that your lyric writing isn't very good	**1 to >0.0 pts Novice** What's up? Your lyric writing is really difficult to follow	**0 pts No Marks**	4 pts
This criterion is linked to a Learning Outcome Musical Interest	**4 to >3.0 pts Expert** I love that you displayed almost professional levels of musical interest	**3 to >2.0 pts Practitioner** I like the level of musical interest that you conveyed in your song—it's very good	**2 to >1.0 pts Apprentice** I'm concerned with how many errors showed up in your song	**1 to >0.0 pts Novice** What's up? Your song seems lacking in musical interest quality	**0 pts No Marks**	4 pts

Criteria	Ratings					Pts
This criterion is linked to a Learning Outcome Creativity	**4 to >3.0 pts Expert** I love that the creativity you displayed could end up on a recording	**3 to >2.0 pts Practitioner** I like that you displayed a very good sense of creativity	**2 to >1.0 pts Apprentice** I'm concerned that your performance did not display very much creativity	**1 to >0.0 pts Novice** What's up? There was really no sense of creativity in your music	**0 pts No Marks**	4 pts
Total Points: 12						

While I have focused this rubric on lyric writing, musical interest, and creativity, you might focus this lesson on any number of musical qualities and characteristics. Everything is on the table for you as an artist teacher to utilize. If you are a teacher in North America and you want these rubric focal points to be specific National Content Standard areas, you can make that happen. The same thing is true if you are working within the Australian Curriculum and you want to align these assessments with your national assessments areas.

Further Reading/Resources

- Using word ladders to help write songs: https://www.youtube.com/watch?v=tWS99kAxa04.
- Tips for using word ladders: https://howtowritesongs.org/tag/word-ladders/.
- On the utility of nouns and verbs: https://austinkleon.com/2020/12/09/nouns-and-verbs/.
- A game from Lewis Carroll: https://www.dltk-kids.com/crafts/music/word-ladder.htm.
- Check out Jeff Tweedy, *How to Write One Song* (New York: Dutton, 2020).

Start with a Riff

WATER: "Walk This Way"

Aerosmith's iconic riff for "Walk This Way" is one of the most recognizable of all time. According to singer Steven Tyler, the tune's funky groove grew out of some pre-show goofing around among himself, drummer Joey Kramer, and guitarist Joe Perry. "The song started at a sound check at HRC in Honolulu," Tyler told NME.[3] "It was a real rhythmical thing. Our drummer Joey Kramer played with a funk band and was always pushing James Brown. He brought funk to the table. And Joe picked up on it and brought that 'Walk This Way' lick." "The groove kind of lent itself to rap," he added. "It kind of pissed me off at first that they weren't following the lyrics, but they were following the rhythm. But I would scat, and then write the lyrics in after. I wrote them on the hallway wall." Guitarist Joe Perry, in an interview with the *Wall Street Journal*,[4] said Aerosmith "were heavily into funk and soul. Jeff Beck had turned me on to the Meters, and I loved their riffy New Orleans funk, especially 'Cissy Strut' and 'People Say.' "

Your students will have similar kinds of "aha" moments when they are allowed time to mess around with creating riffs. Some will have immediate smashing success, while others will have to be coached a bit more. Musically, riffs seem to fall out of particular voicings and fingerings on the instruments that we use to accompany our voices—guitar and keys primarily. The same is true of the riff from "Walk This Way."

SUNLIGHT: Most Memorable Riffs of All Time

Here is a list of some of the most memorable guitar riffs of all time:[5]

1. Nirvana: "Smells Like Teen Spirit" (1991)
2. Chuck Berry: "Johnny B Goode" (1958)
3. The Rolling Stones: "(I Can't Get No) Satisfaction)" (1965)
4. Deep Purple: "Smoke on the Water" (1972)
5. Guns N' Roses: "Sweet Child o' Mine" (1988)
6. Link Wray: "Rumble" (1958)
7. Led Zeppelin: "Whole Lotta Love" (1969)
8. The Jimi Hendrix Experience: "Purple Haze" (1967)
9. ZZ Top: "La Grange" (1973)
10. The Kinks: "You Really Got Me" (1964)

Here is a list of the most memorable non-guitar-based hooks from popular music over the past decade:

1. Robyn: "Dancing on My Own" (1982)
2. Rihanna: "We Found Love" (2011)
3. Carly Rae Jepsen: "Call Me Maybe" (2012)
4. Beyoncé: "Love on Top" (2011)
5. Lorde: "Royals" (2013)
6. Taylor Swift: "We Are Never Getting Back Together" (2012)
7. Katy Perry: "Last Friday Night (T.G.I.F.)" (2011)
8. Icona Pop feat. Charli XCX: "I Don't Care" (2012)
9. Luis Fonsi feat. Daddy Yankee: "Despacito" (2017)
10. Carly Rae Jepsen: "Cut to the Feeling" (2016)

These lists can be helpful when thinking about giving our students examples of what riffs or hooks could sound like. Start building your own playlists of memorable riffs and hooks and see what those lists can do for you as you help students create their own.

Materials

- A room full of accompaniment instruments including but not limited to: guitar, keyboard, bass guitar, drum kit, drum sequencer, ukulele, and so forth. You can use a digital audio workstation (DAW) with various keyboard and pad controllers as instruments as well. You can also use homemade instruments and/or body percussion.
- A playlist full of songs that contain some of the most memorable riffs.
- Examples of prior songs written in your class by using riffs.
- Some way of displaying your riffs (digital or otherwise).
- Songwriting journals for every student.

Context

This is a beginning songwriting lesson that leverages our propensity to respond to catchy riffs. In this seed we start with musical aspects that we will later add lyrics to. Remember, something must come first, whether it is music or lyrics. From that beginning, you work up the rest of the song. Riffs come most of the time from our instruments and tend to be easily played by notes that are under our fingers when we play simple chords. The best riffs of all time tend to be pretty easy to play, which adds to their desirability—someone with very little musical skill or experience can pick up an instrument and learn how to play them.

Jamming. You need to give your students time to mess around in a band instrumental context. Remember that "Walk This Way" started out with a musical groove from the drummer (Figure 11.5) that spawned a riff on the guitar (Figure 11.6). The song was born when the musical creativities of a small group of musicians was given time to play off one another. Provide time for this to happen in your class. Follow up this time with opportunities to take some of the lyric writing session ideas (noun/

Figure 11.5 "Walk This Way" drum riff

Figure 11.6 "Walk This Way" guitar riff

verb ladders, object writing, etc.) to the next level. This lesson starts with musical ideas with the knowledge that later on you will bring in lyrics.

Lesson Time

This lesson can take place in one 45-minute class. However, you will most likely have to extend it over multiple classes depending on what you would like to do with the song—special recording or performance. You will start with the jamming to discover a memorable riff to structure a song around. Set a timer and ask them to jam for five minutes to search for a memorable riff (you probably will need longer, but start with five minutes just to see how they respond). Have them perform their riffs for each other. Take one of the riff ideas and do a mock-up songwriting session on that riff to show how you can build an entire song upon a musical riff idea.

Lesson Instructions

Preparation (10 minutes)

Gather the class and give them a short lesson on creating word ladders. Share with them the results of prior riffs sessions. If you don't have other examples (i.e., this is the first time that you have ever tried this), use the example that I have provided here. Talk about how everyone comes up with ideas that you can share as you come up with ideas for a song together. Demonstrate how the results of riffs sessions are used to produce lyrics later. Talk about how you are not looking for rhyming lyrics at this point, only ideas that you will later use to come up with other ideas. Share some songs that were written using this strategy. I have provided you with the song "Walk This Way" just in case this is the first time that you are trying out this strategy.

Riffs (5 minutes or longer)

This is the part of the lesson where you give them time to write. Make sure that this time is quiet and focused.

Pull Together Ideas (10 minutes or most likely much more)

This is where you will need to tap into your skills of inspiration, imagination, and creativity. All the time that you spend making music yourself will help you do this part well. You field their ideas and copy them into one central location that you will later draw from to come up with lyrics that pull everything together.

Write Lyrics to a Verse and/or Chorus (Another Class Period)
When coming up with lyrics, I like to have some sort of musical idea or musical fragment to build around. I like to start with a beat (or sometimes a bass line) that encapsulates the feel of the song. Another way that I have done this lesson is to start with a chord progression on the guitar or piano. In the performance of the progression is the feel of the verse or chorus that helps provide the backdrop for how the lyrics should sound. So it matters how you perform it. You can have a student who has a progression perform it at this point. Ultimately, you just want to demonstrate a creative process that started with riffs and led to the writing of a song.

Record (Another class period or multiple class periods)
I suggest that you record the song along the way, as you write it. As soon as you know the overall structure, establish a tempo and lay out the various sections in a DAW. Rather than thinking of production elements later—as an afterthought—include them up front as ideas come. You can think of what Findeisen (2015) has to say in *The Addiction Formula* from the beginning. You are wielding energy en route to telling the most impactful story as you come up with your song. Recording can and should come before performance in most cases.

Perform (Another class period or multiple class periods)
It is time to perform the song. This might come in increments before the song exists in a recorded form. Depending on how long it has been since you did the riffs, it might be a good idea for you to show them the initial riffs so that they can remember where you started. From beginning to end, especially for this first riffs seed, try to have the entire shell of the song written in two class sessions or less. I have written an entire song in one day with classes. This can be very inspirational for them, especially if the song has catchy or memorable elements.

Modifications for Learners

Let Them Work in Pairs
Some of the best riffs sessions of all time happened with John Lennon and Paul McCartney trying to outwit one another and pushing the overall quality of their combined work to new heights.

Word Ladders in Private
Some students will have severe apprehension for sharing their riffs brainstorming with their classmates. Allow them to take their work home and share it with only you. Try to encourage them to open up. Remember, though, that a lifetime of songwriting is a marathon and not a sprint. Growth is what you are about. You can see growth in private as much as you can in public.

Have Them Write for Others in the Class

It is entirely possible and probable that you will have students who have a knack for songwriting but who are not at all about performing. Perhaps you can let them be great at what they are great at and encourage performance, but not hang their success or failure on it. Think of the Swedish music culture, or Motown, where people specialize in particular aspects of the music-making enterprise.

Learning Outcomes

- Complete a riffs writing session.
- Translate riffs lesson work into lyrics of a song (verse, chorus, and/or bridge).
- Work out a creative arrangement, either solo or within a group setting.
- Identify and internalize the conventions of song structure.
- Perform and record your original song for yourself and/or peers.

Assessment Considerations

Informal Assessment. How did they respond to the lesson? Were there any gains that are difficult to categorize in a rubric? Sometimes lessons don't look like a success on paper, but when you gauge the interest and enthusiasm in the room, accomplishment and student achievement can clearly be seen. The success of a riffs lesson as a starting point for songwriting is seeing the value of generating ideas around a topic that does not initially have to be tied to lyrics.

There are times when I have taught a lesson that didn't work very well with a class as a whole, but one student made such massive gains that inspired the rest of the class to up their game in some way. Be careful with how you wield the assessment hammer. Your primary goal is that when your students leave your care, they continue writing, recording, and performing their songs. Your assessments should be formative and fair enough that they want to continue practicing their craft. These are tricky waters to navigate. Be careful.

Formal Assessment. Here is a rubric that you might adapt and use as a way of helping your students develop their songwriting craft:

Criteria	Ratings					Pts
This criterion is linked to a Learning Outcome Lyric Writing	**4 to >3.0 pts** **Expert** I love that your lyricism is approaching professional quality	**3 to >2.0 pts** **Practitioner** I like that you demonstrated very good lyric writing technique (including many strategies discussed in class)	**2 to >1.0 pts** **Apprentice** I'm concerned that your lyric writing isn't very good	**1 to >0.0 pts** **Novice** What's up? Your lyric writing is really difficult to follow	**0 pts** **No Marks**	4 pts

Criteria	Ratings					Pts
This criterion is linked to a Learning Outcome Musical Interest	**4 to >3.0 pts Expert** I love that you displayed almost professional levels of musical interest	**3 to >2.0 pts Practitioner** I like the level of musical interest that you conveyed in your song—it's very good	**2 to >1.0 pts Apprentice** I'm concerned with how many errors showed up in your song	**1 to >0.0 pts Novice** What's up? Your song seems lacking in musical interest quality	**0 pts No Marks**	4 pts
This criterion is linked to a Learning Outcome Creativity	**4 to >3.0 pts Expert** I love that the creativity you displayed could end up on a recording	**3 to >2.0 pts Practitioner** I like that you displayed a very good sense of creativity	**2 to >1.0 pts Apprentice** I'm concerned that your performance did not display very much creativity	**1 to >0.0 pts Novice** What's up? There was really no sense of creativity in your music	**0 pts No Marks**	4 pts
Total Points: 12						

While I have focused this rubric on lyric writing, musical interest, and creativity, you might focus this lesson on any number of musical qualities and characteristics. Everything is on the table for you as an artist teacher to utilize. If you are a teacher in North America and you want these rubric focal points to be specific National Content Standard areas, you can make that happen. The same thing is true if you are working within the Australian Curriculum and you want to align these assessments with your national assessments areas.

Further Reading/Resources

- Using word riffs to help write songs: https://www.youtube.com/watch?v=Y5u66I-92fk
- Tips for using riffs: https://www.youtube.com/watch?v=v0aGoltdZpM
- On the utility of riffs: https://www.youtube.com/watch?v=ydEVH2KcsSY
- How to turn a guitar riff into a song: https://www.youtube.com/watch?v=EHZ2VAvFFoY
- How to create riffs from scales: https://www.youtube.com/watch?v=jeSXGRl0tQc

12

Intermediate Songwriting Seeds

Using "Song Maps"

Materials

- A room full of accompaniment instruments including but not limited to: guitar, keyboard, bass guitar, drum kit, drum sequencer, ukulele, and so forth. You can use a digital audio workstation (DAW) with various keyboard and pad controllers as instruments as well. Considering using homemade instruments and/or body percussion. Musical accompaniment can come from a variety of different places. Orchestration need not be complex to be highly effective at conveying the meanings of a song.
- A playlist of songs like the ones that I have mentioned in the section on Hawkins's "Song Maps" in Chapter 1.
- Check out *It All Begins with a Song* (2020), a documentary on the life and creative work of songwriters in Nashville.
- Examples of songs that fit into the "Song Maps" way of thinking about form and narrative.
- Percussion instruments, including but not limited to drum set (snare drum tuned high), timbale, egg shaker, cajon, djembe, boomwackers, congas, maracas, bongos, and so forth.

Context

This is an intermediate lesson that should be used to extend early experiences covering songs and first attempts at writing songs. It pushes students out of their comfort zones creatively with respect to lyrics, getting them to use particular song maps to organize their lyrical content. The lesson idea is presented by Simon Hawkins in his book Song Maps (2016) as an exercise to assist in lyric writing. The idea will transform your students' creativity regarding narrative arc and meaningful form. It is one of the most used tools in my classroom. Here is a list again of the seven maps:

Map 1: Tension/Response (Ex. Kelly Clarkson "Breakaway").
Map 2: Problem/Declaration (Ex. Miley Cyrus "The Climb").

Growing Songwriting. Clint Randles, Oxford University Press. © Oxford University Press 2024.
DOI: 10.1093/oso/9780197693216.003.0012

Map 3: Timezones (Ex. Five for Fighting "100 Years").
Map 4: Places (Ex. Taylor Swift "Love Story").
Map 5: Roles (Ex. Third Day "I Need a Miracle").
Map 6: Twist (Ex. Michael Bublé "It's a Beautiful Day").
Map 7: Literal Figurative (Ex. Kelsey Ballerini "Peter Pan").

The maps are general ways that songwriters have gone about organizing the structure of their songs. You can use all of them in separate lessons, or have students choose one. I can imagine an entire semester or year of songwriting lessons that utilize each of the maps. Take this idea and use it as you see fit to grow songwriting in your specific classroom. Remember, you are the master gardener who knows how your plants (students) might best grow.

WATER: Keep It Simple

The following bit of advice for songwriters was offered up by Taylor Swift in an interview for *Harper's Bazaar* magazine:[1]

> "Songwriting is still the same uncomplicated process it was when I was 12 years old writing songs in my room," said Taylor Swift in a recent interview with Harper's BAZAAR magazine.
>
> She said: "There are definitely moments when it's like this cloud of an idea comes and just lands in front of your face, and you reach up and grab it.
>
> "A lot of songwriting is things you learn, like structure, cultivating that skill and knowing how to craft a song. But there are mystical, magical moments—inexplicable moments—when an idea that is fully formed just pops into your head."
>
> Instead of allowing ideas to bubble to the surface naturally from their subconscious, many new writers tend to try too hard and end up forcing the creative process. They try to cram too much into a song—making it way too long and unnecessarily complicated, and leaving the listener feeling confused.
>
> As Taylor Swift suggests, it is important to avoid over-thinking or over-writing your songs. Sometimes, the chords, melodies and lyrics that come to you instinctively are the right ones. So don't spend forever searching for the perfect melody or lyrics. Don't keep on going until you end up with way too many notes and words.
>
> Just make sure your song form is clear, predictable and easy to follow. Keeping it simple will make it easier for people to remember the song.
>
> In other words, know when to quit.
>
> As Sting once remarked: "Songs have to be simple. It's not like you have a huge canvas to paint on or a novel length to fill. You've got to tell the story in two verses, a chorus and a coda and that takes some skill."

The idea of just telling a story on some verses and a chorus is helpful when considering how song maps can help you write better songs. The seven different maps are ways that other people have told a story working with a similar simple formal structure.

SUNLIGHT: Following a Recipe

Here are some tips on cooking that might be helpful to you as you consider making use of Hawkins's (2016) *Song Maps*. When you read them, think of what recipes provide for those who prepare food for others to eat. As I write this section, I have just eaten a wonderful Thanksgiving feast prepared by my wife (see Figure 12.1). There is a useful analogy of people preparing songs for listening to people preparing food to be consumed by others:[2]

1. **Choose the recipe wisely**. Keep in mind your experience and abilities in the kitchen when you choose a recipe to prepare for the first time.
2. **Make a copy of it**. Print out a copy of your recipe so that you can consult it at every step of the process.
3. **Read and reread it**. Take a quiet moment to read your recipe through from beginning to end. Breathe, read slowly, focus on each ingredient, and the sequence of instructions.

Figure 12.1 Pecan pie . . . the highlight of my Thanksgiving feast

4. **Gather and prepare your ingredients**. Before you start beating, chopping, and sautéing, get everything you need out of the cabinets and fridge. Make sure you have enough of each ingredient, and that you have the necessary equipment—bowls, pans, utensils, appliances, and so forth.
5. **Follow instructions to the letter and in order**. You have your hard copy of the recipe at hand (see Tip 2); now follow it carefully, step by step. If you are one of those natural rule-breaker types, try to suppress that urge, at least the first time you make the dish.
6. **Take Notes (and Keep Them)**. Throughout the cooking process, write down anything you'd like to remember for later—what ingredient gave you trouble, which knife worked well (or badly) for a particular purpose, any step that took longer than you expected, and so forth.

Do you see how the analogy works? Your students will choose a song map just as they would choose a recipe. They will consult the Chapter 1 examples about how each map works and how each provides a lens through which they can see a completed and successful song lyric. Then they will utilize all of the tips here given for chefs as they fill in the verses, chorus, and maybe bridge of their song lyric. They will take notes on how the process goes in their songwriting journal.

Lesson Time

This lesson can take place in part over one 45-minute class. However, you will most likely have to extend it over multiple classes depending on what you would like to do with the song—special recording or performance. Students will need a list of the song maps and a rationale for what each of them achieves. You will need examples of songs for each of the maps in both audio and written lyric form. This lesson is a seed that will take you in many different directions if you allow it to. You could make this an individual lesson or you could work it into an entire album or performance. You might use the songwriting workgroups idea that I introduce in Chapter 10 to split the class up and keep sections of the class continuing with other lesson seeds as you introduce this one to your idea generation group. As with the other lesson seeds, it helps if you have spent time working out your own songs utilizing the strategies that I bring you here. Use the work of prior classes to inspire your students. The longer you teach songwriting, the more examples you have to offer.

Lesson Instructions

Preparation (10 minutes)

Gather the class and give them a short lesson on the song maps. Choose one of them to work on generating an example for them. Demonstrate how the verses across the

Box 12.1 The chorus of "Radical Empathy"

Chorus
Moving now
Vulnerability
Changing practice
Taking action
Creating change
Building trust
Opening up to our shared experience

It's radical empathy

song connect to the specific song map. Remember, the strength of the song map idea is in how it helps connect the content of the verses across the song. Comp some chords on an accompaniment instrument as you do this to help you drum up some harmonic inspiration. Write down lyrics that jump out at you as having potential. Make a list of the phrases that fit your melody. It works best if you precede this seed with prior object writing sessions (see Chapter 1 and the beginning lesson that makes use of object writing as a place to start with lyric idea generating). Doing this will help give you a focal point for the primary narrative arc for the song. I chose the "Problem/Declaration" song map. I started writing a declaration for a song that would eventually be called "Radical Empathy." The narrative focuses on the idea that we need a lot more empathy in the world.

I then tried to think of three other ways to approach the problem of how we need a lot more empathy in the world. The "face of love" was an image that I thought that I could sing about after the song was written. You have to ask yourself when you are writing whether you would be willing to say the things that you are writing. Do you believe in them enough to write it? I then talk about how it's easier to feel than to say. The payoff of the song is the spoken third verse where it all comes together. Each of the verses supports the chorus (see Boxes 12.1–12.2).

The highlight of the song for me is the excellent tenor saxophone work by one of my former students Jazmin Ghent. Have a listen to the song in the online content. You can also stream the song in all the places where streamed music can be found under my artist listing.

Time to Work (10–15 minutes or longer)

Give them some time to work on doing what you just demonstrated. The dynamic will be different if you have them do this solo or with others in a group. This could take a lot of time or not, depending upon the group and their dynamics. Help them only when they need your help; otherwise, stay out of the way. They come

Box 12.2 Verses of "Radical Empathy"

Verse 1
Imagining the face of love
Looking on and really seeing me
Understanding what can be if we share life
Transforming light reveals

Verse 2
Easier to feel than say
Sometimes we fail to listen more than speak
Finding voice in the art that can unite
Strangers become friends

Verse 3 (spoken)
Long overdue for a time of grace and peace
For a love that reaches to our pain
Wiping tears of generations past
Replacing fear

to you with diverse opinions and highly developed taste for what they like. Let them lead the way. You will sometimes have to move them away from music with explicit content. You know your school culture and what is allowed/tolerated. Monitor the activity in the room carefully to make sure that it stays productive.

Work on the Song (30 minutes or most likely much more)
Allow them time to work on the song. This can be complicated if they are working on band arrangements of the song in groups. If they are working on the song individually, you will have a different series of considerations. Help when you need to help. Get out of the way when you need to get out of the way. You can sometimes help by demonstrating techniques that would help all the groups locate songs better. Positivity needs to be the mantra in your classroom for students to feel safe trying out song ideas and stylistic pathways. Model singing and performing in front of them. Celebrate as they form closer and closer approximations to their musical goals.

Perform (Another class period)
Depending on how many groups/individuals you want to perform in class, you will have to leave time for all students who want to perform. Work with students with severe performance anxiety. For them you will have to create alternate performance opportunities. They could record their performances and submit them electronically to you from home. You could make the band collaborate that way

as well, adding their parts to the recording video/audio. If you have a small performance stage in your class, this would be an excellent opportunity to utilize it. Celebrate their success, be positive, and provide them with a clear path to what they will need to improve—basically, they will need to continue practicing the process. Let their student peers be the first to provide feedback. Provide guidelines for the feedback: for example, give one positive comment and a comment that they could use to improve by (Kratus, 2016).

Record (Another class period or multiple class periods)
Record their performances. They learn by engaging in practice and reflection upon their practice. Self-assessment for musicians is essential. Critically listening to their performances will help them develop their craft. You can be meticulous and professional about recording or not depending upon your expertise with recording arts. An audio interface with an XY-configured microphone pattern would capture the sound of a room well. If you have a computer at each station that your small groups are in, you could multitrack-record their performance and engineer the audio for matching with your video. You could simply use your phone or tablet to record the performances with the built-in microphone.

Modifications for Learners

Recording at Home Modification
For those of your students with performance anxiety, allow them to record their performances at home on their phones or with their computers with DAWs. Many times their desire to make use of this modification has nothing to do with their interest in your class or the lesson but everything to do with their anxiety toward performing in front of their peers. Allow them to record at home. Doing so still means that they are developing a connection to the real world of people making music in the world. They could come around to the possibility of performing in front of their peers when they develop a bit more confidence. You should encourage them to share their videos with the class as a way of encouraging their live performance prowess.

You Perform with Them Modification
If performing the accompaniment is too difficult a task for them, you can always sit in and perform an accompaniment for their singing. This is a widely used accommodation by me when I am working with younger students. It is not easy to play an instrument and sing at the same time. Remember, though, as you are working on developing this skill in your students that singing and playing together is wrapped up in quite a lot of cultural capital. They will gain skills that can last a lifetime with these abilities.

Learning Outcomes

- Write a song by utilizing the idea of song maps.
- Work out a creative arrangement either solo or within a group setting.
- Identify how song lyrics are made better through the use of the song maps idea.
- Identify some influential lyricists whose songs fall into these map forms.
- Perform and record your original music.

Assessment Considerations

Informal Assessment. How did they respond to the lesson? Were there any gains that are difficult to categorize in a rubric? Sometimes lessons don't look like a success on paper, but when you gauge the interest and enthusiasm in the room, accomplishment and student achievement can clearly be seen. The success of a songwriting lesson that centers on stretching their lyricism might best be gauged by how well all are engaged when trying to seek out lyrics that match their melodic ideas in a book. Do some of them get really good ideas? If so, then the lesson was a success. Those students will use the technique in the future. Will some of them not get as much out of the lesson? Most likely. That is okay.

There are times when I have taught a lesson that didn't work very well with a class as a whole, but one student made such massive gains that inspired the rest of the class to up their game in some way. Be careful with how you wield the assessment hammer. Your ultimate goal is that when your students leave your care, they continue writing, recording, and performing their songs. Your assessments should be formative and fair enough that they want to continue practicing their craft. These are tricky waters to navigate. Be careful.

Formal Assessment. Here is a rubric that you might adapt and use as a way of helping your students develop their songwriting craft:

Criteria	Ratings					Pts
This criterion is linked to a Learning Outcome Lyric Writing	**4 to >3.0 pts Expert** I love that your lyricism is approaching professional quality	**3 to >2.0 pts Practitioner** I like that you demonstrated very good lyric writing technique (including many strategies discussed in class)	**2 to >1.0 pts Apprentice** I'm concerned that your lyric writing isn't very good	**1 to >0.0 pts Novice** What's up? Your lyric writing is really difficult to follow	**0 pts No Marks**	4 pts

Criteria	Ratings					Pts
This criterion is linked to a Learning Outcome Musical Interest	**4 to >3.0 pts** **Expert** I love that you displayed almost professional levels of musical interest	**3 to >2.0 pts** **Practitioner** I like the level of musical interest that you conveyed in your song—it's very good	**2 to >1.0 pts** **Apprentice** I'm concerned with how many errors showed up in your song	**1 to >0.0 pts** **Novice** What's up? Your song seems lacking in musical interest quality	**0 pts** **No Mark**	4 pts
This criterion is linked to a Learning Outcome Creativity	**4 to >3.0 pts** **Expert** I love that the creativity you displayed could end up on a recording	**3 to >2.0 pts** **Practitioner** I like that you displayed a very good sense of creativity	**2 to >1.0 pts** **Apprentice** I'm concerned that your performance did not display very much creativity	**1 to >0.0 pts** **Novice** What's up? There was really no sense of creativity in your music	**0 pts** **No Mark**	4 pts
Total Points: 12						

While I have focused this rubric on lyric writing, musical interest, and creativity, you might focus this lesson on any number of musical qualities and characteristics. Everything is on the table for you as an artist teacher to utilize. If you are a teacher in North America and you want these rubric focal points to be specific National Content Standard areas, you can make that happen. The same thing is true if you are working within the Australian Curriculum and you want to align these assessments with your national assessments areas.

Further Reading/Resources

- Check out Simon Hawkins, *Song Maps* (London: Create Space Independent Publishing Platform, 2016).
- Check out Pat Pattison, *Writing Better Lyrics*, 2nd ed. (Cincinnati: Writer's Digest Books, 2009).
- Check out this resource from Berklee Online for writing better lyrics: https://online.berklee.edu/takenote/how-to-write-better-lyrics/.
- As a way of fueling your creative process, consider making use of song lyric-generators: https://online.berklee.edu/takenote/song-lyrics-generators-are-they-good-for-songwriters/.

A Song in the Style of Reggae

Materials

- A room full of accompaniment instruments including but not limited to: guitar, keyboard, bass guitar, drum kit, drum sequencer, ukulele, and so forth. You can use a digital audio workstation (DAW) with various keyboard and pad controllers as instruments as well. You can also use homemade instruments and/or body percussion.
- A playlist full of songs in the style of reggae. Some famous performances of Bob Marley and The Wailers, Desmond Dekker, Toots and The Maytals, and Sizzla.
- The One Love Peace Concert is a great example of reggae music being performed live.
- Examples of musical artists who have crossed over into reggae: Shabba Ranks, Shaggy, Eric Clapton, Amy Grant, Sean Paul, and Diana King.
- Percussion instruments used to accompany reggae, including drum set (snare drum tuned high), timbale, egg shaker, cajon, djembe, boomwackers, congas, maracas, bongos, and so forth.

Context

This is an intermediate lesson that should be used to extend early experiences covering songs. It pushes students out of their comfort zones, taking songs that they know well from their musical heroes and seeds them to cover them in the style of reggae. This lesson should be used only when they have covered songs the way they want to, choosing their own musical material and creative processes.

WATER: Bob Marley's Inspiration for "Three Little Birds"

Bob Marley was inspired by many of the things around him. His friend Tony Gilbert was around at the time he was writing the song and said: "Bob got inspired by a lot of things around him, he observed life. I remember the three little birds. They were pretty birds, canaries, who would come by the windowsill at Hope Road." So being attentive to the things around you might attune you to lyrical content that will resonate with a diverse audience. In your songwriting journal, make sure that you keep notes of things that inspire you. Write down as many different inspirations as you can think of, and when describing them try to be as fluent and flexible in your descriptions as possible. Your reflections just might become the foundation of a lyric that reaches your audience in a powerful way.

SUNLIGHT: Chronicling the Best Reggae Songs of All Time

In order to write a good reggae song, we must be students of the best reggae songs that have been written. Here are a few of them that should be a part of your playlist as you internalize this important genre:

1. "One Love"—Bob Marley and the Wailers
2. "Legalize It"—Peter Tosh
3. "The Tide Is High"—The Paragons
4. "Bam Bam"—Sister Nancy
5. "I Shot the Sherriff"—Bob Marley and the Wailers
6. "Hold Me Tight"—Johnny Nash
7. "I've Got to Go Back Home"—Bob Andy
8. "Many Rivers to Cross"—Jimmy Cliff
9. "Now We've Found Love"—Third World
10. "Talk about Love"—Pat Kelly
11. "Stealing Love"—Carlene Davis
12. "Mr. Boombastic"—Shaggy
13. "Black Woman"—Judy Mowatt

Study the lyrical content. Where do these artists find the stories behind their songs? Where might you find similar stories in your own lives? Why do you think these songs have risen to the top among all of the reggae songs ever written? Does anything surprise you as you listen to them?

Lesson Time

This lesson can take place in one 45-minute class. However, you will most likely have to extend it over multiple classes depending on what you would like to do with the song—special recording or performance. You will need to allow time for students to search for a song that might sound good in reggae style. This lesson is a seed that will take you in many different directions if you allow it to. You could make this an individual lesson or you could work it into an entire album or performance. You might take multiple class periods to teach some about the style and have them play around with it utilizing familiar songs. Take some of the songs that you have used in class up to that point and arrange them in the style of reggae. It might also be worth class time to take a reggae song and take the reggae elements out to make it sound like a ballad or rock song (other styles). Doing so will help students better recognize what makes a song sound reggae. Figure 12.2 shows some of the most common reggae drum beats. They can be a helpful tool for you as you begin to help students internalize this widely used style of music.

Figure 12.2 Some of the most common reggae drum beats

Lesson Instructions

Preparation (10 minutes)

Gather the class and give them a short lesson on reggae style. Share with them sound bites from some of the best reggae artists of all time. Talk about how they make you feel when you hear them, how they can alter your mood for the better. Demonstrate how you perform basic reggae accompaniments. Comp some chords of songs like "Three Little Birds," "Red Red Wine," or "I Shot the Sherriff." Show them some of the techniques employed by Bob Marley to create syncopated guitar accompaniments. Have a student volunteer who you think can internalize the style of reggae to sit in on the drum set and play along as you comp chords on either guitar or keyboard and sing a song in reggae style that you can pull off well. You could even demonstrate a song that is currently trending to demonstrate the style.

Choose the Song (10–15 minutes or longer)

Give them some time to search for a song to cover. They will have to agree on which one that they want to do. This could take a lot of time or not, depending upon the group and their dynamics. Help them only when they need your help; otherwise, stay out of the way. They come to you with diverse opinions and highly developed taste for what they like. Let them lead the way. You will sometimes have to move them away from music with explicit content. You know your school culture and what is allowed/tolerated. Monitor the activity in the room carefully to make sure that it stays productive.

Work on the Song (30 minutes or most likely much more)

Allow them time to work on the song. This can be complicated if they are working on band arrangements of the song in groups. If they are working on the song individually, you will have a different series of considerations. Help when you need to help. Get out of the way when you need to get out of the way. You can sometimes help by demonstrating techniques that would help all of the groups locate songs better. Positivity needs to be the mantra in your classroom for students to feel safe trying out song ideas and stylistic pathways. Model singing and performing in front of them. Celebrate as they form closer and closer approximations to their musical goals.

Perform (Another class period)

Depending on how many groups/individuals you want to perform in class, you will have to leave time for all students who want to perform. Work with students with severe performance anxiety. For them you will have to create alternate performance opportunities. They could record their performances and submit them electronically to you from home. You could make the band collaborate that way as well, adding their parts to the recording video/audio. If you have a small performance stage in your class, this would be an excellent opportunity to utilize it. This is meant to be an intermediate exercise, so these performances should be better put together than beginner performances, taking into account that they will be working within a genre that might be unfamiliar. Celebrate their success, be positive, and provide them with a clear path to what they will need to improve—basically, they will need to continue practicing the process. Let their student peers be the first to provide feedback. Provide guidelines for the feedback: for example, give one positive comment and a comment that they could use to improve by.

Record (Another class period or multiple class periods)

Record their performances. They learn by engaging in practice and reflection upon their practice. Self-assessment for musicians is essential. Critically listening to their performances will help them develop their craft. You can be meticulous and professional about recording or not depending upon your expertise with recording arts. An audio interface with an XY-configured microphone pattern would capture the sound of a room well. If you have a computer at each station that your small groups are in, you could multitrack-record their performance and engineer the audio for matching with your video. You could simply use your phone or tablet to record the performances with the built-in microphone.

Modifications for Learners

Close to Reggae but Not Quite Modification

It is possible that they could miss the mark completely in trying to cover a song in the style of reggae. You are going to want to reward their adventures outside their comfort zone, though. The goal with all of these seeds is to provide you with various places to start creative work utilizing music that your students love. If they take one of their favorite songs in a direction that they had not intended because you introduced a new style and it helped give them a fresh perspective that moved that song to a new and interesting place—GOOD. That was the point. The lesson was a success. You may be more or less comfortable with this way of working in your classroom. Do what is best for your students, and what best fits you as a teacher.

Recording at Home Modification

For those of your students with performance anxiety, allow them to record their performances at home on their phones or with their computers with DAWs. Many times their desire to make use of this modification has nothing to do with their interest in your class or the lesson but everything to do with their anxiety toward performing in front of their peers. Allow them to record at home. Doing so still means that they are developing a connection to the real world of people making music in the world. They could come around to the possibility of performing in front of their peers when they develop a bit more confidence. You should encourage them to share their videos with the class as a way of encouraging their live performance prowess.

You Perform with Them Modification

If performing the accompaniment is too difficult a task for them, you can always sit in and perform an accompaniment for their singing. This is a widely used accommodation by me when I am working with younger students. It is not easy to play an instrument and sing at the same time. Remember, though, as you are working on developing this skill in your students that singing and playing together is wrapped up in quite a lot of cultural capital. They will gain skills that can last a lifetime with these abilities.

Learning Outcomes

- Choose a cover song that will sound good in the style of reggae.
- Work out a creative arrangement, either solo or within a group setting.
- Identify what makes a song reggae.
- Identify some influential reggae artists and their best-known songs.
- Perform a favorite song in the style of reggae for peers and or for public performance.

Assessment Considerations

Informal Assessment. How did they respond to the lesson? Were there any gains that are difficult to categorize in a rubric? Sometimes lessons don't look like a success on paper, but when you gauge the interest and enthusiasm in the room, accomplishment and student achievement can clearly be seen. The success of a cover song in the style of reggae lesson might be in how very different students make their songs but appropriate to the style requirement. Lauren Daigle, a giant in the world of contemporary Christian music at the moment, does a great cover of the song "Turn Your Eyes upon Jesus" in the style of reggae with 808-styled beats that is unlike any version that I have ever heard of the song. That is what makes it great.

There are times when I have taught a lesson that didn't work very well with a class as a whole, but one student made such massive gains that inspired the rest of the class to up their game in some way. Be careful with how you wield the assessment hammer. Your ultimate goal is that when your students leave your care, they continue writing, recording, and performing their songs. Your assessments should be formative and fair enough that they want to continue practicing their craft. These are tricky waters to navigate. Be careful.

Formal Assessment. Here is a rubric that you might adapt and use as a way of helping your students develop their songwriting craft:

Criteria	Ratings					Pts
This criterion is linked to a Learning Outcome Lyric Writing	**4 to >3.0 pts Expert** I love that your lyricism is approaching professional quality	**3 to >2.0 pts Practitioner** I like that you demonstrated very good lyric writing technique (including many strategies discussed in class)	**2 to >1.0 pts Apprentice** I'm concerned that your lyric writing isn't very good	**1 to >0.0 pts Novice** What's up? Your lyric writing is really difficult to follow	**0 pts No Marks**	4 pts
This criterion is linked to a Learning Outcome Musical Interest	**4 to >3.0 pts Expert** I love that you displayed almost professional levels of musical interest	**3 to >2.0 pts Practitioner** I like the level of musical interest that you conveyed in your song—it's very good	**2 to >1.0 pts Apprentice** I'm concerned with how many errors showed up in your song	**1 to >0.0 pts Novice** What's up? Your song seems lacking in musical interest quality	**0 pts No Marks**	4 pts

Criteria	Ratings					Pts
This criterion is linked to a Learning Outcome Creativity	**4 to >3.0 pts Expert** I love that the creativity you displayed could end up on a recording	**3 to >2.0 pts Practitioner** I like that you displayed a very good sense of creativity	**2 to >1.0 pts Apprentice** I'm concerned that your performance did not display very much creativity	**1 to >0.0 pts Novice** What's up? There was really no sense of creativity in your music	**0 pts No Marks**	4 pts
Total Points: 12						

While I have focused this rubric on lyric writing, musical interest, and creativity, you might focus this lesson on any number of musical qualities and characteristics. Everything is on the table for you as an artist teacher to utilize. If you are a teacher in North America and you want these rubric focal points to be specific National Content Standard areas, you can make that happen. The same thing is true if you are working within the Australian Curriculum and you want to align these assessments with your national assessments areas.

Further Reading/Resources

- Roger Steffens, *So Much Things to Say: The Oral History of Bob Marley* (New York: W. W. Norton, 2018).
- Lloyd Bradley, *This Is Reggae Music: The Story of Jamaica's Music* (New York: Grove Press, 2002)
- *Roots, Reggae, Rebellion* (BBC documentary): https://www.youtube.com/watch?v=PQ1BNJpVS5M.
- Muthoni Drummer Queen on African styles (including reggae): https://www.ted.com/speakers/muthoni_drummer_queen.

Stealing Words from a Book

Materials

- A room full of accompaniment instruments including but not limited to: guitar, keyboard, bass guitar, drum kit, drum sequencer, ukulele, and so forth. You can use a digital audio workstation (DAW) with various keyboard and pad controllers as instruments as well. Considering using homemade instruments and/or body percussion. Musical accompaniment can come from a variety of different places. Orchestration need not be complex to be highly effective at conveying the meanings of a song.

- A playlist full of songs that masterfully weave together lyrics. Consider the work of Bob Dylan, Nas, Joni Mitchell, Bruce Springsteen, Tupac, Carole King, and the Notorious B.I.G.
- Check out *No Direction Home* (2005), a documentary on the life and creative work of Bob Dylan.
- Examples of songs that reach a next level status lyrically: Billy Joel, "Vienna"; Hamilton, "Who Lives, Who Dies, Who Tells Your Story"; Jimmy Eat World, "Delivery."
- Percussion instruments, including but not limited to drum set (snare drum tuned high), timbale, egg shaker, cajon, djembe, boomwackers, congas, maracas, bongos, and so forth.

Context

This is an intermediate lesson that should be used to extend early experiences covering songs and first attempts at writing songs. It pushes students out of their comfort zones creatively with respect to lyrics, getting them to fish for words out of a book. The lesson idea is presented by Jeff Tweedy in his book *How to Write One Song* (2020) as an exercise to assist in lyric writing. The idea will transform your students' creativity when composing lyrics.

WATER: Nas and Wordsmithing

Nas (Nasir bin Olu Dara Jones), also called Nasty Nas, was born September 14, 1973, in Brooklyn. He is an American rapper and songwriter who became a dominant voice in 1990s East Coast hip-hop. Nasir Jones is the son of a jazz musician and grew up in public housing in Queens. He dropped out of school in the eighth grade and searched for a creative outlet—and hip-hop found him. His song "Half Time" (credited to Nasty Nas) appeared on the soundtrack to the film *Zebrahead* and was a huge success. Columbia Records signed him to a contract, and he recorded his debut, *Illmatic* (1994), which drew widespread critical acclaim.

Nas says this about rhyming in his lyric writing:[3]

> A rhythmic pattern is another way of saying a style. So your rhythmic pattern would be whatever you choose. And you can stay into that pattern. In your bars, you can rap (RAPPING) this, that, this, that, this, this, that, this, or that, or you could chain it to (RAPPING) this and that, and this and that, and this and this, this, that, that. It's the pattern you use. Sometimes you bore people when the pattern is the same thing too long, so you switch up your pattern throughout the rhyme, throughout the verse, to show how many ways you're capable of rapping.

Some people can only rap in one style, one rhythmic pattern. But the more you have shows that you are the better emcee.

As I have shared throughout this book, one of your primary missions is to get your students listening outside of their normal patterns and routines. Listen both broadly and deeply to artists who break new ground lyrically. You cannot go wrong listening to Nas, especially to the way that he crafts his lyrics.

SUNLIGHT: Rhyming Dictionary Bliss

It is no surprise; I have said it over and over again throughout this book. A rhyming dictionary is one of your number tools as a lyricist. You will discover the many ways that having numerous options for these will encourage your creative processes. Here is a list of some of the more beneficial online rhyming dictionary platforms:

1. Rhyme Zone: https://www.rhymezone.com/
2. Rhymer: https://www.rhymer.com/
3. Rhyme Finder: https://www.rhymefinder.net/
4. Rhyming Dictionary: https://rhyming.wordhippo.com/
5. Kenn Nesbitt's Poetry4Kids: https://poetry4kids.com/rhymes/
6. Rhyme Brain: https://rhymebrain.com/en
7. WikiRhymer: https://wikirhymer.com/
8. Word Central: https://www.merriam-webster.com/kids
9. Rhymes & Chimes: https://www.rhymes.com/

Finding and using even one of these resources will transform your lyrical creativity. I enjoy using Rhyme Zone regularly. I find that I cannot live without it. It is a literal lifesaver when it comes to getting outside of my own vocabulary in effective ways. The true test of whether these tools are effective or necessary is what your students say about them.

Lesson Time

This lesson can take place in one 45-minute class. However, you will most likely have to extend it over multiple classes depending on what you would like to do with the song—special recording or performance. Students will need a book to browse and steal words from. Of course, the book can be in a digital format or not. This lesson is a seed that will take you in many different directions if you allow it to. You could make this an individual lesson or you could work it into an entire album or performance. You might use the songwriting workgroups idea that I introduce in Chapter 10 to split the class up and keep sections of the class continuing with other lesson seeds as you introduce this one to your idea generation group. As with the other lesson seeds, it helps if you have spent time working out your own songs utilizing the strategies that I bring you here. Use the work of prior classes of students as well to inspire your students. The longer you teach songwriting, the more examples you have to offer.

Lesson Instructions

Preparation (10 minutes)

Gather the class and give them a short lesson on how Jeff Tweedy steals words from books to write lyrics (see Table 12.1). [smile] That sentence sounded criminal as I wrote it. I just stole the first column of words/phrases from the Declaration of Independence. I then used a rhyming dictionary to generate the five columns after the first one. Then, I generated lyrical ideas (see Box 12.3) based on pairings of the lyrical ideas. A story emerges about Anna and her lifelong love for the hero of the song! You will want to share with them sound bites from some Wilco songs. Talk about the artistry to the lyric writing. Demonstrate how to hum a melody in your mind while combing through book pages to audition lyrics. Comp some chords

Table 12.1 Example of phrases pulled from a book that fit a particular melodic idea

changed for light	great foresight	day or night	mate for life	your right	war might
times of peace	wand of peace	kiss of peace	Divine Caprice	delightful piece	dime apiece
powers of	our love	founders of	empowers us	flowers hung	devour us
requires	desires	conspires	spiders	heifers	denials
candid world	had a word	Anna turned	afterward	candle burned	glance upward

Box 12.3 Lines pieced together from stolen book words and their rhyming children words

Anna turned
Day or night mate for life
Afterword
Kiss of peace Divine Caprice

Had a word
Great foresight changed for life
Candid world
Requires desires

on an accompaniment instrument as you do this to help you drum up inspiration. Write down lyrics that jump out at you as having potential. Make a list of the phrases that fit your melody. Working this way will get you out of your own language and free up your creative process for pleasant surprises.

Book Work (10–15 minutes or longer)
Give them some time to work on doing what you just demonstrated. The dynamic will be different if you have them do this solo or with others in a group. This could take a lot of time or not, depending upon the group and their dynamics. Help them only when they need your help; otherwise, stay out of the way. They come to you with diverse opinions and highly developed taste for what they like. Let them lead the way. You will sometimes have to move them away from music with explicit content. You know your school culture and what is allowed/tolerated. Monitor the activity in the room carefully to make sure that it stays productive.

Work on the Song (30 minutes or most likely much more)
Allow them time to work on the song. This can be complicated if they are working on band arrangements of the song in groups. If they are working on the song individually, you will have a different series of considerations. Help when you need to help. Get out of the way when you need to get out of the way. You can sometimes help by demonstrating techniques that would help all of the groups locate songs better. Positivity needs to be the mantra in your classroom for students to feel safe trying out song ideas and stylistic pathways. Model singing and performing in front of them. Celebrate as they form closer and closer approximations to their musical goals.

Perform (Another class period)
Depending on how many groups/individuals you want to perform in class, you will have to leave time for all students who want to perform. Work with students with severe performance anxiety. For them you will have to create alternate performance opportunities. They could record their performances and submit them electronically to you from home. You could make the band collaborate that way as well, adding their parts to the recording video/audio. If you have a small performance stage in your class, this would be an excellent opportunity to utilize it. Celebrate their success, be positive, and provide them with a clear path to what they will need to improve—basically, they will need to continue practicing the process. Let their student peers be the first to provide feedback. Provide guidelines for the feedback: for example, give one positive comment and a comment that they could use to improve by (Kratus, 2016).

Record (Another class period or multiple class periods)
Record their performances. They learn by engaging in practice and reflection upon their practice. Self-assessment for musicians is essential. Critically listening to their performances will help them develop their craft. You can be meticulous and professional about recording or not depending upon your expertise with recording arts.

An audio interface with an XY-configured microphone pattern would capture the sound of a room well. If you have a computer at each station that your small groups are in, you could multitrack-record their performance and engineer the audio for matching with your video. You could simply use your phone or tablet to record the performances with the built-in microphone.

Modifications for Learners

Recording at Home Modification

For those of your students with performance anxiety, allow them to record their performances at home on their phones or with their computers with DAWs. Many times their desire to make use of this modification has nothing to do with their interest in your class or the lesson but everything to do with their anxiety toward performing in front of their peers. Allow them to record at home. Doing so still means that they are developing a connection to the real world of people making music in the world. They could come around to the possibility of performing in front of their peers when they develop a bit more confidence. You should encourage them to share their videos with the class as a way of encouraging their live performance prowess.

You Perform with Them Modification

If performing the accompaniment is too difficult a task for them, you can always sit in and perform an accompaniment for their singing. This is a widely used accommodation by me when I am working with younger students. It is not easy to play an instrument and sing at the same time. Remember, though, as you are working on developing this skill in your students that singing and playing together is wrapped up in quite a lot of cultural capital. They will gain skills that can last a lifetime with these abilities.

Learning Outcomes

- Write a song using words that you steal from a book to fuel your creative process.
- Work out a creative arrangement, either solo or within a group setting.
- Identify what makes song lyrics unique (unpredictable).
- Identify some influential lyricists who write well lyrically.
- Perform and record your original music.

Assessment Considerations

Informal Assessment. How did they respond to the lesson? Were there any gains that are difficult to categorize in a rubric? Sometimes lessons don't look like a success on paper, but when you gauge the interest and enthusiasm in the room, accomplishment and student achievement can clearly be seen. The success of a songwriting lesson that centers on stretching their lyricism might best be gauged by how well all are engaged when trying to seek out lyrics that match their melodic ideas in a book. Do some of them get really good ideas? If so, then the lesson was a success. Those students will use the technique in the future. Will some of them not get as much out of the lesson? Most likely. That is okay.

There are times when I have taught a lesson that didn't work very well with a class as a whole, but one student made such massive gains that inspired the rest of the class to up their game in some way. Be careful with how you wield the assessment hammer. Your ultimate goal is that when your students leave your care they continue writing, recording, and performing their songs. Your assessments should be formative and fair enough that they want to continue practicing their craft. These are tricky waters to navigate. Be careful.

Formal Assessment. Here is a rubric that you might adapt and use as a way of helping your students develop their songwriting craft:
While I have focused this rubric on lyric writing, musical interest, and creativity, you might focus this lesson on any number of musical qualities and characteristics. Everything is on the table for you as an artist teacher to utilize. If you are a teacher in North America and you want these rubric focal points to be specific National Content Standard areas, you can make that happen. The same thing is true if you are working within the Australian Curriculum and you want to align these assessments with your national assessments areas.

Criteria	Ratings					Pts
This criterion is linked to a Learning Outcome Lyric Writing	**4 to >3.0 pts Expert** I love that your lyricism is approaching professional quality	**3 to >2.0 pts Practitioner** I like that you demonstrated very good lyric writing technique (including many strategies discussed in class)	**2 to >1.0 pts Apprentice** I'm concerned that your lyric writing isn't very good	**1 to >0.0 pts Novice** What's up? Your lyric writing is really difficult to follow	**0 pts No Marks**	4 pts
This criterion is linked to a Learning Outcome Musical Interest	**4 to >3.0 pts Expert** I love that you displayed almost professional levels of musical interest	**3 to >2.0 pts Practitioner** I like the level of musical interest that you conveyed in your song—it's very good	**2 to >1.0 pts Apprentice** I'm concerned with how many errors showed up in your song	**1 to >0.0 pts Novice** What's up? Your song seems lacking in musical interest quality	**0 pts No Marks**	4 pts

Criteria	Ratings					Pts
This criterion is linked to a Learning Outcome Creativity	4 to >3.0 pts **Expert** I love that the creativity you displayed could end up on a recording	3 to >2.0 pts **Practitioner** I like that you displayed a very good sense of creativity	2 to >1.0 pts **Apprentice** I'm concerned that your performance did not display very much creativity	1 to >0.0 pts **Novice** What's up? There was really no sense of creativity in your music	0 pts **No Marks**	4 pts
Total Points: 12						

Further Reading/Resources

- Here's a lyric-writing resource called Lyric Studio: https://lyricstudio.net/.
- Here's a lyric-writing software that you can use to assist your creative processes: https://masterwriter.com/songwriters/.
- Here is a collection of resources that will help you write your best songs: https://theartofsongs.com/songwriting-resources/.
- Check out the Musical Futures guide to songwriting: https://www.musicalfutures.org/resource/songwriting.

13
Advanced Songwriting Seeds

Don't Be Yourself

Materials

- A room full of accompaniment instruments including but not limited to: guitar, keyboard, bass guitar, drum kit, drum sequencer, ukulele, and so forth. You should fill your space with unique instruments as well as these typical accompaniment instruments. The stranger the better.
- Fill your space with unique effects pedals, processors, and synthesizers. These can be expensive, so take advantage of less expensive digital approximations when you can.
- A playlist full of songs that you have written and recorded in the past.
- Clips of some of your prior performances.
- Examples of musical artists who you are not like, but whose work you might like to explore in your own work.
- Percussion instruments of diverse variety and background.

Context

This is an advanced lesson that should be used to extend your style and compositional process to new territory. This lesson is designed to push students out of their comfort zones, taking the personal style that they have been developing in prior songs to new conceptual and performance soil. This lesson should be used when they have written songs the way they want to and have developed a personal voice and artistry through various songwriting processes.

WATER: Becoming Ziggy Stardust

David Bowie created an alter ego when he birthed "Starman" on Top of The Pops dressed like glamorous aliens to perform the song of the same name.[1]

> To introduce Great Britain to *Ziggy Stardust and The Spider From Mars* with three-and-a-half minutes of perfect pop. Bowie played his blue acoustic guitar

Growing Songwriting. Clint Randles, Oxford University Press. © Oxford University Press 2024.
DOI: 10.1093/oso/9780197693216.003.0013

like a prop and pointed his finger seductively down the camera. Ronson's wailing guitar soared. Bolder's intergalactic bass throbbed as his silver sideburns swayed. Woody's drumbeat kept it all together. Ronson and Bowie shared the mic, as they often did in the studio. When they'd been to the BBC bar earlier, everyone thought they were Doctor Who extras. They were different. They were weird.

Bowie was a trailblazer in the world of pop music, without a doubt, constantly reinventing himself with each successive album that he released over the four decades that he made albums. His creation of the alter ego Starman opened the door for other artists to free themselves creatively by becoming someone else in their music. Here are some artists and their alter egos:

1. Hank Williams as Luke the Drifter.
2. The Beatles as Sgt. Pepper's Lonely Hearts Club Band.
3. Prince as Camille.
4. Bono as The Fly.
5. Garth Brooks as Chris Gaines.
6. Damon Albarn as Murdoc.
7. Beyoncé as Sasha Fierce.
8. Kevin Barnes as Georgie Fruit.
9. Miley Cyrus as Hannah Montana.

SUNLIGHT: Seeing through Other People's Eyes

Key to this lesson seed is recognizing the value of seeing yourself through the eyes of other people, OR perhaps setting aside your own history to assume the history of another individual or group that comes in part from your imagination. We all have a tendency to dismiss ideas and concepts that stretch or challenge our accepted beliefs and values. It is human to have opinions and beliefs, and to come across people or groups who think differently than we do. By setting judgments and presuppositions, we can discover ways to create more headroom and flexibility in our creative practices. Each of us experiences our own individual perceptions of reality. By taking off our internal blinders, we can give ourselves permission to consider new concepts, ideas, and knowledge without bias or discrimination. When we do this, something wonderful begins to happen—we find we have a lot more in common with others!

For the duration of this lesson seed, try to model an open mind and acceptance of what you might have even considered silliness before. Try to imagine yourself as objects in the room that you find yourself in right now. What would it like to be your dog for the duration of the day? Can you imagine what it would feel like to be blown into town with the winds of a tropical storm? If you were a make and model of automobile, which one would you be and what would you do this weekend?

Lesson Time

This lesson seed can take place in one 45-minute class. However, you will most likely have to extend it over multiple classes depending on what you would like to do with the song—special recording or performance. You are going to need to inspire them in some way to think differently about their own songwriting style. This lesson is a seed that will take you in many different directions if you allow it to. You could make this an individual lesson or you could work it into an entire album or performance. The main thrust of this seed is taken from Jeff Tweedy's *How to Write One Song* (2020) and centers on writing from the perspective of anyone and/or anything but yourself.

In his book, Tweedy reflects on writing the album *A Ghost Is Born* (2004), taking on the persona of an insect on the song "Company on My Back." It was so freeing to think as an insect with lyrics like:

I attack with love, pure bug beauty
I curl my lips and crawl up on you

And your afternoon
And I've been puking

The song goes into strange and interesting territory because it isn't written from Tweedy's life story. It is purposefully meant to not be him—and that is incredibly freeing for him as a lyric writer. He feels way more secure to say new things when he knows that it isn't him saying it. That is the main point that you need to present to your students when you start with this lesson seed. You want them to write as someone or something else.

Lesson Instructions

Preparation (10 minutes)

Gather the class and give them a short lesson on writing as someone or something else. Use the Tweedy example that I just shared and play the song from *A Ghost Is Born* (2004). Talk about how when they take on the persona of someone or something else they can free up their imagination to say new things. Demonstrate a song that you have written that achieves this end. Comp some chords of songs that achieve this by other artists. Have other students in the room perform some songs that they have written that achieve this end goal. Show them some of the techniques employed by artists to write as other people. Have a student volunteer sit in on the drum set and play along as you comp chords on either guitar or keyboard and sing a song that accomplishes this idea well. Is there a song on the Billboard charts currently that achieves this end goal? If there is, consider using it in your lesson seed.

Make a Plan for the Song (10–15 minutes or longer)

Give them some time to consider how they are going to develop the song. If they are group writing, they will have to agree on the scope and focus of the track. This could take a lot of time or not, depending upon the group and their dynamics. Help them only when they need your help; otherwise, stay out of the way. They come to you with diverse opinions and highly developed taste for what they like. Let them lead the way. In my experience, you best serve them by being inspirational in some way. Bring something new to their thinking. Put some new ideas and musical examples on the table for them. Let their response to your ideas guide how you proceed to meet their needs.

Work on the Song (30 minutes or most likely much more)

Allow them time to work on the song. This can be complicated if they are working on band arrangements of the song in groups or if they are working in songwriting workgroups like the ones that I describe in Chapter 10. If they are working on the song individually, you will have a different series of considerations. Help when you need to help. Get out of the way when you need to get out of the way. You can sometimes help by demonstrating techniques that would help all the groups locate songs better. Positivity needs to be the mantra in your classroom for students to feel safe trying out song ideas and stylistic pathways. Model singing and performing in front of them. Celebrate as they form closer and closer approximations to their musical goals.

Perform (Another class period)

Depending on how many groups/individuals you want to perform in class, you will have to leave time for all students who want to perform. Work with students with severe performance anxiety. For them you will have to create alternate performance opportunities. They could record their performances and submit them electronically to you from home. You could make the band collaborate that way as well, adding their parts to the recording video/audio. If you have a small performance stage in your class, this would be an excellent opportunity to utilize it. This is meant to be an advanced exercise, so these performances should be better put together than beginner performances, taking into account that they will be working within a genre that might be unfamiliar. Celebrate their success, be positive, and provide them with a clear path to what they will need to improve—basically, they will need to continue practicing the process. Let their student peers be the first to provide feedback. Provide guidelines for the feedback: for example, give one positive comment and a comment that they could use to improve by (Kratus, 2016).

Record (Another class period or multiple class periods)
Record their songs. You need to help them create the album version of their song (as well as performed versions of the songs live in class). Follow the procedures that I lay out in Chapter 10 for recording a song as a part of a songwriting workgroup culture. Critically listening to their recordings for production assistance will help them develop their craft. You can be meticulous and professional about recording or not depending upon your expertise with recording arts. Check out *Sound Production for the Emerging Music Teacher Producer* (Randles, Aponte, and Johnson, forthcoming) for help on making your tracks sound better. An audio interface with an XY-configured microphone pattern would capture the sound of a room well. If you have a computer at each station that your small groups are in, you could multitrack-record their songs.

Modifications for Learners

Works in Progress
The reality of creative processes is that sometimes our work takes a long time to finish. Sometimes we are not happy with a particular work until years, even decades later. You can't exactly give them a decade extension for finishing their work! Be that as it may, you will need to be forgiving sometimes when they are not finished when the deadline comes and goes. Some of my most brilliant students never met their deadlines in class, only to finally hit their stride with their songs after they graduated or had moved on past my class. Don't forget that songwriting is something that you want to give them during the contact that you have with them, knowing that they will continue practicing well after their time with you. It is a marathon that you are starting them on, not a sprint.

Recording at Home Modification
For those of your students with performance anxiety, allow them to record their performances at home on their phones or with their computers with DAWs. Many times their desire to make use of this modification has nothing to do with their interest in your class or the lesson but everything to do with their anxiety toward performing in front of their peers. Allow them to record at home. Doing so still means that they are developing a connection to the real world of people making music in the world. They could come around to the possibility of performing in front of their peers when they develop a bit more confidence. You should encourage them

to share their videos with the class as a way of encouraging their live performance prowess.

Others (Including You) Perform with Them Modification
If performing the accompaniment is too difficult a task for them, others (including you) can always sit in and perform an accompaniment for their singing. This is a widely used accommodation by me when I am working with younger students. It is not easy to play an instrument and sing at the same time. Remember, though, as you are working on developing this skill in your students that singing and playing together is wrapped up in quite a lot of cultural capital. They will gain skills that can last a lifetime with these abilities. Encourage them to do it themselves, but help them when they need some help.

Learning Outcomes

- Write a song utilizing the perspective of someone or something else.
- Work out an arrangement, either solo or within a group setting of the song.
- Identify how the lyrics represent the experiences of someone or something else.
- Identify some influential artists who have done this in their own songwriting.
- Perform a song that they have written that employs this writing strategy.
- Record a song that they have written that employs this writing strategy.

Assessment Considerations

Informal Assessment. How did they respond to the lesson? Were there any gains that are difficult to categorize in a rubric? Sometimes lessons don't look like a success on paper, but when you gauge the interest and enthusiasm in the room, accomplishment and student achievement can clearly be seen. The success of a lesson seed on being and becoming a songwriter who can write on experiences that relate to other people or things can be equally gauged by how well they achieved the end goal of writing as "others" and how they felt about the experience. Do they feel as though they could do it again? Did they enjoy the process? What will they do better next time?

There are times when I have taught a lesson that didn't work very well with a class as a whole, but one student made massive gains that inspired the rest of the class to up their game in some way. Be careful with how you wield the assessment hammer. Your primary goal is to inspire them to continue writing, recording, and performing their songs. Your assessments should be formative and fair enough that they want to continue practicing their craft. These are tricky waters to navigate. Be careful.

Formal Assessment. Here is a rubric that you might adapt and use as a way of helping your students develop their songwriting craft:

Criteria	Ratings					Pts
This criterion is linked to a Learning Outcome Lyric Writing	**4 to >3.0 pts Expert** I love that your lyricism is approaching professional quality	**3 to >2.0 pts Practitioner** I like that you demonstrated very good lyric writing technique (including many strategies discussed in class)	**2 to >1.0 pts Apprentice** I'm concerned that your lyric writing isn't very good	**1 to >0.0 pts Novice** What's up? Your lyric writing is really difficult to follow	**0 pts No Marks**	4 pts
This criterion is linked to a Learning Outcome Musical Interest	**4 to >3.0 pts Expert** I love that you displayed almost professional levels of musical interest	**3 to >2.0 pts Practitioner** I like the level of musical interest that you conveyed in your song—it's very good	**2 to >1.0 pts Apprentice** I'm concerned with how many errors showed up in your song	**1 to >0.0 pts Novice** What's up? Your song seems lacking in musical interest quality	**0 pts No Marks**	4 pts
This criterion is linked to a Learning Outcome Creativity	**4 to >3.0 pts Expert** I love that the creativity you displayed could end up on a recording	**3 to >2.0 pts Practitioner** I like that you displayed a very good sense of creativity	**2 to >1.0 pts Apprentice** I'm concerned that your performance did not display very much creativity	**1 to >0.0 pts Novice** What's up? There was really no sense of creativity in your music	**0 pts No Marks**	4 pts
Total Points: 12						

While I have focused this rubric on lyric writing, musical interest, and creativity, you might focus this lesson on any number of musical qualities and characteristics. Everything is on the table for you as an artist teacher to utilize. If you are a teacher in North America and you want these rubric focal points to be specific National Content Standard areas, you can make that happen. The same thing is true if you are working within the Australian Curriculum and you want to align these assessments with your national assessments areas.

Further Reading/Resources

- Jeff Tweedy, *How to Write One Song* (New York: Dutton, 2020).
- *A Ghost Is Born* (2004) by the band Wilco.

- “Wilco’s *A Ghost is Born* Turns 15—Anniversary Retrospective”: https://albumism.com/features/wilco-a-ghost-is-born-turns-15-anniversary-retrospective.
- Barack Obama introducing Wilco at Farm Aid 2005: https://www.youtube.com/watch?v=nmR32cFfGTQ.

Experimental Rhymes

Materials

- A room full of accompaniment instruments including but not limited to: guitar, keyboard, bass guitar, drum kit, drum sequencer, ukulele, and so forth. You should fill your space with unique instruments as well as these typical accompaniment instruments. The stranger the better.
- Fill your space with unique effects pedals, processors, and synthesizers. These can be expensive, so take advantage of less expensive digital approximations when you can.
- A playlist full of songs that you have written and recorded in the past.
- A rhyming dictionary.
- Examples of lyrics that either do not rhyme or rhyme in strange and unique ways.
- Percussion instruments of diverse variety and background.

Context

This is an advanced lesson that should be used to extend your style and compositional process to new territory lyrically. This lesson is designed to push students out of their comfort zones with regard to rhyming. This lesson should be used when they have written songs from object writing sessions and within songwriting workgroups. This is a lesson seed that focuses on stretching their conception of what rhyming accomplishes in the lyric writing process. Jeff Tweedy in *How to Write a Song* (2020) motivates readers to resist predictable rhymes by figuring out how to use seemingly unrelated rhyming words in song lyrics.

WATER: Approaching 8-Mile

Eminem was just recently inducted into the Rock and Roll Hall of Fame (November 2022). He has come to be known as a MASTER of rhyme. In his induction speech he recalls how rhyming has been an essential part of his life. This was printed in the Detroit News after the ceremony:[2]

Eminem: Hip-hop saved my life

Can y'all hear me? I can't hear me. Can you hear me?

This s—t's crazy. So I wrote some s—t down tonight that I'm never going to f—-ing remember, so I had to read it off the paper and s—t, but it's from the heart. I realize what an honor it is right now for me to be up here tonight, and what a privilege it is to do the music that I love, and the music that basically saved my life.

Where'd the man, where did Dre go? The man who saved my life, ladies and gentlemen, Dr. other—-in' Dre. So I'm going to try to make this as quick and painless as possible. I'm f—-ing stuttering and s—t, I mean Jesus Christ.

So I'm probably not supposed to actually be here tonight because of a couple of reasons. One of them that I'm a rapper, and this is the Rock and Roll Hall of Fame. And there's only a few of us right now that have been inducted in already, but there's only a few of us.

Secondly, I almost died from an overdose in 2007, which kind of sucked. Hailie, plug your ears: because drugs were f—ing delicious, and I thought we had a good thing going man, but I had to go and f—- it all up and take too many. God d—n. OK Hailie.

OK, so. Hold on, I lost my motherf—in' spot. Paul, did I say, I said drugs were delicious, right? And finally, I had to really fight my way through man to try and break through in this music, and I'm so honored and I'm so grateful that I'm even able to be up here doing hip-hip music, man, because I love it so much.

And they say you won't work a day if you love your job and s—t. This part I'm not crazy about? But, OK.

My musical influences are many, and they say it takes a village to raise a child. Well it took a whole genre and culture to raise me.

They say success has many fathers, and that's definitely true for me. So whatever my impact has been on hip-hop music, I never would have or could have done this s—t without some of the groundbreaking artists that I'm about to mention right now.

And this is a list man, I put this list together yesterday. And I kept adding to the s—t, adding to the s—t, and if I forget anybody, I apologize. But these were my teachers right here:

I'm gonna start with the 2 Live Crew, 2Pac, 3rd Bass, Alliance, Apache, Audio Two—Milk Dee, what up!—Awesome Dre, the Beastie Boys, Big Daddy Kane, Big Pun, Big L, Biz Markie, the Notorious B.I.G. of course, Black Moon, the Boogie Monsters, Brand Nubian, Brother J from X Clan, Buckshot, Casual from Heiroglyphics, Chill Rob G, Chubb Rock, Chuck D and Public Enemy, Cypress Hill, D-Nice, Dana Dane, De La Soul—now I'm about a third of the way done.

How are you addressing hip-hop music in your curriculum? What could you do to grow your students' capacity to rhyme lyrics? Find some inspiration in the life of Eminem.

SUNLIGHT: Dreaming and Scheming

Here are the most popular four-line rhyme schemes used by songwriters, as presented by Musician on a Mission:[3]

#1: AABB

An AABB rhyme scheme is made up of four lines. The first two lines are a pair, as are the last two lines.

Each of the pairs has a different rhyme. This type of end rhyme is also referred to as a couplet.

You can see this at work in Simon and Garfunkel's "The Sound of Silence."

Hello darkness, my old friend
I've come to talk with you again
Because a vision softly creeping
Left its seeds while I was sleeping

The end rhyme of the first pair, or couplet, is "friend" with "again." That's our A rhyme.

The second couplet also rhymes. But it uses a different sounding rhyme—"creeping" with "sleeping"—and that's the B rhyme.

This scheme also unites each new idea with a couplet. Once the rhyming couplet finishes, a new couplet (and idea) starts. Have another look:

Idea 1—the A rhyme

Hello darkness, my old friend
I've come to talk with you again

Idea 2—the B rhyme

Because a vision softly creeping
Left its seeds while I was sleeping

This way of moving your ideas through the song (particularly the verses) is called topic movement.

It's a key reason why rhyme schemes are so well used in song. We hear rather than read the words.

#2: ABAB

This very popular scheme has interlocking rhymes. ABAB is also known as alternate rhyme.

Here is how you can write it:
Rhyme the first line with the third.
Rhyme the second line with the fourth, but use a different vowel sound.
A good example is "Scarborough Fair." This is a traditional English folk tune made evergreen by Simon and Garfunkel.

> Are you going to Scarborough Fair?
> Parsley, sage, rosemary, and thyme
> Remember me to one who lives there
> For once she was a true love of mine

#3: AAAA

This scheme has all the lines ending with the same rhyme. It's also known as monorhyme.

Using this scheme is harder to keep sounding fresh, but it's great for creating a buildup.

Here's Sam Smith's "Latch":

> You lift my heart up when the rest of me is down
> You, you enchant me even when you're not around
> If there are boundaries, I will try to knock them down
> I'm latching on, babe, now I know what I have found

#4: ABBA

This rarer scheme works as a sandwich. It's called an enclosed or envelope rhyme.

You rhyme the first line with the last one. Then the two lines between them rhyme with each other, but the rhyme sounds different.

Here's James Taylor's "Sweet Baby James":

> There is a young cowboy, he lives on the range
> His horse and his cattle are his only companions
> He works in the saddle and he sleeps in the canyons
> Waiting for summer his pastures to change

#5: AAAB

Everything rhymes except for the very last line in the verse. Often, this last line has a completely different number of syllables as the three lines before it.

Here's Coldplay with the verse scheme from "Fix You":

When you try your best but you don't succeed
When you get what you want but not what you need
When you feel so tired but you can't sleep
Stuck in reverse

When the tears come streaming down your face
'Cause you lose something you can't replace
When you love someone but it goes to waste
What could be worse?

The next three schemes (well, four really) have more relative freedom and flexibility. They mix rhyming lines (A) and non-rhyming lines (X).

The first one is the most popular.

#6: XAXA

In XAXA, you have two lines that do not rhyme with others and two that do.

Make sure that lines 1 and 3 do not rhyme with each other or with any other line.

Line 2 and line 4 do rhyme with each other.

This scheme's less predictable because it has two lines that don't rhyme with anything, but it allows the potential for a more natural, conversational way of writing. That makes it a real favorite with contemporary songwriters.

The XAXA scheme is used by The Police in "Everything Little Thing She Does Is Magic":

I resolved to call her up
A thousand times a day
Ask her if she'll marry me
In some old-fashioned way

#7: AXAA and AAXA

With both these schemes, you need to rhyme only three out of four lines.

It is another great opportunity to get a little bit more freedom.

You can vary where that unpredictable unrhymed line turns up. Makes it a little edgy.

Here's Bruno Mars using an AAXA scheme in "Grenade":

> I would go through all this pain
> Take a bullet straight through my brain
> Yes, I would die for you, baby
> But you won't do the same

Here's Joni Mitchell in "Both Sides Now," varying it to AAAX to highlight her last line.

> Rows and flows of angel's hair
> And ice cream castles in the air
> And feathered canyons everywhere
> I've looked at clouds that way

#8: AXXA

This rhymes the first line with the last one, like in the envelope scheme ABBA. However, it leaves two unrhymed lines in the middle.

Lesson Time

This lesson seed can take place in one 45-minute class. However, you will most likely have to extend it over multiple classes depending on what you would like to do with the song—special recording or performance. You will make a list of words that you would like to work with, taken from a rhyming dictionary. This lesson is a seed that will take you in many different directions if you allow it to. You could make this an individual lesson or you could work it into an entire album or performance. The main thrust of this seed is taken from Jeff Tweedy's *How to Write One Song* (2020) and centers on writing lyrically from a list of nonsensical words and making them work together and rhyme.

In his book, Tweedy reflects on writing down words that he picked somewhat randomly out of a book that he was reading and then pulled them together and used them to write a song. Working this way, suggests Tweedy, makes the subject matter of the songs start at an interesting left-of-center sort of place. Ultimately, we want all the songs that we write to have some sort of narrative arc. By starting with random words pulled from a book that you are reading, or from a newspaper, or from your favorite blog, you add particular ingredients to the pie that when prepared and cooked contribute significantly to what you and others will take away from it. The particular words chosen will certainly affect the outcome. That is what is exciting about working this way.

Lesson Instructions

Preparation (10 minutes)
Gather the class and give them a short lesson on selecting words from a book, newspaper, blog, Tweet, Instagram post, or some other place. Use an example list. Here's one that I just created just now by pulling words from *Music Teacher as Music Producer* (Randles, 2022):

subwoofers
vibe
diverse
overdriven
perform
mixer
gift
externalize

Talk about how when they pull random words from some external source it frees up their imagination to say new things. There are excellent resources for generating rhyming words; free website services use algorithms to generate possible rhyming words and phrases. Demonstrate a song that you have written that achieves this end. Here is the list of words that I pulled from *Music Teacher as Music Producer* along with some rhyming words/phrases that I pulled from RhymeZone:

subwoofers	the butcher	brown sugar	scrubwoman	much fuller
vibe	tribe	subscribe	prescribe	jibe
diverse	reverse	rehearse	immerse	disperse
overdriven	overridden	covert mission	power driven	over women
perform	transform	reform	warmth	storms
mixer	elixir	fix her	trickster	miss her
gift	adrift	shift	twist	pissed
externalize	verbalize	paternal lines	dull eyes	internal rhymes

Now, take the words and start thinking about how they go together. Look across columns and see what you can come up with. Here are some groupings of words that I put together just now as I'm writing this lesson:

the butcher . . . . . . pissed
vibe . . . . . . trickster
gift . . . . . . fix her
externalize . . . . . . reverse
diverse . . . . . . paternal lines
storms . . . . . . miss her
perform . . . . . . dull eyes
subwoofers . . . . . . internal rhymes

Comp some chords of songs that achieve excellent rhyming complexity by other artists. Have other students in the room perform some songs that they have written that achieve this end goal. Consult the "Dreaming and Scheming" SUNLIGHT section above. Here is my creative arrangement of the rhyming words that I pulled from *Music Teacher as Music Producer* and found rhyming words for what feels at least initially like a chorus:

You perform to her your song, bright eyes
While all around storms miss her
Subwoofers pump out internal rhymes
Maybe your gift will fix her
She plays the butcher, trickster, pissed
Maybe your gift will fix her

Play around with the song in a DAW, with an accompaniment instrument—the ones that hopefully are lining the walls of your room. Harmonic and/or melodic inspiration can come from MANY places. Practice in front of your students. Be vulnerable. Your imperfection will not be seen as a fault . . . it will exactly what you want to project . . . A CREATIVE PROCESS.

Have a student volunteer sit in on the drum set and play along as you comp chords on either guitar or keyboard and sing a song that accomplishes this idea well. Is there a song on the Billboard charts currently that might be inspirational as far as interesting rhyming words go? If there is, consider using it as you realize this lesson seed. Then, give them time to do what you just did. If they are working in songwriting workgroups, have the lyric-generating workgroup get to work doing what I just demonstrated for you here. You might also work on the chorus as a full group and then have individual groups write the verse lyrics. There so many ways to use these ideas. Choose a path and see where it leads.

Make a Plan for the Song (10–15 minutes or longer)
Give them some time to consider how they are going to develop the song. If they are group writing, they will have to agree on the scope and focus of the track. This could take a lot of time or not depending upon the group and how they work together. Help them only when they need your help; otherwise, stay out of the way. They come to you with diverse opinions and highly developed taste for what they like. Let them lead the way. In my experience, you best serve them by taking what they bring you and then through your musical and life experiences give them something back that amplifies their creative process. Bring something new to the table. Let their response to your ideas guide how you proceed to meet their needs.

Work on the Song (30 minutes or most likely much more)
Allow them time to work on the song. This can be complicated if they are working on band arrangements of the song in groups or if they are working in songwriting workgroups like the ones that I describe in Chapter 10. If they are working on the

song individually, you will have a different series of considerations. Help when you need to help. Get out of the way when you need to get out of the way. You can sometimes help by demonstrating techniques that would help all of the groups locate songs better. Positivity needs to be the mantra in your classroom for students to feel safe trying out song ideas and stylistic pathways. Model singing and performing in front of them. Celebrate their work it progresses.

Perform (Another class period)
Depending on how many groups/individuals you want to perform in class, you will have to leave time for all students who want to perform. Work with students with severe performance anxiety. Create alternate performance opportunities. They could record their performances and submit them electronically to you from home. You could make the band collaborate that way as well, adding their parts to the recording video/audio. If you have a small performance stage in your class, this would be an excellent opportunity to utilize it. This is meant to be an advanced lesson seed, so these performances might very well be more put together than earlier lesson seed performances. This might not necessarily be the case, though. Celebrate their success, be positive, and provide them with a clear path to what they will need to improve—basically, they will need to continue practicing the process. Let their student peers be the first to provide feedback. Provide guidelines for the feedback: for example, give one positive comment and a comment that they could use to improve by (Kratus, 2016).

Record (Another class period or multiple class periods)
Record their songs. You need to help them create the album version of their song (as well as performed versions of the songs live in class). Follow the procedures that I lay out in Chapter 10 for recording a song as a part of a songwriting workgroup culture. Critically listening to their recordings for production assistance will help them develop their craft. You can be meticulous and professional about recording or not depending upon your expertise with recording arts. Check out *Sound Production for the Emerging Music Teacher Producer* (Randles, Aponte, and Johnson, forthcoming) for help on making your tracks sound better. An audio interface with an XY-configured microphone pattern would capture the sound of a room well. If you have a computer at each station that your small groups are in, you could multitrack-record their songs.

Modifications for Learners

Works in Progress
The reality of creative processes is that sometimes our work takes a long time to finish. Sometimes we are not happy with a particular work until years, even decades later. You can't exactly give them a decade extension for finishing their work! Be that as it may,

you will need to be forgiving sometimes when they are not finished when the deadline comes and goes. Some of my most brilliant students never met their deadlines in class, only to finally hit their stride with their songs after they graduated or had moved on past my class. Don't forget that songwriting is something that you want to give them during the contact that you have with them, knowing that they will continue practicing well after their time with you. It is a marathon that you are starting them on, not a sprint.

Recording at Home Modification
For those of your students with performance anxiety, allow them to record their performances at home on their phones or with their computers with DAWs. Many times their desire to make use of this modification has nothing to do with their interest in your class or the lesson but everything to do with their anxiety toward performing in front of their peers. Allow them to record at home. Doing so still means that they are developing a connection to the real world of people making music in the world. They could come around to the possibility of performing in front of their peers when they develop a bit more confidence. You should encourage them to share their videos with the class as a way of encouraging their live performance prowess.

Others (Including You) Perform with Them Modification
If performing the accompaniment is too difficult a task for them, others (including you) can always sit in and perform an accompaniment for their singing. This is a widely used accommodation by me when I am working with younger students. It is not easy to play an instrument and sing at the same time. Remember, though, as you are working on developing this skill in your students that singing and playing together is wrapped up in quite a lot of cultural capital. They will gain skills that can last a lifetime with these abilities. Encourage them to do it themselves, but help them when they need some help.

Learning Outcomes

- Write a song utilizing random words obtained from a particular text source.
- Work out an arrangement, either solo or within a group setting of the song.
- Identify how the lyrics flow from a creative process of discovering rhyming words.
- Identify some influential artists who have done this in their own songwriting.
- Perform a song that they have written that employs this writing strategy.
- Record a song that they have written that employs this writing strategy.

Assessment Considerations

Informal Assessment. How did they respond to the lesson? Were there any gains that are difficult to categorize in a rubric? Sometimes lessons don't look like a success on paper, but when you gauge the interest and enthusiasm in the room, accomplishment and student achievement can clearly be seen. The success of a lesson seed on being and becoming a songwriter who can write on experiences that relate to other people or things can be equally gauged by how well they achieved the end goal of writing as "others" and how they felt about the experience. Do they feel like they could do it again? Did they enjoy the process? What will they do better next time?

There are times when I have taught a lesson that didn't work very well with a class as a whole, but one student made massive gains that inspired the rest of the class to up their game in some way. Be careful with how you wield the assessment hammer. Your primary goal is to inspire them to continue writing, recording, and performing their songs. Your assessments should be formative and fair enough that they want to continue practicing their craft. These are tricky waters to navigate. Be careful.

Formal Assessment. Here is a rubric that you might adapt and use as a way of helping your students develop their songwriting craft:

While I have focused this rubric on lyric writing, musical interest, and creativity, you might focus this lesson on any number of musical qualities and characteristics. Everything is on the table for you as an artist teacher to utilize. If you are a teacher in North America and you want these rubric focal points to be specific National Content Standard areas, you can make that happen. The same thing is true if you are working within the Australian Curriculum and you want to align these assessments with your national assessments areas.

Criteria	Ratings					Pts
This criterion is linked to a Learning Outcome Lyric Writing	**4 to >3.0 pts** **Expert** I love that your lyricism is approaching professional quality	**3 to >2.0 pts** **Practitioner** I like that you demonstrated very good lyric writing technique (including many strategies discussed in class)	**2 to >1.0 pts** **Apprentice** I'm concerned that your lyric writing isn't very good	**1 to >0.0 pts** **Novice** What's up? Your lyric writing is really difficult to follow	**0 pts** **No Marks**	4 pts
This criterion is linked to a Learning Outcome Musical Interest	**4 to >3.0 pts** **Expert** I love that you displayed almost professional levels of musical interest	**3 to >2.0 pts** **Practitioner** I like the level of musical interest that you conveyed in your song—it's very good	**2 to >1.0 pts** **Apprentice** I'm concerned with how many errors showed up in your song	**1 to >0.0 pts** **Novice** What's up? Your song seems lacking in musical interest quality	**0 pts** **No Marks**	4 pts

Criteria	Ratings					Pts
This criterion is linked to a Learning Outcome Creativity	**4 to >3.0 pts Expert** I love that the creativity you displayed could end up on a recording	**3 to >2.0 pts Practitioner** I like that you displayed a very good sense of creativity	**2 to >1.0 pts Apprentice** I'm concerned that your performance did not display very much creativity	**1 to >0.0 pts Novice** What's up? There was really no sense of creativity in your music	**0 pts No Marks**	4 pts
Total Points: 12						

Further Reading/Resources

- Check out Jeff Tweedy, *How to Write One Song* (New York: Dutton, 2020).
- *RhymeZone Online Rhyming Dictionary*: https://www.rhymezone.com/.
- Listen to *The Marshall Mathers LP* (2000) by Eminem.
- Listen to *All Eyez On Me* (1996) by 2Pac.

Cut-Up Technique(s)

Materials

- A room full of accompaniment instruments including but not limited to: guitar, keyboard, bass guitar, drum kit, drum sequencer, ukulele, and so forth. You should fill your space with unique instruments as well as these typical accompaniment instruments. The stranger the better.
- Fill your space with unique effects pedals, processors, and synthesizers. These can be expensive, so take advantage of less expensive digital approximations when you can.
- A playlist full of songs that you have written and recorded in the past.
- A rhyming dictionary.
- Examples of lyrics that either do not rhyme or rhyme in strange and unique ways.
- Percussion instruments of diverse variety and background.

Context

This is an advanced lesson that should be used to extend your style and compositional process to new territory lyrically. This lesson is designed to push students out of their comfort zones with regard to rhyming. This lesson should be used when they have written songs from object writing sessions and within songwriting workgroups. This is a lesson seed that focuses on stretching their conception of what rhyming accomplishes in the lyric writing process. Jeff Tweedy in *How to Write a Song* (2020) motivates readers to resist predictable rhymes by figuring out how to use seemingly unrelated rhyming words in song lyrics.

WATER: John Lennon's Practice: "You've Got to Hide Your Love Away"

John Lennon has been called a "mercurial figure,"[4] his creative bursts ranging from highly experimental to art rock to songs that were "moody and enigmatic," to more personal works that provided listeners into what he was feeling. Here his songwriting process for "Hide Your Love Away" is described by blogger Keith Hatschek:[5]

> Taking a page from Dylan's approach to songwriting, "You've Got to Hide Your Love Away" uses four basic chords learned by nearly every beginning guitarist: G, D, C, and F. Lennon plays his acoustic guitar part using a Framus 12-string and keeps the G note (first string, third fret) as a common pedal tone between the three main chords (G, D, C) during the song's four brief verses. This makes the D chord a suspended chord, often referred to as a D4 or Dsus4. Whenever he uses the F chord, he makes it an F9 chord by keeping his pinky finger on the same G note.
>
> With this simple technique, Lennon ties together the song's harmonic underpinning neatly and sets up the points in the song where he will stray away from that high G to play a regular D with its chordal third, F♯, tweaking the ear of the listener (e.g. at the end of the song's first verse, at the turnaround after he sings "Feeling two foot small," the chord helps propel the listener right into the second verse).
>
> To provide variety, with economy, Lennon uses one of his favorite techniques at the end of the second and fourth verses to build up tension leading into the punchline and title of the song, which is repeated twice each time. He plays the normal D chord and walks his own 12-string part with Paul's bass down from D-C-B-A, building tension to lead into the song's chorus. It's reported that Pete Shotton, an original member of Lennon's first group, The Quarrymen, was present when Lennon was writing the song at home and suggested he add the emphatic "Hey!" at the start of each line in the chorus. It is an attention-grabbing technique that adds an emotional punch. As for the chords used in the chorus, it's just G, C, and D, but he varies the D chord by using both the D4 from the verse and the D2 versions. It's a simple but effective embellishment, especially on the chime-like 12-string he favored for many of his more acoustic-oriented tracks.
>
> The rest of the group plays understated but perfectly appropriate background parts. Ringo adds a snare part tastefully played with brushes, as well as tambourine which comes in on the second verse and stays steadily on what is essentially

the backbeat for the remainder of this triple meter song. In the brief choruses, he plays a single maraca to give added texture. Paul's bass is way back in the mix and in a nod to the emotional oomph that the lyrics provide, simply play root notes for the folk-sounding piece. George contributes a tasty, understated nylon string guitar part, which beautifully doubles the chorus melody an octave lower, adding subtle power to the title lyric. Although Lennon played harmonica well, the decision was made to not echo Dylan's instrumentation too closely and the band decided on a double tracked flute part to take the song home, performed by studio musician, Johnnie Scott, who played a regular flute onto John's vocal track after his part concluded, then overdubbed an alto flute an octave lower to give the outro its wistful, folk-like feeling. (Remember, the Beatles had only four recording tracks available at this stage of their career.)

Finally, unlike the polished, in your face, three-part vocal harmonies featured on many other Beatles' tracks of this era, "You've Got to Hide Your Love Away" features only John singing with a small amount of effects on his voice. Notably, his performance's emotional coefficient trumps the imperfect break in his voice during the last verse when he sings, "Gather round all you clowns," a simple-to-fix edit easily achieved with a drop in, but the flaw was left intentionally to maintain the integrity and emotion of his performance.

The lyrics of the song, it is rumored, were about The Beatles manager Brian Epstein, who was a closeted gay man. When you hear the song now, think of the sad story that is behind the lyrics.

SUNLIGHT: Cut-Up Technique in Literature

Though neither ever abandoned the ballad, it's significant that two of the 1960s best songwriters, John Lennon and Bob Dylan, drew much of the inspiration for their more experimental songs from poetry—Lennon from an older nonsense tradition in English literature exemplified by Lewis Carroll, and Dylan from T. S. Eliot. The strict realist mold that dominated fiction and poetry for over 100 years broke open in the late nineteenth century with symbolist French poets like Arthur Rimbaud, Stéphane Mallarmé, and Charles Baudelaire.[6] Songwriters started to come on board with this style of writing in the 1960s.

Another form of modernist literature developed in the 1950s and 1960s—"darker and weirder,"[7] though no less traceable to a literary source: William S. Burroughs's surrealist cut-up technique, which he developed with artist Brion Gysin. Cut-up writing is a "montage technique" from painting applied to "words on a page." Words and phrases are cut from newspapers and magazines and the fragments rearranged at random. David Bowie was a musical artist who liked to employ this technique. In a 2008 interview, Bowie explained his use of cut-ups:[8] "You write down a paragraph or two describing different subjects, creating a kind of 'story ingredients' list,

I suppose, and then cut the sentences into four or five-word sections, mix 'em up and reconnect them." The technique allows songwriters, he says, to "get some pretty interesting idea combinations," even if they "have a craven need not to lose control." Bowie did much to advance the genre of "art rock" with his application of avant-garde techniques to conventional song forms and rock 'n' roll.

Lesson Time

The main thrust of this seed is taken from Jeff Tweedy's *How to Write One Song* (2020) and centers on writing lyrically from a list of nonsensical words and making them work together a rhyme. This lesson seed will likely emerge over several classes. However, I have given you some time constraints that could be applied to one class session. Make a list of words that you would like to work with. Generate more words based on those initial words from a rhyming dictionary. Then, take the exercise to the next level by cutting the words into tiny fragments. Lay the word in paper fragment form out on the table. Look at what you can do to piece together a different combination of them to tell the best story that is now available to you since you removed the prior connections that you had made regarding how they are related. You will find that something magical happens when you do this.

Lesson Instructions

Preparation (10 minutes)

Gather the class and give them a short lesson on selecting words from a book, newspaper, blog, Tweet, Instagram post, or some other place. Use an example list. Here's one that I just created just now by pulling words from *To Create* (Randles, 2020):

renaissance
actualization
inclusive
originality
goodness
Telecaster
rock 'n' roll
energy

Talk about how when they pull random words from some external source it frees up their imagination to say new things. There are excellent resources for generating rhyming words; free website services use algorithms to generate possible rhyming words and phrases. Demonstrate a song that you have written that achieves this end. Here is the list of words that I pulled from *Music Teacher as Music Producer* along with some rhyming words/phrases that I pulled from RhymeZone:

renaissance	response	wants	props	chops
actualization	lateralization	naturalization	actual occasion	entire nations
inclusive	elusive	use of	produce in	seduces
originality	personality	humanity	pluralities	vitality
goodness	sureness	madness	lures us	tour bus
Telecaster	develops faster	forever after	clever actor	fell faster
rock 'n' roll	lock and load	please enroll	comic role	stop and go
energy	memory	synergy	treachery	together we

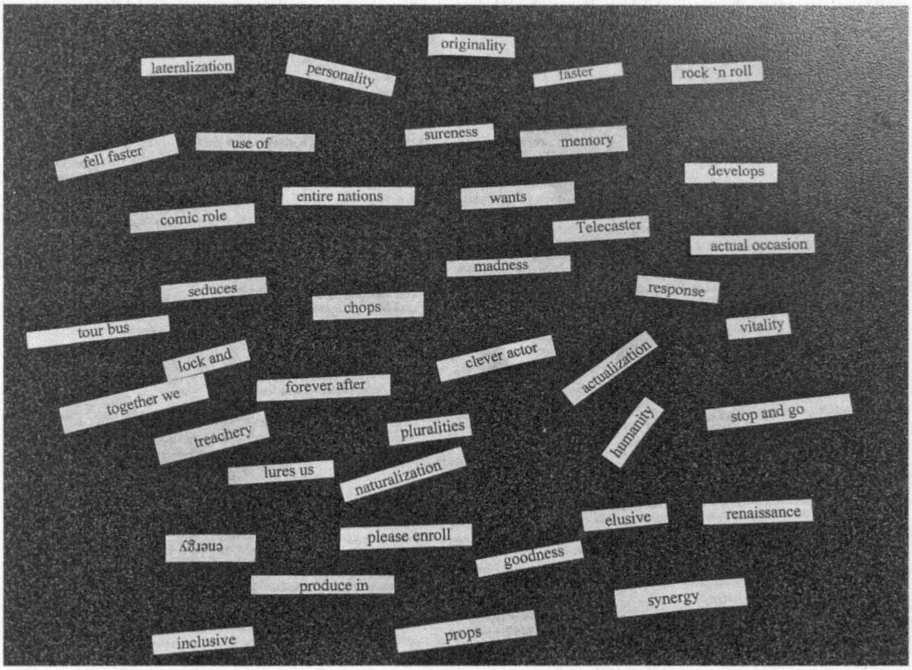

Figure 13.1 Cut-up technique

Now, take the words and print a piece of paper with each word written down. Look across columns and see what you can come up with (see Figure 13.1).

Here are some groupings of words that I put together just now as I'm writing this lesson:

together we . . . stop and go
rock 'n' roll
comic role seduces
forever after

inclusive . . . synergy
please enroll
clever actor . . . wants
humanity
actualization . . . lures us
renaissance
originality . . . tour bus
response

Comp some chords of songs that achieve excellent rhyming complexity by other artists. Have other students in the room perform some songs that they have written that achieve this end goal. Consult the "Dreaming and Scheming" SUNLIGHT section in a prior lesson seed. Here is my creative arrangement of the rhyming words that I pulled from *Music Teacher as Music Producer* and found rhyming words for what feels at least initially like a pair of verses:

Together we stop and we go
Till forever after? We don't know
A comic role seduces
It needs us to enroll

Actualization it lures us
To the originality tour bus
Clever actors desired
Seizing all of our trust

Play around with the song in a DAW, with an accompaniment instrument—the ones that hopefully are lining the walls of your room. Harmonic and/or melodic inspiration can come from MANY places. Practice in front of your students. Be vulnerable. Your imperfection will not be seen as a fault . . . it will exactly what you want to project . . . A CREATIVE PROCESS.

Have a student volunteer sit in on the drum set and play along as you comp chords on either guitar or keyboard and sing a song that accomplishes this idea well. Is there a David Bowie, John Lennon, or Bob Dylan song that you think might inspire them today? If there is, consider using it as you realize this lesson seed. Then, give them time to do what you just did. If they are working in songwriting workgroups, have the lyric-generating workgroup get to work doing what I just demonstrated for you here. You might also work on the verses as a full group and then have individual groups write the chorus lyrics. Maybe you can have the class agree upon the primary narrative takeaway of the song up front. Maybe you can develop a feel for the song within a DAW environment by identifying some reference tracks—songs and/or sounds that you would like your song to sound like.

Make a Plan for the Song (10–15 minutes or longer)
Give them some time to consider how they are going to develop the song. If they are group writing, they will have to agree on the scope and focus of the track. If you did not establish this as a large group, and you are giving more creative freedom to individual groups, then each group will have to make a plan for their song during this time. This could take a lot of time or not depending upon the group and how they work together. Help them only when they need your help; otherwise, stay out of the way. They come to you with diverse opinions and highly developed taste for what they like. Let them lead the way. In my experience, you best serve them by taking what they bring you and then through your musical and life experiences give them something back that amplifies their creative process. Bring something new to the table. Let their response to your ideas guide how you proceed to meet their needs.

Work on the Song (30 minutes or most likely much more)
Allow them time to work on the song. This can be complicated if they are working on band arrangements in groups or if they are working in songwriting workgroups like the ones that I describe in Chapter 10. If they are working on the song individually, you will have a different series of considerations. Help when you need to help. Get out of the way when you need to get out of the way. You can sometimes help by demonstrating techniques that would help all of the groups locate songs better. Positivity needs to be the mantra in your classroom for students to feel safe trying out song ideas and stylistic pathways. Model singing and performing in front of them. Celebrate their work as it progresses.

Perform (Another class period)
Depending on how many groups/individuals you want to perform in class, you will have to leave time for all students who want to perform. Work with the ones with severe performance anxiety. Create alternate performance opportunities. They could record their performances and submit them electronically to you from home. You could make the band collaborate that way as well, adding their parts to the recording video/audio. If you have a small performance stage in your class, this would be an excellent opportunity to utilize it. Celebrate their success, be positive, and provide them with a clear path to what they will need to improve—basically, they will need to continue practicing the process. Let their student peers be the first to provide feedback. Provide guidelines for the feedback: for example, give one positive comment and a comment that they could use to improve by (Kratus, 2016).

Record (Another class period or multiple class periods)
Record their songs. You need to help them create the album version of their work (as well as performed versions of the songs live in class). Follow the procedures that I lay out in Chapter 10 for recording a song as a part of a songwriting workgroup culture. Critically listening to their recordings for production assistance

will help them develop their craft. You can be meticulous and professional about recording or not depending upon your expertise with recording arts. Check out *Sound Production for the Emerging Music Teacher Producer* (Randles, Aponte, and Johnson, forthcoming) for help on making your tracks sound better. An audio interface with an XY-configured microphone pattern would capture the sound of a room well. If you have a computer at each station that your small groups are in, you could multitrack-record their songs.

Modifications for Learners

Works in Progress

The reality of creative processes is that sometimes our work takes a long time to finish. Sometimes we are not happy with a particular work until years, even decades later. You can't exactly give them a decade extension for finishing their work! Be that as it may, you will need to be forgiving sometimes when they are not finished when the deadline comes and goes. Some of my most brilliant students never met their deadlines in class, only to finally hit their stride with their songs after they graduated or had moved on past my class. Don't forget that songwriting is something that you want to give them during the contact that you have with them, knowing that they will continue practicing well after their time with you. It is a marathon that you are starting them on, not a sprint.

Recording at Home Modification

For those of your students with performance anxiety, allow them to record their performances at home on their phones or with their computers with DAWs. Many times their desire to make use of this modification has nothing to do with their interest in your class or the lesson but everything to do with their anxiety toward performing in front of their peers. Allow them to record at home. Doing so still means that they are developing a connection to the real world of people making music in the world. They could come around to the possibility of performing in front of their peers when they develop a bit more confidence. You should encourage them to share their videos with the class as a way of encouraging their live performance prowess.

Others (Including You) Perform with Them Modification

If performing the accompaniment is too difficult a task for them, others (including you) can always sit in and perform an accompaniment for their singing. This is a widely used accommodation by me when I am working with younger students. It is not easy to play an instrument and sing at the same time. Remember, though, as you are working on developing this skill in your students that singing and playing together is wrapped up in quite a lot of cultural capital. They will gain skills that can last a lifetime with these abilities. Encourage them to do it themselves, but help them when they need some help.

Learning Outcomes

- Write a song utilizing random words obtained from a particular text source that are then cut up and reorganized as a part of the creative process.
- Work out an arrangement, either solo or within a group setting of the song.
- Identify how the lyrics flow from a creative process of discovering rhyming words utilizing a rhyming dictionary.
- Identify some influential artists who have done this in their own songwriting processes.
- Perform a song that they have written that employs this writing strategy.
- Record a song that they have written that employs this writing strategy.

Assessment Considerations

Informal Assessment. How did they respond to the lesson? Were there any gains that are difficult to categorize in a rubric? Sometimes lessons don't look like a success on paper, but when you gauge the interest and enthusiasm in the room, accomplishment and student achievement can clearly be seen. The success of a lesson seed on utilizing cut-up techniques during the creative process should center on how it positively benefited someone or even a small sub-section of the class. Did any of them find the technique liberating? Did anyone really enjoy the process? How would they adjust the process next time to make it work even better for them?

There are times when I have taught a lesson that didn't work very well with a class as a whole, but one student made massive gains that inspired the rest of the class to up their game in some way. Be careful with how you wield the assessment hammer. Your primary goal is to inspire them to continue writing, recording, and performing their songs. Your assessments should be formative and fair enough that they want to continue practicing their craft. These are tricky waters to navigate. Be careful.

Formal Assessment. Here is a rubric that you might adapt and use as a way of helping your students develop their songwriting craft:

Criteria	Ratings					Pts
This criterion is linked to a Learning Outcome Lyric Writing	**4 to >3.0 pts** **Expert** I love that your lyricism is approaching professional quality	**3 to >2.0 pts** **Practitioner** I like that you demonstrated very good lyric writing technique (including many strategies discussed in class)	**2 to >1.0 pts** **Apprentice** I'm concerned that your lyric writing isn't very good	**1 to >0.0 pts** **Novice** What's up? Your lyric writing is really difficult to follow	**0 pts** **No Marks**	4 pts

Criteria	Ratings					Pts
This criterion is linked to a Learning Outcome Musical Interest	**4 to >3.0 pts Expert** I love that you displayed almost professional levels of musical interest	**3 to >2.0 pts Practitioner** I like the level of musical interest that you conveyed in your song—it's very good	**2 to >1.0 pts Apprentice** I'm concerned with how many errors showed up in your song	**1 to >0.0 pts Novice** What's up? Your song seems lacking in musical interest quality	**0 pts No Marks**	4 pts
This criterion is linked to a Learning Outcome Creativity	**4 to >3.0 pts Expert** I love that the creativity you displayed could end up on a recording	**3 to >2.0 pts Practitioner** I like that you displayed a very good sense of creativity	**2 to >1.0 pts Apprentice** I'm concerned that your performance did not display very much creativity	**1 to >0.0 pts Novice** What's up? There was really no sense of creativity in your music	**0 pts No Marks**	4 pts
Total Points: 12						

While I have focused this rubric on lyric writing, musical interest, and creativity, you might focus this lesson on any number of musical qualities and characteristics. Everything is on the table for you as an artist teacher to utilize. If you are a teacher in North America and you want these rubric focal points to be specific National Content Standard areas, you can make that happen. The same thing is true if you are working within the Australian Curriculum and you want to align these assessments with your national assessments areas.

Further Reading/Resources

- Jeff Tweedy, *How to Write One Song* (New York: Dutton, 2020).
- *RhymeZone Online Rhyming Dictionary*: https://www.rhymezone.com/.
- Listen to *The Rise and Fall of Ziggy Stardust and the Spiders from Mars* (1972) for inspiration.
- Listen to *Blood on the Tracks* (1975) by Bob Dylan.
- Read "The Waste Land" (1922) by T. S. Eliot.

OUTRO

14
A Whole New World of Original Songs

SUNLIGHT: Viktor Frankl and Living a Meaningful Life

Viktor Frankl was an influential Austrian psychologist who survived the Holocaust (1942–1945), being detained in Auschwitz and three other camps over that period. By the end of the war, his pregnant wife, his parents, and his brother had been murdered. Only he and his sister survived from his immediate family. When he was able to escape the war, he wrote his most influential work titled *Man's Search for Meaning* (1946/1985). Here are some excerpts that might help us think about songwriting:

> We can discover this meaning of life in three different ways: (1) by creating a work or doing a deed; (2) by experiencing something or encountering someone; and (3) by the attitude we take toward unavoidable suffering. The first, by way of achievement or accomplishment, is quite obvious. The second and third need further elaboration.
>
> *The Meaning of Love*
> Love is the only way to grasp another human being in the innermost core of his personality. No one can become fully aware of the essence of another human being unless he loves him. By his love he is enabled to see the essential traits and features of the beloved person; and even more, he sees that which is potential in him, which is not yet actualized but yet ought to be actualized. Furthermore, by his love, the loving person enables the beloved person to actualize these potentialities. By making him aware of what he can be and of what he should become, he makes these potentialities come true. . . .
>
> The third way of finding a meaning in life is by suffering.
>
> *The Meaning of Suffering*
> We must never forget that we may also find meaning in life even when confronted with a hopeless situation, when facing a fate that cannot be changed. For what then matters is to bear witness to the uniquely human potential at its best, which is to transform a personal tragedy into triumph, to turn one's predicament into a human achievement. When we are no longer able to change a situation—just think of an incurable disease such as inoperable cancer—we are challenged to change ourselves.

Growing Songwriting. Clint Randles, Oxford University Press. © Oxford University Press 2024.
DOI: 10.1093/oso/9780197693216.003.0014

In songwriting we find an activity that leverages our capacity to do all three of these things. We create works, share them with the world, and ultimately change ourselves through the daily work of turning our failures into opportunities to learn more about ourselves and others. The topic of suffering deserves more time than I can treat it here.

WATER: Stevie Wonder and Spirituality

Rolling Stone magazine lists Stevie Wonder as the tenth greatest songwriter of all time.[1] His longevity and enduring qualities make him an excellent source of inspiration:

> "I feel there is so much through music that can be said," Wonder once observed, and the songs he's been writing for a half-century have more than lived up to that idea. Whether immersing himself in social commentary ("Higher Ground," "Living for the City"), unabashed sentimentality ("You Are the Sunshine of My Life," "I Just Called to Say I Love You"), jubilant love ("Signed, Sealed, Delivered I'm Yours") or gritty disses ("You Haven't Done Nothin'"), Wonder has consistently tapped into the sum of human emotions and happenings. He was already writing his own songs as a childhood prodigy at Motown during the Sixties (including the 1966 smash "Uptight (It's Alright)."
>
> As he hit his artistic stride on albums like 1972's *Talking Book* and 1973's *Innervisions*, he used the recording studio as his palette to create groundbreaking works of soulful self-discovery. "Like a painter, I get my inspiration from experiences that can be painful or beautiful," he has said. "I always start from a feeling of profound gratitude—you know, 'Only by the grace of God am I here'— and write from there. Most songwriters are inspired by an inner voice and spirit." Combined with melodies that can be jubilant, funky or simply gorgeous, Wonder's songs are so enduring that they've been covered by everyone from Sinatra to the Backstreet Boys.[2]

WATER: U2 and Longevity

Bono, the Edge, Larry Mullen Jr., and Adam Clayton have been a band with top-selling albums for four decades—the only band to ever achieve this status, earning twenty-two Grammy awards to date. Their songwriting centers on spiritual longing and finding inner peace. The band was formed in 1976 when Larry Mullen Jr. put an advertisement on the wall in their high school—Mount Temple Comprehensive School (MTCS)—and Bono and the Edge replied. I spoke with Don Moxman, their high school history teacher at MTCS when I was visiting Dublin to present a paper at St. Patrick's College several years ago. He said that they sounded terrible when they started. Larry was the only one who could play an instrument. Since the music teacher wouldn't let them use the music room, they had to practice in his history classroom.

Within four years, they had signed with Island Records and released their debut album, *Boy* (1980). Subsequent work such as their first UK number-one album, *War* (1983), and the singles "Sunday Bloody Sunday" and "Pride (In the Name of Love)" helped establish U2's reputation as a politically and socially conscious group. By the mid-1980s, they had become renowned globally for their live act, highlighted by their performance at Live Aid in 1985. The group's fifth album, *The Joshua Tree* (1987), made them international superstars and was their greatest critical and commercial success. Topping music charts around the world, it produced their only number-one singles in the United States to date: "With or without You" and "I Still Haven't Found What I'm Looking For."

Finding Your Way

So what do you do now? Assess your situation. What do you know? What can you observe in your classroom? In your community? How are your own songwriting skills? These questions and their answers will push you into new territory. The purpose of this book is to grow songwriting, both as a curricular offering and as an activity that is well known and established as a pathway for humanity to engage in the practice of living meaningful lives. With our works, with our love, and through our suffering we can give back to the planet more than we have taken. These are serious matters.

In order to leverage the benefits that engaging in ongoing creative practice in music provides, music educators need to create an alternate universe, a place for songwriting to grow. The idea of making music in school in more of the ways that people make music in the world is big and beautiful. Why can't we diversify the curriculum to include more playing by ear, more contemporary instrumentation, and more small group collaboration? There are technological ways to make these ideas more achievable (Randles, 2022). However, the pedagogical ideas presented here throughout this book can happen in places with no technology.

Tech or No Tech

I gave a research presentation to an international music education audience in Turkey this past week, focusing on *Music Teacher as Music Producer* (2022) and ideas regarding the role of technology in facilitating an expanded vision of what music education can be. At the end of my talk a local music teacher from Sivas, Turkey, shared about how difficult it is to get these types of technologies in Turkey because of their cost and availability. This has challenged me to think about how a Music Teacher as Music Producer classroom can work in terms of very limited resources. I feel that I have a duty to share what is possible with technology, so that people can be inspired to explore this end of possibility. But

I feel an urge now to consider what these pedagogies might look like with no technology.

You have heard in various ways across the pages of this book how some of the greatest and most influential songwriters go about their daily work. MANY of them utilize songwriting journals, mainly paper and pencil versions, to collect their life's work. That is pretty low-tech. They learn how to perform their songs by accompanying their singing on a keyboard or guitar. They share their work with members of their collaborative communities. This leads to further collaboration where members of bands add their own flavor to the creative process, and songs become the synthesis of multiple creative minds (Gardner, 2011) working together.

A Lowell Mason Spirit

You need to adopt a pioneer spirit, the kind that Lowell Mason must have had when he played a key role in leading a movement to make music a school subject in Boston in the 1830s (Mark & Gary, 2007). The first thing that you can appropriate from Mason is his vision. Public school in the United States was relatively new in the 1830s. While educational systems had been created that featured music as an essential part of the education of boys (and sometimes girls) as far back as 400 BC in Greece (Mark & Gary, 2007) and China (Fung, 2018), as of the early 1830s it had not been incorporated into our collective idea of the education of the masses. That changed when leadership in Boston moved to justify a place for it. They needed to capture the curiosity of the multitudes in Boston to make this happen. They did that by suggesting that music education could help the quality of singing in church services. It worked!

Secondly, Mason was strategic. His persistence was a vital part of our records of how he went about leading a movement to create a place for school music education in Boston. He organized performances of his boys' choir for the school board (Mark & Gary, 2007). He followed these performances with discussions about how singing was good for one's moral development and great for the overall health of the body (intellectually and physically). That body-and-soul way of thinking about health struck a chord in the hearts of the public as well as the school board. There was no refusing this choirmaster. The proof was in the sound and the good spirit that those performances displayed.

Thirdly, the father of school music education in the United States was able to demonstrate his pedagogical skills as a music teacher. Mason walked the walk as much as he talked the talk. He has been described as possessing a P. T. Barnum sort of circus-promoter personality. When he spoke, people naturally wanted to listen. Reports from the Boston Musical Gazette's performances of Mason's 400-member choirs indicate that the quality of their singing was profoundly impressive to everyone in attendance. People could not believe that the choir progressed at the rate that they did. Once music was adopted as a core subject in August 28, 1838, Mason was able to demonstrate mastery in performance in a short period. The public and administration felt that the incorporation of music into the curriculum was well worth their financial investment.

Baseline Musicianship

I write this book at the end of the COVID-19 pandemic. The open-mic night community that I am a part of here in my hometown stopped meeting for a period of a little over a year and a half. Since things have started up again, I have tried to remember what it was like to not have this creative outlet in my life. I have observed the camaraderie that comes from peoples' ability to share their music with each other. My friends in this space live for the ten minutes they get every week to stand up in front of a group of mostly friends but also some strangers and perform cover songs and original songs that convey a sense of where they are at this moment in time. It is a release that is healthy and very much necessary. I can't help thinking that the world would have much better social/emotional health if they could only do something like this regularly.

What would it mean to society if the baseline for musicianship was covering your favorite songs and writing your own original songs based on the sonic qualities of your musical heroes? So every person's experience of school music education would include opportunities to make the music that they most admired, to see themselves as people who not only appreciate music, but as people who ARE music makers. If more people saw themselves as part of the club, then more people would want to support the activities of the club. If everyone was a member of the club, there would be no need to justify the existence of the club to everyone since EVERYONE is a member. There is already buy-in. No need to have to convince people of why the thing that they love, the essential part of their lives, is important. It just is at that point. Professional orchestras and concert bands start to look more necessary as well, as a natural outgrowth of people who see themselves as musical.

What is music, and is it important? What makes people love it (or not)? In my experience, you have to teach people to not like music, as all of us come wired to be curious by it. I mean to say that we all love music until someone teaches that we really don't. Our curiosity with organized sound is either fed the right way and it grows, or it is stymied and it decays. No one sets out to destroy curiosity pertaining to particular points of interest in people—at least in most cases. However, by focusing our attention on less potent aspects of music, we do tend sow our seeds in less-generative soil. We need to embrace the questions that this paragraph started with and focus on the creativities that emerge from their answers. It is there that we will find the most high-yielding soil from which to grow our plants (thinking of the metaphor that is featured throughout this book). Music educators need to focus much attention on the baseline musicianship that we want to grow.

SUNSHINE: George Washington Carver's Focus on Science and the Arts

I gleaned the following story of wisdom and innovation from the Henry Ford Museum in Detroit[3]. You can see a Lowell Mason kind of spirit in the life of one of the greatest scientists of all time:

Throughout George W. Carver's life, he balanced two interests and talents that may seem at odds—the creative arts and the natural sciences. Skills of observation, experimentation, replication, and communication applied to both art and science, making Carver as comfortable in the sciences as in the arts.

> From a child I had an inordinate desire for knowledge,
> and especially music, painting, flowers, and the sciences.
> —George W. Carver

The Artist's Eye, the Scientist's Hands, and the Possibilities of Plants

Understanding plants required Carver to collect them, as he had during his childhood, and relocate them from their natural habitats to conservatories. Carver used weeding tools to extract specimens with roots intact, necessary for substantial study. While living in Kansas, Carver amassed a "collection of about five hundred plants [housed] in a neat conservatory adjoining the residence of his employer." His knowledge of plants translated into practical uses, particularly as natural remedies or as patent medicine ingredients. The fledgling botanist held the secrets that purveyors of patent medicines sought as they concocted cure-alls from organics and marketed them to consumers seeking relief from maladies.

In fact, one of the growth industries of the late nineteenth century related to innovation in plant science: plant fibers had commercial uses. In 1880, both the Walter A. Wood Harvesting Machine Company and the Deering Harvester Company began selling a self-tying binder that used twine rather than metal to tie bundles of grain. Not to be outdone, McCormick Company put its binder on the market in 1881. A blend of sisal and henequen, both plants in the same family as the yucca, became the preferred material in twine. Carver likely encountered farmers and harvest crews with twine binders in the years he spent homesteading 160 acres near Beeler, Kansas, in the late 1880s. He later recalled that he based his painting *Yucca and Cactus* on his memories of the Western plains.

Carver's mentor at Iowa State, Louis H. Pammel, had documented yucca pollination in a report on flower pollination. It appeared in the 1891 report of the Iowa State Horticulture Society. Carver researched the cultivation and management of cacti and presented his findings at the 1892 meeting. Both these factors could have inspired him to paint the larger-than-life-size *Yucca and Cactus*. This painting received the first major public viewing of his work, appearing alongside that of other

Iowa artists in the Iowa State Building during the Columbian Exposition in 1893. It received an honorable mention.[4]

Teaching Farm Families and Children

Carver moved to the Tuskegee Institute in 1896. He illustrated his messages to black farmers with his own drawings of plant physiology, cultivation techniques, and soil treatments. These helped him convince farmers to change their farming practices with a goal toward improving their standard of living. Carver believed poor farmers could accomplish this by raising crops and livestock that could help them vary their diet from the routine "meat, meal, and molasses" that many poor farm families ate, and that would provide additional marketable products.

Carver advocated for careful observation of nature throughout his career, joining a larger movement supporting nature study. In Progressive Nature Study, a pamphlet published in 1897, Carver explained that "the study of Nature . . . is the only true method that leads up to a clear understanding of the great natural principles which surround every branch of business in which we may engage." He encouraged teachers to provide each student a slip of plain white or manila paper so they could make sketches. Neatness mattered—and proved no easy feat given the lack of pencils with erasers. As Carver explained, the grading scale "only applies to neatness, as some will naturally draw better than others." Encouraging students to explore and document their natural surroundings increased self-awareness but could also result in ways to diversify farm incomes.[5]

The Power of Collaboration

Every student who comes to our classrooms is a single puzzle piece in the larger puzzle that is your class. Each life interacts with all the others and the sum total of the pieces creates the full picture. You cannot have any idea what the puzzle will look like by looking at one piece! You have to put them together to see the big picture. Our music classrooms work like this. The process of seeing the puzzle pieces come together, sometimes with our help and sometimes without our help, is endlessly rewarding to be a part of. Just like when you open a puzzle and lay it out on the table in your living room, and spread the pieces out to see what it is that you actually need to try to accomplish, you take a look at all of the pieces when they come to you. Then, you begin to imagine how they might be brought together.

The puzzle analogy works well to a certain extent. However, the real-world result is even more dramatic as each puzzle piece contributes something like a chemical substance to the whole. The way that the chemicals combine and recombine over the course of creative processes is nothing short of magic. They are unpredictable in how they will react to the other parts.

WATER: Linkin Park and Jay-Z

"Numb/Encore" is a song by rapper Jay-Z and rock band Linkin Park from their EP *Collision Course* (2004). It was released as a single on December 13, 2004, by Warner Bros., Machine Shop, Def Jam, and Roc-A-Fella Records. The song is a mashup that fuses rock and hip-hop, combining lyrics from "Numb" by Linkin Park and "Encore" by Jay-Z, both released in 2003. It is known as one of the best musical collaborations of all time.[6] This is about children who are sick of living up to the high expectations their parents set for them. The lyric "Every step that I take is another mistake to you" is about how they feel as though they can't do anything to make their parents proud. In the spirit of rockers Aerosmith and rappers Run DMC, Linkin Park and Jay-Z created a track that we will all remember fondly for the pure fun that it induces.

SUNLIGHT: About Chemical Reactions

We can learn a lot about our students and our music classrooms by studying how chemicals react with one another. Table 14.1 summarizes some of the ways that chemicals react and how that might be applied to your thinking about your students and classrooms.

Combination Reaction

When two or more substances combine to form one compound you have a combination reaction. Something new is created by lumping together chemicals that were before separate. When students self-select their bands in your classroom they take part in combination reactions. The puzzle pieces analogy that I used earlier is a lot like that. The sum of the chemicals is greater than the existence of each chemical in isolation.

Decomposition Reaction

The opposite of a combination reaction is a decomposition reaction. This occurs when chemicals that were once together separate. Bands break up all the time. They will in your classroom as well. Sometimes this is for the better. Sometimes it is not. We might think of decomposition as moving against the natural progression of the universe that I talk about in other work (Randles, 2020). However, decomposition presents opportunities for other combination reactions that would not have occurred had the decomposition not occurred. Why do I start to think like a divorce lawyer when thinking through combination and decomposition?!

Table 14.1 Types of chemical reactions

Types of Chemical Reactions	Explanation	General Reaction
Combination reaction	Two or more compounds combine to form one compound.	$A + B \rightarrow AB$
Decomposition reaction	The opposite of a combination reaction—a complex molecule breaks down to make simpler ones.	$AB \rightarrow A + B$
Precipitation reaction	Two solutions of soluble salts are mixed, resulting in an insoluble solid (precipitate) forming.	A + Soluble salt B → Precipitate + soluble salt C
Neutralization reaction	An acid and a base react with each other. Generally, the product of this reaction is salt and water.	Acid + Base → Salt + Water
Combustion reaction	Oxygen combines with a compound to form carbon dioxide and water. These reactions are exothermic, meaning they give off heat.	$A + O_2 \rightarrow H_2O + CO_2$
Displacement reaction	One element takes place with another element in the compound.	$A + BC \rightarrow AC + B$

Precipitation Reaction

This is a chemical reaction that involves the formation of an insoluble product (precipitate; solid) from two or more soluble products. As far as music teachers are concerned, this chemical reaction is one where two or more things come together and something completely new emerges. There are so many examples of this in the history of music! The quirky drum beats of Meg White against Jack White's catchy riffs, the brilliance of Easy-E's politically charged lyrics with Dr. Dre's musical sensibilities and pension for creating sick beats, the sass that emerged when sat met pepa, the bombastic drum playing of John Bonham joining Jimmy Page's thunderous guitar playing, the musical artistry of Billy Eilish and the musical production savvy of her brother Finneas, and Flea's bass playing against the funky guitar work of Hillel Slovak (and then John Frusciante). Music is full of precipitation reactions.

Neutralization Reaction

Acids and bases produce salt and water. Interestingly enough, bands are made up of people who are acids and bases. An example of this is the combustible acids Sting and Stewart Copeland coming together with the base Andy Summers in The Police. They neutralized each other and produced new-to-the-world and loved-by-the-world music. Acids Don Henley and Glen Frey came together with bases Bernie

Leadon and Randy Meisner to form the first iteration of The Eagles. Bands need both acids and bases to function to the best of their abilities.

Combustion Reaction

This type of reaction produces heat! The genius of Jay-Z has helped launch Notorious B.I.G. (Biggie Smalls) and DMX, Rihanna, Justin Timberlake, Missy Elliott, Mariah Carey, Pharrell Williams, Justin Timberlake, Big Sean, Mary J. Blige, Ja Rule, Drake, Snoop Dogg, and Foxy Brown. Certain people seem to ignite creativity in their collaboration efforts. John Lennon and Paul McCartney produced some of the most enduring songs of all time that were made great with George Harrison and Ringo Starr. The genius of Willie Nelson has collaborated with countless artists over the years to surprisingly wonderful results: Waylon Jennings, Toby Keith, Merle Haggard, Kenny Chesney, Johnny Cash, Julio Iglesias, Chris Young, Lionel Richie, Dolly Parton, Miranda Lambert, Loretta Lynn, Carrie Underwood, Rosanne Cash, Wynonna Judd, Sheryl Crow, Mavis Staples, and Norah Jones. People coming together produces friction when they come together musically, and often that friction produces heat.

Displacement Reaction

I laughed as I wrote the definition of a displacement reaction for Table 14.1: one element takes place with another element in the compound. I thought immediately of the Fleetwood Mac album *Rumours*—the band's most successful of all time. During the recording of the album, Stevie Nicks and Lindsey Buckingham broke up AND John McVie and Christine McVie did as well. Nicks has suggested that Fleetwood Mac created their best music when they were in the worst shape. Many times, tensions between band members informed the recording process and led to the whole being more than the sum of the parts. It was rumored that at one time Stevie Nicks was shacking up with drummer Mick Fleetwood. So, displacement reactions occur as well. Sometimes they produce quite memorable results. This, like the other reactions, emerges because human beings are complex and messy in their interactions with one another. Music teacher producers have to be aware of and make the most of this.

WATER: The Motor City Five (MC5)

Formed in suburban Detroit in 1965 as a bar band that played mostly cover songs, the MC5 (Motor City Five) developed a chaotic, heavy, explosive sound that borrowed from avant-garde jazz, rock, and rhythm and blues. The original band lineup consisted of vocalist Rob Tyner, guitarists Wayne Kramer and Fred "Sonic" Smith, bassist Michael Davis, and drummer Dennis Thompson. Their fame peaked in 1969 with the release of their controversial live album *Kick Out the Jams*. They were contemporaries of The Stooges—a Detroit band that formed in Ann Arbor, Michigan, in the 1960s as Beatlemania cooked up and spilled over into popular culture. Both The Stooges and MC5 would contribute significantly to the heavier grungier-sounding rock music that would come later (the 1970s) and much later (the 1990s). The Seattle "Grunge" rock sound that bands like Nirvana, Alice in Chains, and Soundgarden championed was taken up in the ashes of the likes of MC5.

The band also heavily influenced The White Stripes in the late 1990s. There's no denying that Jack and Meg White knew their city's musical history. The White Stripes even covered MC5's "Looking at You," streamlining out some of the original grooves as they channeled the band's fiery, recklessly controlled playing. While the MC5's Tyner and Jack White can howl with the best of 'em, and both bands tended to call on the blues, the biggest similarity between MC5 and the White Stripes is their improvisational foundation. Kramer and Smith were bold personalities who could shift the direction of a song in a heartbeat. The White Stripes were built around Jack White's musical groove finding. Meg White actually went on to marry Jackson Smith, the son of Patti Smith and the MC5's Fred Smith.

SUNLIGHT: Thomas Edison, Henry Ford, and a Love of Plants

Thomas Edison, America's greatest inventor, and Henry Ford, the father of the moving assembly line and his namesake car company, had a massive love of growing plants.[7] Edison enjoyed bamboo and thought it might make the perfect filament for his new electric light bulb. He liked to surround his New Jersey home with native and unusual trees.

Henry Ford was fascinated by soybeans, an up-and-coming crop in the early 1900s. He used soybeans to make car-horn buttons and ornamentation on gearshift knobs and even wore a suit made out of soybean fiber—always looking to experiment! He once tried Spanish moss as stuffing in some of his Model T seats, only to find that chiggers ("red bugs") often infested the organic material. That made riding in those seats fairly uncomfortable.

Ford's wife, Clara, also enjoyed growing plants. She planted 10,000 roses in a five-acre rose garden on their Michigan estate. It was in Florida, though, that she really had the right growing conditions. Both the Edisons and the Fords wintered in Fort Myers. Their massive gardens can still be seen in the remaining vestiges on the grounds of the 20-acre Edison and Ford Winter Estates, one of America's most visited historic-home sites. Edison and Ford actually had homes right next to one another in Fort Myers. Edison bought 13 acres of land along the Caloosahatchee River in 1885 and built a lodge, study, and wintertime lab there. He and his wife, Mina, added a guest house next to the main house and enjoyed winters there for decades.[8]

In 1914, Edison invited Ford and his family to Fort Myers. They liked the site so much that they bought the Craftsman home next to Edison's guest house two years later. Ford's home was called "The Mangoes" for the grove of mangoes that grew in the front yard. Ford reportedly loved to sit on the front porch and look out over the mango trees.

As you read through the following analogies of the systems of an automobile—one of the great mechanical accomplishments of the twentieth century, try not to think of Henry Ford and Thomas Edison as innovators who were only about machines. The reality is that they, like many of us now, took a great deal of satisfaction from the natural world. Technology and innovation can work hand in hand with a love of the earth, soil, water, sunlight, planting, growing, and harvesting. For inspiration on growing songwriting, we can look to the successes of the city of Detroit and the automobile.

Study the Systems: An Automobile Analogy

I am from Michigan, and consequently am endlessly inspired by the city of Detroit and its roots as the Motor City. Chrysler, Ford, and General Motors are still based in Detroit. In the fall of 2021 I became the owner of a 1973 Corvette that has been in my family since 1982 (see Figure 14.1). I purchased the car from my uncle Dan Randles, who owned and drove the car for most of my life. I remember being a young child riding in the passenger seat of the car as he liked to throw my siblings and me back in our seats with the car's take-off speed—it was a drag racing champion at the Central Michigan Dragway (now known as the Mid-Michigan Motorplex) in Stanton, Michigan, in the 1980s beating out old and then-new Corvettes with its 400 cui racing engine. To own a car such as this one, I discovered that I needed to become

Figure 14.1 The author's 1973 Corvette as a race car in the 1980s and today

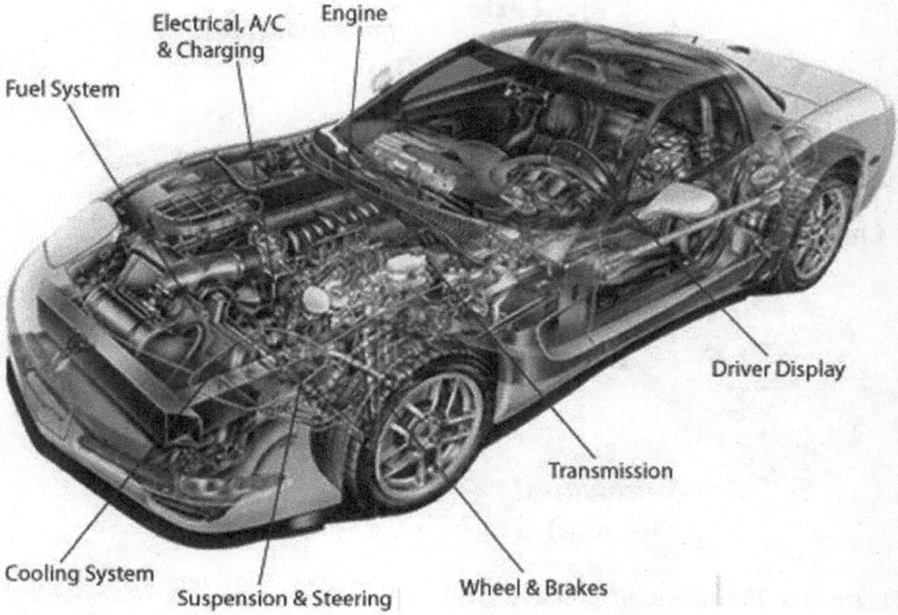

Figure 14.2 The systems of an automobile

an automotive mechanic to maintain the car. That meant that I had to study how the car systems work (see Figure 14.2) so that I would be able to make updates to it and fix issues that were sure to arise with fifty-year-old cars. Below are some things that I have learned about the systems of classic cars and how that knowledge can help you in a classroom centered on bringing out the creativities in your students.

Drive Train

The drive train comprises the engine, transmission, drive shaft, and differential of an automobile (see Figure 14.3). It is what makes a car move. The machine cannot work without the other systems, though. That is important to consider when reading through this section. The drive train of your classroom where songwriting is concerned is the creative processes of your students. I always tell my PhD students that they should be concerned with the content of the classes that I teach, but they should never lose track of their own agenda for what they would like to accomplish with their research projects and career goals. The creative processes that propel your students forward are the most important aspects of your classroom time. Engaging in these activities will move them down the road and keep you reaching your ultimate goal—revealing to your students roads that will be accessible for their entire lifetime. You need to make sure that the drive train is always up and running. Paying attention to the other systems will help you manage that.

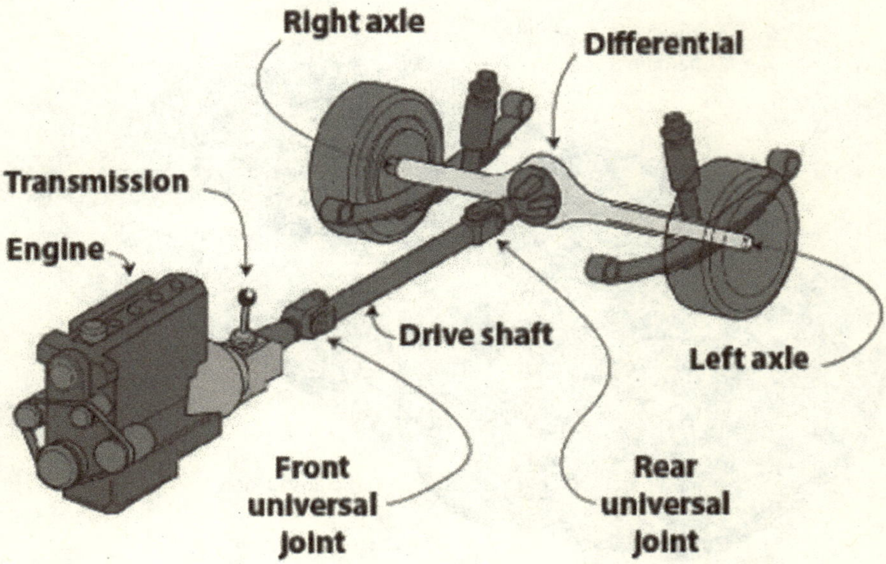

Figure 14.3 The drive train of an automobile

Fuel System

The fuel system provides your drive train with the fluid that, when ignited, creates a combustion reaction that moves the pistons in your car's engine. Without the fuel system, the drive train (creative process) does not work. The fuel system cannot do its job without the ignition system. Fuel without fire does not produce a combustion reaction. Similarly, fire without fuel does not create a combustion reaction. You need both! In terms of your classroom, you need to provide them with lesson seeds. These beginnings of cover, middle ground, and songwriting lessons provide your students with places to start in the creative process. Fuel provides the drive train with the right stuff to be able to take advantage of the combustion reactions required to move forward. Keep fuel always close at hand. Always be thinking about where the next source of fuel is going to come from. As we move into the future, alternate sources of fuel are going to be really important—we need sustainable sources of fuel. Stay imaginative and open to new discoveries.

Ignition System

The ignition system is the fire part of the fuel + fire = combustion reaction = drive train moves forward equation. The ignition system comprises an ignition coil, a distributor, spark plug wires, and spark plugs. Electrical current from the battery (electrical system) provides power to the ignition coil, which serves to convert the low current from a car battery into enough power to ignite the fuel and start the engine. An ignition coil is like a preamp to an audio signal—it boosts it. The distributor then sends electrical energy to specific cylinders of the car where it meets the spark plugs, creating fire that when combined with fuel causes a combustion reaction that moves the pistons that turn the crankshaft that moves the wheels/tires and propels the automobile forward. In many cases, YOU THE TEACHER are the ignition system. You provide sunlight and water that helps the plants in your room grow. Your efforts help them produce their own spark! Sometimes you are the electric current, sometimes you are the spark plugs, sometimes you are the distributer diverting power from place to place around your room. We are at our best, most inspirational selves, when we provide the ignition system within our classroom.

Electrical System

The systems of a car start with some sort of electrical current to the starter that turns the flywheel that turns the distributer and the engine valves that open and close around the combustion reactions that occur within each cylinder. My 1973 Corvette engine fires in a 1–8–4–3–6–5–7–2 cylinder order. As I have shared, pistons move the crankshaft that moves the wheels/tires and the automobile is sent into motion. That's probably too much information for those of you who are automobile novices. That is okay. When we think of the music classroom, this activity is like a music teacher being keenly aware of the power dynamics of students and how they have worked best together over time. There's no substitution for knowing where power is coming and going. You want to give power to them in a way that maximizes their potential and keeps them firing on all cylinders. As with fuel, you will constantly need to be aware of where you can get power. In Florida I have to replace the batteries in my cars regularly as the heat wears them down quicker. Always be on the lookout for power sources in your classroom. It will help ensure that you will be able to provide adequate water and sunlight for their growth.

Cooling System

The cooling system is what cools the engine of a car. A coolant mixture of antifreeze and water is pumped through the engine block (where the pistons and valves are working) into the radiator that has a fan that blows cool air across it. The cycling of coolant along with the cooling elements of radiator and electric fan (mechanical on my fifty-year-old classic) lowers the temperature of the engine block. The cooling system works to warm up the engine when it is cold as well. The thermostat keeps antifreeze from circulating until the engine warms to 185 degrees. It should stay running around 185 degrees to not do damage to the engine. In your classroom, you will have to work to keep the temperature at a normal level. Personalities can and will clash at times. It is your job to bring the temperature down to a level where everyone can do their best work. Experience and careful reflection can help put you in the right frame of mind to know how to keep the temperature down in your classroom environment.

Braking System

It is a matter of safety that when you drive an automobile you need to be able to stop. That is where the braking system becomes a necessity. Brake fluid works by hydraulics to compress a caliper that clamps down brake pads on a metal rotor. Squeezing the rotor with ceramic brake pads stops the car. Music teachers use their experience and best instinct to determine when they must utilize the braking system to stop activity in the classroom. We try to keep things moving. We even postpone bringing things to a halt sometimes just to let students learn valuable lessons. However, as the persons responsible for keeping everyone safe and healthy, sometimes we need to bring everything to a stop. The braking system also slows down the pace of the automobile. As teachers, we must do THAT sometimes as well. Constantly monitor the goings-on in your classroom. As much as possible, let students lead the pace, but do not be afraid to use the brakes when necessary to do so.

Suspension System

The suspension system of a car is what makes it ride smoothly and turn well. If your suspension system is working properly, when you go over bumps it levels out and is not jarring to you and your passengers. If your suspension system is well tuned, you are able to make wide turns without feeling as though you are going to fly off the road. To a large extent, you the teacher act as the suspension system. You have to smooth things out when there is conflict among members of your community. You act as a counselor when someone needs one. You smooth out bumps that will naturally occur among community members, parents, and administrators. Experience, reflection, and some good fortune help you know how to handle adverse situations—for instance, inclement weather on the road. With time and careful reflection, you will be able to handle anything that the road presents you with.

Steering System

There is no doubt that the steering system, as the part of the car that makes it go any direction that you want it to, is essential for getting around. This might be the clearest analogy to what a music teacher does in a classroom. You steer the automobile to places where it is safe and secure and able to be the best version of itself that it can be. I can't help pondering the main themes of this book—water + sunlight + good soil = growth. Since we are all about growing songwriting in this book, you as the teacher will need to steer your class toward the best possible conditions for growing. Being able to steer the vessel toward excellent growing conditions means first being aware of where the best conditions are. This requires vision, imagination, and creativity. Nurture each of these aspects of your teacher personality. You are going to need them.

Master Gardener Similitude

As I have suggested throughout this book, being a gardener is healthy, beautiful, and rewarding. A master gardener is a gardener who is interested in both the art and science of gardening. Teaching is an art—*expression or application of creative skill and imagination*—and a science—*systematic study of the natural world through observation and experiment.* We are all working together to create opportunities for our students to grow through songwriting, all the while growing songwriting as a school curricular offering. Education is and should be all about *the process* of growing. As I have said, our assessments should be *formative* and *tentative.*

You should strive to be an artist teacher. Go about each day looking for ways to exercise your own creative imagination. You are a musician who will need to stretch yourself in new and interesting ways, always looking to grow and move forward. You have come to realize the power of creative activity in your life and so you work to nurture it in your students. Your excitement can be seen by your students who would like to actualize their own creative potential. They have begun to see a person who in some cases they would like to be just like in some ways. You have been vulnerable in front of them. You now understand the value of being creative along with your students.

As I said in Chapter 1, scientifically minded teachers look constantly for ways to improve their teaching and undertake daily reflection about how things are going, while constantly experimenting with better ways of doing what they do. *Everything is an experiment.* They use their artistic powers of creative imagination to help them discover the best questions to ask with regard to daily practice. I challenge you to adopt this kind of mindset. In this way, art and science combine to propel them to the best possible practice for themselves and their students. Thoughtful reflection goes a long way toward your becoming the best version of your teacher self in a Music Teacher as Music Producer form of classroom.

Focusing on Healthy Plants

Maintain your focus on the idea of growing the healthiest plants that you possibly can. The seeds, water, and sunlight presented throughout the book will help you get started teaching songwriting. You will find that doing so will promote musical health and well-being in the lives of your students. It ignites and engages their creative imagination. It taps into their human experience. It fulfills a longing that we all have to take simpler things and make them more complex, to put our signature on something that we have made (Randles, 2009a). We seek to grow songwriting as a curricular practice. We seek to grow our skill as songwriters so that we better help our students do the same.

Our goal is to plant and provide the right conditions for seeds to grow while they are in our care. Growth is the singular goal. There are lots of quantitative and qualitative ways to measure growth. We need to become experts in ways of doing this. I have provided MANY ways of doing that here, and you will have to always be on the lookout for more refined ways that fit well the culture of your classroom and the specific interests of your students. Growth conditions change constantly. You will have to monitor the change and be a constant reflector on what is working and not working in your classroom. Adjust your water and sunlight as you plant seeds and move your students to the most fertile soil based on the feedback that they provide you with.

As I said in Chapter 1, in some cases, you will have to tend to removing weeds that can grow around your plants. You will have to think of both the short term—How can I help this group finish a song without damaging their creative vision?—and long term—How can I provide feedback on a particular song that will provide forward momentum for a songwriter who is graduating or moving to another state? The best predictor of long-term success and continuation is healthy success and continuation while in your classroom. Healthy perspectives on growth and lifelong learning can be instilled in your students that, when given proper root, can last a lifetime.

Skill-Building: Spend Your Time Wisely

This book taps into the working lives of professional songwriters, the working lives of practicing music teachers who have taught songwriting, and teacher educators to work to teach pre-service music teachers to do this. I am partly all of these things in my job as a professor, but I don't have all of the answers. My job as director of contemporary worship at a church in Tampa, Florida, leverages much of the content that I have presented here in these pages (see Figure 14.4). I have gathered many of the best ideas from the best sources that I have used over the years. Use them, transform them, and make them your own. Let me know what has worked and/or not worked from what I have shared here.

Remember foremost that songwriting and creativities for that matter resist linear paths. Start with cover songs. Use preexisting forms and write original lyrics. Use improvisation for motivation and inspiration, then follow the joy of your students. Break down the task of writing a song to:

1. discovering grooves
2. finding harmonic progressions

Figure 14.4 The author as director of contemporary worship in Tampa, Florida

3. discovering melodies
4. writing lyrics

I have shared with you how to develop these areas in your daily practice throughout the pages of this book. What are they, and what will they do for the health of your students in being and becoming songwriters? Let me jump back into that discussion before I set you free to practice these ideas in your classroom.

Discovering Grooves

A considerable amount of your classroom time needs to be devoted to improvising. We need as musicians to get back to that Johann Sebastian Bach kind of musicianship. We need to be inspired by the playfulness that was the start to so much of the music that has endured across time. Jazz, rock, and hip-hip started as freewheeling fun among friend groups. The themes of each of those genres centered on giving voice to longings of the human soul. Each of these genres was originally the music of Black America, with 400 years of oppression and injustice pushing and prodding innovation and excellence. Music at the base level moves us in some way. It touches us to the bone. We can latch on to the innovation and excellence that gave a particular music birth when we play around with its themes, riffs, and tonalities just as its originators did. Although we can look at each of them as an artistic art form of the highest caliber, when they were conceived of they were musical experiments of human beings with something important to say. Tap into that experimental nature and improvise more with your students every day.

Finding Harmonic Progressions

The guitar is my favorite instrument to explore harmonies on. You can move shapes around the neck easily and sometimes break free of our tendency to land on I–IV–V progressions prematurely. Harmonic progressions in the form of lead sheets end up being the framework upon which we hang the lyrical and melodic content of our songs. Harmonic progressions sometimes come before and sometimes after we have lyrics for our songs. One thing is certain, though: the harmonic progression that we work with will do a lot to determine the overall feel of a song and the scope of the melodic content that we end up using. Just as with all of the areas listed above, we should create far more harmonic progressions than we will actually use. Most artists work this way. Of course, there are exceptions to this rule. Mozart and Led Zeppelin seemed to use everything that they ever worked on. Most of the rest of us will create lots of things that don't quite work, and some that do. The process of always creating something is what will lead us to eventually creating something that is really good.

Discovering Melodies

I have written in these pages about how Jeff Tweedy likes to hum over harmonic progressions to help him discover melodies. Your melodic content might fall out of specific voicing on your guitar or keyboard. Your melodic content can come from specific riffs that you have created, OR your riffs can come from particular melodic ideas that you come up with. Melodies can come from birdsong—a pair of zebra finches once inspired a melody that I wrote during the pandemic. A lot of times we borrow parts of melodies from other songs that we know and love. Of course, we have to be careful not to borrow TOO MUCH of the melodies from the songs that we know as to infringe on copyright laws! Basically, though, we live in a world that is full of melodic content. We bathe in it. We breath it in. To discover melodies, we need to (1) open our ears and listen; (2) be diligent to sometimes listen outside of our normal life circumstances; and (3) be disciplined enough to get down on paper/screen/DAW those melodic ideas. Again, we need to come up with far more melodies than we will actually use to eventually land on something great. Be wild and free as a bird and as diligent as a soldier as you go about this.

Writing Lyrics

This is new territory for music education. We have not been people on a large scale who spend much time writing lyrics. That can change, though. That is why you chose to read this book. I have shared tricks and tips from sources that I have used in the past. In some cases I have shared creative processes that I have used in my classes (K–16). You might have ideas that I have not shared here. That is great. Can you let me know about them so that I can help other people with your ideas? Considered together, our work can be highly effective for creating a more secure place for songwriting in the curriculum. Object writing is where it is at. You should do this every day in your classroom. Collaborative writing works well. You should do that every day in your classroom. Your students should keep a journal. There they can keep everything from song lyrics to beginnings of ideas that can be more fully fleshed out at a later time. Everything is tentative, so you want to capture even germinal ideas so that they have a chance to grow at a later time. That is part of being and becoming a master gardener for your students.

Final Words

We will not cure cancer by writing songs or providing more and more time in the school curriculum for songwriting. However, we can help people live more meaningful lives by giving them a way to create works, connect with greater humanity, and make sense of their own suffering. That is no small task or meaningful pursuit. We need not displace the other ways that people have used music in schools to do good works. What we need to focus on at this point is creating an alternate universe of music education that focuses on leveraging the power of all the music that happens in the world, and ways of being musical that give that music life. We have done a good job of positioning the making of music from Western Classical notation in large and small groups. So what is next?

As I write this book, I partner with all of the wonderful people in music education who have championed growing songwriting in the curriculum over the past decades. I am inspired to this work in no small part by the inspiration that they have provided. I think most notably of John Kratus, my thesis and dissertation advisor at Michigan State University in the early 2000s who opened a whole world of questioning the status quo in music education to my daily thought processes. This work would not have happened if he had not planted seeds, watered them, and provided endless opportunities for sunlight over the years. When I was a teacher in Michigan taking Dr. Kratus's classes, my students benefited from his work and leadership. Now my students' students benefit from it. Thank you so much, my dear mentor.

To pre-service music teachers everywhere: we have important work to do to bring these ideas into common practice. To pre-service music teacher educators: we have important work to give our future teachers opportunities to do the things that I have presented in this book in their classes for their degree. To music teachers everywhere: we need to practice doing the techniques and strategies that I have mentioned in this book. Everyone who reads this: be and become a songwriter yourself so that you can help other people do it. We owe diligent practice and attention to detail to all of the innovators across the history of music: Louis Armstrong, Sister Rosetta

Tharpe, James Brown, and Taylor Swift. Our students will be able to tap into their favorite music and end up drawing from a well of musical creativities that will stay with them for their entire lifetime. That, in some ways, is better than a cure for cancer. It will lead to more widespread self-expression through music in ways that are natural, self-sustaining, and refreshing. We can do this! We will succeed together.

Resources Worth Exploring

Source	Expertise	URL
Berklee Online's Music Business Handbook	You can download a PDF of tips for thinking about the business side of being a songwriter	https://cloud.info.berklee.edu/bol-music-business
Songwriting: Essential Guide to Lyric Form and Structure: Tools and Techniques for Writing Better Lyrics	Here is a guide from Pat Pattison (1991) on how to organize your lyric writing	https://www.amazon.com/Songwriting-Essential-Structure-Techniques-Writing/dp/0793511801/
How to Write a Song That Matters	Dar Williams gives us some great things to think about as we work with lyrics and melody for a purpose	https://www.amazon.com/How-Write-Song-that-Matters/dp/0306923297/
The Philosophy of Modern Song	Bob Dylan writes his first book on songwriting in over twenty years. This is a must-have for your library	https://www.amazon.com/dp/1451648707
The Song in My Head: Songwriter Cards	This is a deck of 110 cards that are meant to be inspirational fuel for your creative processes	https://www.amazon.com/Song-My-Head-Inspirational-Songwriting/dp/1527249077
It All Begins with a Song	Documentary on the working lives of Nashville's songwriting scene	https://www.amazon.com/All-Begins-Song-Garth-Brooks/dp/B085R9H36Q

Notes

Chapter 1

1. https://www.ted.com/talks/brene_brown_the_power_of_vulnerability?language=en
2. https://www.inc.com/lolly-daskal/how-improv-can-make-you-a-better-leader.html.
3. https://www.masterclass.com/articles/how-to-write-a-melody.
4. https://www.udiscovermusic.com/stories/yesterday-beatles-song-story/.
5. https://www.masterclass.com/articles/how-to-write-a-melody.
6. https://www.masterclass.com/articles/how-to-write-a-melody.
7. https://www.youtube.com/watch?v=OP9_lG3nslA.
8. https://splice.com/blog/tips-writing-better-lyrics/.
9. https://www.spin.com/2017/08/taylor-swift-songs-explanation-guide.
10. https://www.songfacts.com/facts/michael-buble/its-a-beautiful-day.

Chapter 2

1. https://bippermedia.com/how-to-find-new-music-and-diversify-your-listening-habits/.
2. https://www.npr.org/2020/04/07/828115972/kendrick-lamar-thinks-like-a-jazz-musician.
3. https://www.thisisdig.com/feature/most-influential-musicians-changed-music/.
4. https://wmich.edu/mus-theo/courses/keys.html.
5. https://soundsorceress.wordpress.com/2012/09/25/six-benefits-i-got-from-learning-cover-songs/.
6. https://www.coverbandcentral.com/10-tips-for-playing-a-cover-song/.

Chapter 3

1. https://faroutmagazine.co.uk/r-e-m-everybody-hurts-story-behind-the-song/.
2. https://faroutmagazine.co.uk/r-e-m-everybody-hurts-story-behind-the-song/.

Chapter 4

1. https://americansongwriter.com/the-white-stripes-seven-nation-army/.

Chapter 5

1. https://www.npr.org/2010/02/26/124078116/american-remembered-rick-rubin-on-johnny-cash.

Chapter 6

1. https://albumism.com/features/tribute-celebrating-50-years-of-michael-jackson-debut-solo-album-got-to-be-there.
2. https://www.almanac.com/video/how-create-year-round-vegetable-garden.
3. https://www.campanellas.com/blog/5-tips-to-keep-comfortable-during-long-road-trips.
4. https://www.masterclass.com/articles/how-to-make-a-mashup.
5. https://open.spotify.com/album/59Zojf7w3RNklTOR9HGMrh.
6. https://serato.com/artists/kittens.
7. https://www.digitaldjtips.com/rock-the-dancefloor/the-basic-djing-technique/.
8. https://www.rollingstone.com/music/music-news/how-the-beastie-boys-made-their-masterpiece-186788/.
9. https://www.allmusic.com/style/golden-age-ma0000012011.

Chapter 7

1. https://www.thefader.com/2022/03/03/fireboy-dml-sickick-remix-madonna-frozen.

Chapter 8

1. https://www.mtv.com/news/i8ctty/kanye-west-blood-on-leaves-strange-fruit.
2. https://www.nme.com/features/the-best-samples-in-music-ever-2667649.

Chapter 9

1. Gary Ewer (2016), webpage, available at: https://www.secretsofsongwriting.com/2016/07/14/ideas-for-keeping-a-songwriting-journal/
2. https://www.secretsofsongwriting.com/2016/07/14/ideas-for-keeping-a-songwriting-journal/.
3. https://www.ajournalofmusicalthings.com/ongoing-history-daily-eddie-vedders-notebooks/.
4. https://www.noise11.com/news/music-news-elton-john-explains-his-songwriting-process-20160120.
5. https://jonimitchell.com/library/print.cfm?id=43.
6. https://songexploder.net/netflix.
7. https://www.researchgate.net/profile/John-Kratus/publication/297899046_Songwriting_A_New_Direction_for_Secondary_Music_Education/links/5a01d11c0f7e9bfd74601073/Songwriting-A-New-Direction-for-Secondary-Music-Education.pdf.
8. https://www.abbeyroad.com/news/in-remembrance-of-legendary-recording-engineer-geoff-emerick-2436.
9. https://www.the-paulmccartney-project.com/artist/geoff-emerick/#:~:text=Geoffrey%20Emerick%20(5%20December%201945,The%20Beatles%20and%20Abbey%20Road.
10. https://www.billboard.com/music/rock/the-beatles-abbey-road-alan-parsons-giles-martin-on-the-classic-8530991/
11. https://www.abbeyroad.com/news/the-genius-of-alan-parsons-as-told-by-abbey-roads-cameron-colbeck-2716.
12. https://www.abbeyroad.com/news/the-genius-of-alan-parsons-as-told-by-abbey-roads-cameron-colbeck-2716.

13. https://www.rockhall.com/inductees/glyn-johns.
14. https://www.rockhall.com/inductees/glyn-johns.
15. https://www.keepitonthelo.com/bio.
16. https://www.keepitonthelo.com/bio.
17. https://www.synchroarts.com/synchroartists/vocaligning-hip-hop-vocal-takes-for-dr-dre-s-record-label..
18. https://www.synchroarts.com/synchroartists/vocaligning-hip-hop-vocal-takes-for-dr-dre-s-record-label.
19. https://plus.pointblankmusicschool.com/pbla-presents-running-aftermath-studios-with-paul-montes-april-28/.
20. https://streamondemandathome.com/the-wrecking-crew-documentary-dvd-blu-ray-vod/.
21. https://streamondemandathome.com/the-wrecking-crew-documentary-dvd-blu-ray-vod/.

Chapter 10

1. https://www.rollingstone.com/feature/red-hot-chili-peppers-blood-sugar-sex-magik-10-things-you-didnt-know-121474/.
2. https://www.songwriting.net/blog/7-beatles-secrets.
3. https://www.nme.com/blogs/nme-blogs/steve-tyler-how-i-wrote-aerosmith-run-dmcs-walk-this-way-22763.
4. https://www.wsj.com/articles/how-aerosmith-created-walk-this-way-1410275586.
5. https://www.udiscovermusic.com/stories/best-guitar-riffs/.

Chapter 11

1. https://thehitformula.com/tag/taylor-swift/#:~:text=Don't%20keep%20on%20going,people%20to%20remember%20the%20song.
2. https://comboplate.net/6-tips-for-following-a-recipe/.
3. https://www.masterclass.com/classes/nas-teaches-hip-hop-storytelling/chapters/rapping-and-rhyme-schemes.

Chapter 12

1. https://www.nme.com/blogs/nme-blogs/star-man-the-story-of-bowies-ziggy-stardust-763290.
2. https://www.detroitnews.com/story/entertainment/music/2022/11/06/eminems-very-long-thank-you-list-his-full-rock-hall-induction-speech/69623621007/.
3. https://www.musicianonamission.com/rhyme-schemes/.
4. https://blog.discmakers.com/2017/09/songwriting-lessons-from-john-lennon/
5. https://blog.discmakers.com/2017/09/songwriting-lessons-from-john-lennon/
6. https://www.openculture.com/2015/02/bowie-cut-up-technique.html.
7. https://www.openculture.com/2015/02/bowie-cut-up-technique.html.
8. https://www.openculture.com/2015/02/bowie-cut-up-technique.html.

Chapter 13

1. https://www.rollingstone.com/interactive/lists-100-greatest-songwriters/#stevie-wonder.

2. https://www.rollingstone.com/interactive/lists-100-greatest-songwriters/#stevie-wonder.
3. https://www.thehenryford.org/explore/stories-of-innovation/what-if/george-washington-carver/.
4. https://www.thehenryford.org/explore/stories-of-innovation/what-if/george-washington-carver/.
5. https://www.thehenryford.org/explore/stories-of-innovation/what-if/george-washington-carver/.
6. https://mixedinkey.com/captain-plugins/wiki/the-10-greatest-musical-collaborations-of-all-time/.
7. https://georgeweigel.net/georges-current-ramblings-and-readlings/edison-and-ford-were-into-plants.
8. https://georgeweigel.net/georges-current-ramblings-and-readlings/edison-and-ford-were-into-plants.

References

Baker, F. (2016). *Therapeutic Songwriting: Developments in Theory, Methods, and Practice.* New York: Springer.

Buchholz, C., and B. Aerssen. (2020). *The Innovator's Dictionary.* Boston: De Gruyter.

Burnard, P. (2012). *Musical Creativities in Practice.* New York: Oxford University Press.

Campbell, J. (2008). *The Hero with a Thousand Faces.* Novato, CA: New World Library.

Citron, S. (2008). *Songwriting: A Complete Guide to the Craft.* Milwaukee, WI: Hal Leonard.

Cremata, R., J. M. Pignato, B. Powell, and G. D. Smith. (2017). *The Music Learning Profiles Project: Let's Take This Outside.* New York: Routledge.

Draves, T. J. (2008). "Music Achievement, Self-Esteem, and Aptitude in a College Songwriting Class." *Bulletin of the Council for Research in Music Education* 178 (Fall): 35–46.

Dylan, B. (2005). *Chronicles.* Vol. 1. New York: Simon & Schuster.

Dylan, B. (2022). *The Philosophy of Modern Song.* New York: Simon & Schuster.

Errico, M. (2022). *Music, Lyrics, and Life.* Lanham, MD: Backbeat Books.

Findeisen, F. (2015). *The Addiction Formula.* Enschede, Netherlands: Albino Publishing.

Frankl, V. E. (1985). *Man's Search for Meaning.* New York: Simon & Schuster.

Freedman, B. (2013). *Teaching Music through Composition: A Curriculum Using Technology.* New York: Oxford University Press.

Fung, C. V. (2018). *A Way of Music Education: Classic Chinese Wisdoms.* New York: Oxford University Press.

Gardner, H. (2011). *Creating Minds: An Anatomy of Creativity Seen through the Lives of Freud, Einstein, Picasso, Stravinsky, Eliot, Graham, and Gandhi.* New York: Civitas.

Green, L. (2017a). *How Popular Musicians Learn: A Way Ahead for Music Education.* London: Routledge.

Green, L. (2017b). *Music, Informal Learning and the School: A New Classroom Pedagogy.* London: Routledge.

Hawkins, S. (2016). *Song Maps: A New System to Write Your Best Lyrics.* London: Create Space Independent Publishing Platform.

Hughes, D., and S. Keith. (2019). "Aspirations, Considerations and Processes: Songwriting in and for Music Education." *Journal of Popular Music Education* 3, no. 1 (March): 87–103.

Johansson, O. (2020). *Songs from Sweden: Shaping Pop Culture in a Globalized Music Industry.* Singapore: Palgrave Pivot.

Kratus, J. (2007). "Music Education at the Tipping Point." *Music Educators Journal* 94, no. 2 (November): 42–48.

Kratus, J. (2016). "Songwriting: A New Direction for Secondary Music Education." *Music Educators Journal* 102, no. 3 (March): 60–65.

Kratus, J. (2019). "A Return to Amateurism in Music Education." *Music Educators Journal* 106, no. 1 (September): 31–37.

Mark, M., and C. Gary. (2007). *A History of American Music Education.* 3rd ed. Lanham, MD: Rowman & Littlefield.

McIntyre, P. (2008). "Creativity and Cultural Production: A Study of Contemporary Western Popular Music Songwriting." *Creativity Research Journal* 20, no. 1: 40–52.

Moore, R. (1992). "The Decline of Improvisation in Western Art Music: An Interpretation of Change." *International Review of the Aesthetics and Sociology of Music* 23, no. 1 (June): 61–84.

Pattison, P. (1991). *Songwriting: Essential Guide to Lyric Form and Structure: Tools and Techniques for Writing Better Lyrics.* Boston: Berklee Press.

Pattison, P. (2009). *Writing Better Lyrics*. 2nd ed. Cincinnati: Writer's Digest Books.
Perricone, J. (2018). *Great Songwriting Techniques*. New York: Oxford University Press.
Randles, C. (2009a). "'That's My Piece, That's My Signature, and It Means More . . .': Creative Identity and the Ensemble Teacher/Arranger." *Research Studies in Music Education* 31, no. 1 (June): 52–68.
Randles, C. (2009b). "Student Composers' Expressed Meaning of Composition with Regard to Culture." *Music Education Research International* 3: 44–56.
Randles, C. (2013). "Being an iPadist." *General Music Today* 27, no. 1 (October): 48–51.
Randles, C. (2020). *To Create: Imagining the Good Life through Music*. Chicago: GIA Publishing.
Randles, C. (2022). *Music Teacher as Music Producer: How to Turn Your Classroom into a Center for Musical Creativities*. New York: Oxford University Press.
Randles, C., N. Aponte, and S. Johnson. (forthcoming). *Music Production for the Emerging Music Teacher Producer*. New York: Oxford University Press.
Randles, C., and P. Burnard, eds. (2022). *The Routledge Companion to Creativities in Music Education*. New York: Oxford University Press.
Randles, C., and M. Sullivan. (2013). "How Composers Approach Teaching Composition: Strategies for Music Teachers." *Music Educators Journal* 99, no. 3 (March): 51–57.
Reinhert, K. (2019). "Lyric Approaches to Songwriting in the Classroom." *Journal of Popular Music Education* 3, no. 1 (March): 129–139.
Reinhert, K. & Gulish, S. (2020). *Songwriting for music educators: Practical strategies for embracing personal creativity while exploring songwriting in the classroom*. Philadelphia: F-Flat Books.
Tobias, E. S. (2013). "Composing, Songwriting, and Producing: Informing Popular Music Pedagogy." *Research Studies in Music Education* 35, no. 2 (December): 213–237.
Tweedy, J. (2019). *Let's Go (So We Can Get Back): A Memoir of Recording and Discording with Wilco, Etc*. New York: Penguin.
Tweedy, J. (2020). *How to Write One Song*. New York: Dutton.
Vogler, C. (2007). *The Writer's Journey*. Studio City, CA: Michael Wiese Productions.
Watson, S. (2011). *Using Technology to Unlock Musical Creativity*. New York: Oxford University Press.
Williams, D. A. (2014). "Another Perspective: The iPad Is a REAL Musical Instrument." *Music Educators Journal* 101, no. 1 (September): 93–98.

Index

For the benefit of digital users, indexed terms that span two pages (e.g., 52–53) may, on occasion, appear on only one of those pages.
Figures are indicated by *f* following the page number.